POLITICAL PARTIES

AND GENERATIONS IN

paraguay's

LIBERAL ERA,

1869–1940

POLITICAL PARTIES

AND GENERATIONS IN

paraguay's

LIBERAL ERA,

1869–1940

by Paul H. Lewis

THE UNIVERSITY OF NORTH CAROLINA PRESS

CHAPEL HILL AND LONDON

Publication of this book was aided by
a grant from the Murphy Institute of
Political Economy, Tulane University.

Library of Congress Cataloging-
in-Publication Data

Lewis, Paul H.

  Political parties and generations in
Paraguay's Liberal era, 1869–1940 / by
Paul H. Lewis.

   p. cm.

   Includes bibliographical references and
index.

   ISBN 0-8078-2078-4

   1. Paraguay—Politics and government—1870–1938. 2. Paraguay—
Politics and government—1938–
1954. 3. Political parties—Paraguay—
History. I. Title.

F2688.L49   1993

989.2'06—dc20   92-21164

                                 CIP

97 96 95 94 93
5 4 3 2 1

For Anne

contents

Preface   ix

Maps   xi

Introduction   1

one   The Family Origins   15

two   From Familial Politics to *Personalismo*   32

three   The Emergence of a Two-Party System   50

four   The Colorado Era   68

five   Realignment and Regime Change   84

six   The Radical Liberals in Power   104

seven   The Climax of Radical Liberal Rule   123

eight   The Rise of Nationalism   144

nine   Revolutionary Paraguay   160

         Summary and Conclusion   184

         Notes   195

         Bibliography   213

         Index   221

preface

This study is by no means a comprehensive history of Paraguay during the Liberal Era. It concentrates upon only a few aspects of political life and much research remains to be done before students of Paraguay will have a clear understanding of those times. Piecing together a complete picture will not be easy, because so many of the primary sources were lost during the many violent upheavals. Those that do exist are often buried away in private archives. The present work had to rely mostly on secondary sources. To offset that disadvantage, I have consulted a wide range of those, with the help of financial support from the Murphy Institute of Political Economy at Tulane University, a summer research grant from the Organization of American States, and a year's sabbatical leave from Tulane. I am very grateful for such assistance and hope that this book will justify it.

Paul H. Lewis
New Orleans

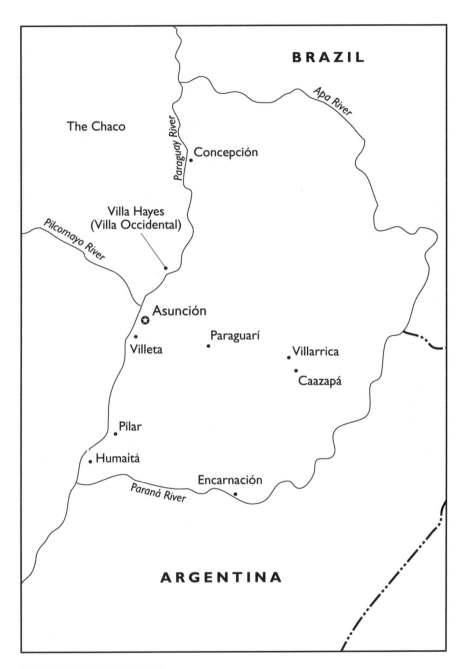

MAP 1. EASTERN PARAGUAY

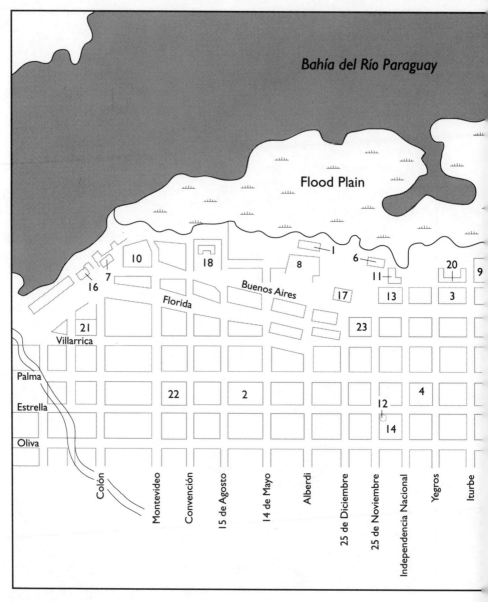

Bahía del Río Paraguay

Flood Plain

Buenos Aires

Florida

Villarrica

Palma

Estrella

Oliva

Colón

Montevideo

Convención

15 de Agosto

14 de Mayo

Alberdi

25 de Diciembre

25 de Noviembre

Independencia Nacional

Yegros

Iturbe

MAP 2. DOWNTOWN ASUNCIÓN

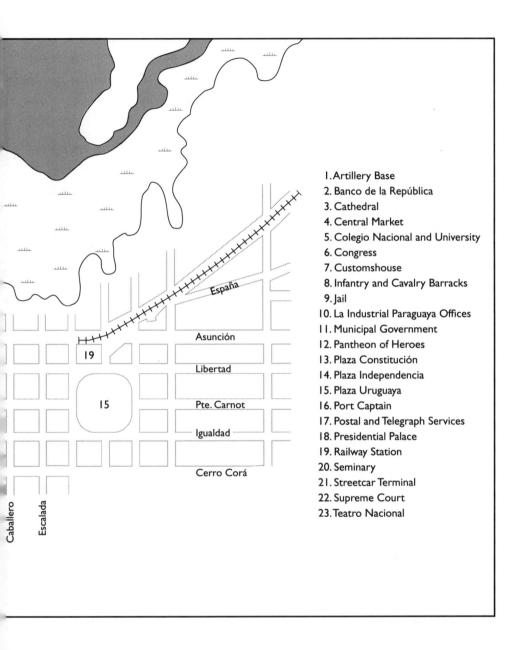

1. Artillery Base
2. Banco de la República
3. Cathedral
4. Central Market
5. Colegio Nacional and University
6. Congress
7. Customshouse
8. Infantry and Cavalry Barracks
9. Jail
10. La Industrial Paraguaya Offices
11. Municipal Government
12. Pantheon of Heroes
13. Plaza Constitución
14. Plaza Independencia
15. Plaza Uruguaya
16. Port Captain
17. Postal and Telegraph Services
18. Presidential Palace
19. Railway Station
20. Seminary
21. Streetcar Terminal
22. Supreme Court
23. Teatro Nacional

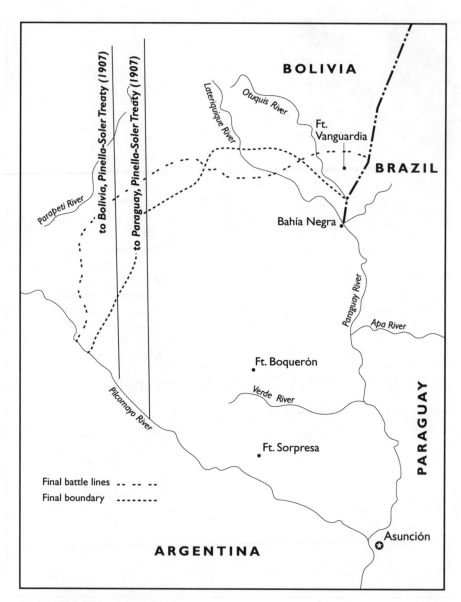

BOLIVIA

Otuquis River

Lateriquique River

Ft.
Vanguardia

BRAZIL

to Bolivia, Pinella–Soler Treaty (1907)

to Paraguay, Pinella–Soler Treaty (1907)

Parapeti River

Bahía Negra

Paraguay River

Apa River

PARAGUAY

Pilcomayo River

Ft. Boquerón

Verde River

Ft. Sorpresa

Final battle lines -- -- --
Final boundary ....

Asunción

ARGENTINA

MAP 3. THE CHACO DISPUTE

POLITICAL PARTIES

AND GENERATIONS IN

paraguay's

LIBERAL ERA,

1869–1940

INTRODUCTION

Writing about the Liberal Era in Paraguayan history, Diego Abente observed, correctly, that

> The Paraguayan liberal republic, spanning from the end of the War of the Triple Alliance to the end of the Chaco War, is one of the most under-researched and probably one of the most undervalued periods of Paraguayan history and has only recently elicited some scholarly interest. During this period capital accumulation developed exclusively in the private domain, economic policies were informed by *laissez-faire* doctrines, and the political arena embodied, if mostly theoretically, the liberal principles of public contestation and elite competition. Those basic and distinctive traits, and in that particular order, are found in no other period of Paraguayan history. It therefore makes conceptual sense to speak of the liberal republic as a distinct period in Paraguayan history.[1]

It also is true that this period, from roughly 1869 to 1940, was the seedtime of Paraguay's two major political parties, the Colorado Party (officially, the National Republican Association) and the Liberal Party. Both of them date their formal beginnings to the year 1887, which makes them among the oldest continuously functioning parties in the world. What is more, those formal organizations that were started in 1887 had their precursors in a number of political clubs, the earliest of which was founded in 1858. Thus, Paraguay is an exception (along with Colombia and Uruguay) to the general rule that political party systems in Latin America are of relatively recent origin and consist to a great extent of ephemeral organizations built around personalities. In this book I describe how Paraguay's major parties evolved out of those clubs and how they consolidated their organizations to create an essentially two-party system that has persisted down to the present.

To say that the parties grew out of political clubs implies stages of evolution, and indeed Paraguay did move from preparty politics to party politics, a process that did not differ much from that of more industrialized nations in Europe or North America. Samuel Huntington offers a general scheme of development by which parties as we know them today emerged.[2] He outlines a four-step process that corresponds very closely to what actually happened in Paraguay.

In the first stage, politics revolve around factions, or cliques.[3] The difference between a faction and a party is that the former has little durability or structure. For Huntington, factions are usually just "projections of individual ambitions in the context of personal and family rivalries and affiliations." Whether they originate, as Duverger says, either as parliamentary cliques or as revolutionary conspiracies, they usually involve a small number of people who "form and re-form in a confusing series of permutations and combinations which are no less factions for being equipped with ponderous names and lengthy manifestoes." And, Huntington adds, "In and of itself the competition of factions—legislative or revolutionary—tends to be a closed system, an endless round of interminable maneuvering in which the actors continually shift partners and antagonists without ever enlarging the number of participants."[4]

William Nesbit Chambers, in his study of the emergence of American political parties offers a useful set of criteria for distinguishing between factions and parties. Like Huntington, he views parties as having more or less permanent structures, whereas factions are the transitory results of frequently shifting alliances. Furthermore, although both factions and parties may adopt procedures for nominating candidates, campaigning, and issuing propaganda, parties carry those out in a more coordinated, continuous, and visible fashion. Again, like Huntington, Chambers notes that parties embrace a larger number of individuals and interests, and he adds that they generate deeper and more lasting loyalty to their party symbols and traditions. Finally, because parties are able to generate such an emotional identification from their members, they are better than factions at coordinating different branches of government and managing public affairs.[5]

According to Huntington, the crucial turning point, or "take-off," by which a political system begins to move from factional to party politics happens when some issue arises—or different issues become linked—so as to polarize the factions in a more or less permanent manner. Then, instead of a constantly changing kaleidoscope of alliances, "reasonably stable groupings" emerge. There is a tendency, when this happens, for those "groupings" to reach out beyond the traditional political class and enlist the support of broader "social forces."

The third step in the evolutionary process is simply a continuation of the tendency to expand the scope of participation. Each side in the political struggle will try to recruit more and more people until participation becomes universal. In the meantime, each grouping strives to improve its organization so as to mobilize its supporters more effectively. This eventually results in the fourth and final stage, in which the parties are fully institutionalized.

Paraguay's political parties evolved in stages closely approximating those in Huntington's theory. Chapter 1 of this study traces the origins of both the Liberal and Colorado parties to revolutionary clubs that formed in exile in the late 1850s and early 1860s. Those clubs were initiated and dominated by certain prominent families. After returning to Paraguay in 1869, those families struggled with each other to control the government, beginning a process of rapidly shifting alliances. Gradually, however, family heads were replaced by powerful individuals—*caudillos*—at the center of the contest. Politics was still a matter of competing factions, but those factions came to be more personalistic than familial. That process is described in Chapter 2.

The move from family-based politics to personalism was a significant step in the evolution of Paraguay's parties. Familial politics is, by its very nature, restrictive; personalism is highly open and fluid. In the Spanish American version, *caudillismo*, leaders often recruit their following from lower-class *mestizo* ("half-breed") elements, which gives it a populist character. According to Eric Wolf and Edward C. Hansen, *caudillo* factions are armed patron-client sets, cemented by personal ties of domination and submission, and by a common desire to obtain wealth by the force of arms. Greed, not ties of blood or marriage, cements the bond; therefore, personalistic leadership is highly unstable. If a *caudillo* is beaten, or fails to deliver on his followers' expectations of booty, he risks being overthrown or seeing his faction disintegrate. Consequently, he must always search for new sources of wealth to distribute among his following and so there is an inner dynamic to *caudillo* politics that drives it forward.[6] Eventually one *caudillo* wins out over all the rest, eliminating his rivals by either murder or bribery and establishing a national dictatorship that is really just a personal machine.

Paraguay's experience indicates that national machine politics is the next phase by which factions begin to turn into parties. That is the subject of Chapter 3, which describes how one *caudillo*, General Bernardino Caballero, came to control the national government. In time, however, his rule generated an opposition, which in July 1887 organized itself as the Centro Democrático, later renamed the Liberal Party. To meet that challenge, Caballero and his clique formalized their own political organization a month later. It was called the National Republican Association, but it became popularly known as the Colorado Party because of its red banner. With those two events, Paraguay's politics entered a new phase.

The last stage of party development, according to Huntington, concerns the system's institutionalization. This has to do with how many permanently established parties eventually occupy space in the political system. There are at least four possible scenarios: (1) one party may eliminate all others; (2) one party may emerge dominant over one or more minor parties; (3) two parties may compete more or less equally for power, with or without the presence of minor parties; and (4) many parties may compete. In the last case, a multiparty system may result either from the splintering of the larger parties, or by the emergence of wholly new parties that represent recently emergent political interests. According to Huntington, these outcomes will be determined by the manner in which the expansion of political participation takes place.[7] Beyond that, he does not venture into specifics.

Obviously, however, institutionalization implies two kinds of processes. First, there must be a growing sense of collective identity among the members of a given party if its organization is to achieve permanence. At the same time, the party must create an effective relationship with the broader society, addressing itself to the main issues of the times, enlisting support, and drawing new talent into its ranks. Failure in any of these things may result in the loss of political ground and even the fragmenting of the party organization.

Angelo Panebianco's comparative study of parties helps to illuminate how a sense of collective identity can come about. At first, party activists have no strong feelings about the organization because it is too new to inspire sentiments of loyalty and affection. Instead, people join it for purely instrumental reasons and view it as merely a "tool" for realizing certain ends; but if the organization holds together, eventually the experience of battles fought together, perhaps of sharing power or even persecution, brings about a qualitative change in the activists' attitudes. "The organization slowly loses its character as a tool: it becomes valuable in and of itself."[8] It acquires a history, replete with heroes, martyrs, slogans, and symbols.

Institutionalization may result either in highly cohesive, tightly disciplined organizations or in much looser, flexible federations. The former type of a "strongly institutionalized" party often results from long periods of persecution, as in the case of European socialist and communist parties. With them, ideology is an additional binding force that separates members from "outsiders." Conversely, an emphasis on centralization and discipline may be a response to intense competition from a mass-based rival, as in the case of the British Conservatives. In either case, strongly institutionalized parties are highly bureaucratized, with finances, recruitment, and campaigning controlled from the top. Weakly institutionalized parties, on the other hand, conform more to Maurice Duverger's concept of a "cadre" party. Their leadership tends to be poorly integrated because it consists chiefly of people who enjoy their own local power bases, composed of their personal followings. Ideology, if it exists at all, is extremely fuzzy.[9]

Paraguay's political parties are, and always have been, "weakly organized." Essentially they are federations of local notables. Personal fights and factional rifts are common to both of them. Nevertheless, as Panebianco points out himself, weakly organized parties are not necessarily at a disadvantage so far as longevity is concerned. They have the charm of flexibility, both in terms of leadership recruitment and program, whereas bureaucratic and doctrinaire parties frequently suffer permanent splits. Most of the fights inside the Liberal and Colorado parties of Paraguay get patched over in the course of time. Party dissidents eventually are reincorporated by their *co-religionarios* and the ranks close once more, with fraternal *abrazos* all around.

The other aspect of party institutionalization involves the number of competing organizations. One-party systems are fairly easy to explain, since they tend to arise from revolutionary situations in which all opposition is suppressed. It is much more difficult to say why some countries have two-party systems while others have multiparty systems. Ever since Duverger's classic study, political scientists usually begin by looking at the type of electoral regime. Single-member district systems, especially those with no runoff, are expected to produce two-party systems, whereas a multimember district system with proportional representation is likely to result in many small parties competing for power.[10] This theory, whatever its merits, is irrelevant to Paraguay for the simple reason that fair elections are practically unknown there.

Another explanation that Duverger offered was that two-party systems are "natural" because of basic contradictory tendencies in human nature and because politics usually requires the choice between two alternatives: clericals versus anticlericals, free markets versus planned economies, or tradition versus innovation. So-called compromise solutions always lean in one direction or the other. In fact, Duverger insists that the center does not really exist: it is simply the point at which the moderates from either side meet, and its fate is "to be torn asunder, buffeted, and annihilated."[11] If two-party systems are natural, then there must be some intervening variables that explain the existence of multiparty systems. For example, activists professing the same ideology may nevertheless differ over tactics, thus dividing their movement into an extremist party and a moderate one. New parties also may form when issues overlap, creating more intricate but highly passionate cleavages.

In Paraguay, only two parties, the Liberals and the Colorados, have any reasonable chance of winning power. Moreover, party identification seems to be very strong, especially among the more educated and politically active population. American writers on Paraguay often have tried to explain this strong partisan feeling that seems to pervade the society. Byron Nichols, in an opinion survey conducted in the late 1960s, found that only a small minority of Paraguayans would ever consider changing their parties, and that many of them considered party affiliation in choosing their friends and even their mates. Frederick Hicks, in another study from about the same time period, failed to find any great ideological differences between the two parties and concluded that the ferocity of their struggles was motivated by the need to control the government as the only way to escape poverty. For him, family loyalties and inherited hatreds from over a century of bitter struggles lay at the bottom of Paraguay's strong partisan attachments. He conceded, nevertheless, that those partisan attachments were ubiquitous and that politically neutral individuals were treated with suspicion.[12] Whatever the reasons, today, more than a hundred years after the formal creation of the two major parties, it is considered a serious matter to change one's affiliation.

It is difficult to pinpoint the source of the two major parties' vitality. Their membership is drawn from all the classes, while at the same time Paraguay, ethnically, is a relatively homogeneous society. Its possession of a unique bilingualism, based on the Guaraní language, is a source of strong national identity. Thus, the usual bases for ideological conflict—class, race, language, and regionalism—are absent. At the same time, it is hard to believe that such deep-seated party attachments could persist over so many generations if the main differences were only a matter of "ins" versus "outs," even with the notion of revenge thrown in. Such a situation could not possibly keep masses of followers from deserting when party fortunes declined. Although the "spoils system" is certainly a central feature of Paraguay's political life, it is obvious that partisan conflict is more than a mere scramble among opportunists.

One simple explanation, which V. O. Key offered to explain the persistence of two-party dominance in the United States, is the ability of parties, like all other human institutions, to perpetuate themselves. Among American parties, the initial lines of cleavage arose over whether to adopt the Constitution.[13] Similarly, in England, the struggle between king and Parliament gave rise to the original Tories and Whigs. So in Paraguay the contest between Caballero's incumbent Colorados and the oppositionist Liberals was followed by a bitter, protracted struggle that created emotional attachments to the parties that outlived the initial issues.

Additionally, Key argued, a presidential system of government, with popular participation in choosing a leader, tends to favor a two-party system because only one person can win and therefore it becomes necessary to seek the broadest possible support. Two large coalitions, or parties, are the result.[14] This is essentially a variant of Duverger's single-member district explanation, but one that is much more applicable to Paraguay.

It was by no means inevitable that Paraguay would have a two-party system, however, or that the Liberals and Colorados would be the two dominant parties. Both of the major parties fragmented, time and again; nevertheless, their history seems to bear out Duverger's contention that the center is an artificial position doomed to be annihilated. At various times moderates of both parties attempted to find a middle ground and even work together to establish a new governing coalition. Every such attempt ended in failure. The centrists either abandoned the effort and, after a suitable time of penance, reentered the parent party's ranks, or else gravitated to the other party. Such a factional "realignment" was responsible for ending the period of Colorado dominance in 1904 and ushering in Liberal Party rule.

The monopoly of political space by Liberals and Colorados was nearly overturned by the 1936 "February Revolution." As with the 1904 revolution, it brought to an end a long period of dominance by one of the two major parties. In this case, three decades of Liberal Party rule were interrupted a revolt of nationalistic military officers and war veterans who rejected the essentially liberal, laissez-faire principles embraced by mainstream Liberals and Colorados alike. For a year and a half Paraguay experimented with land reform and labor reform under a revolutionary dictatorship. What is more, the regime sought to establish a one-party state by outlawing all political activity except that carried on under the aegis of the official Unión Nacional Revolucionaria, forerunner of today's Febrerista Party—a minor party in the democratic socialist camp. Although the February Revolution was ended by another coup in August 1937 and the Liberal Party was restored to power, the military was now the real arbiter of who would rule. In 1940 the Liberals, badly divided and increasingly unpopular, were ousted again by nationalistic officers.

The achievement, as well as the loss, of party dominance occurs particularly in two-party systems, and it reveals another aspect of the institutionalization process. Duverger offers it as a universal rule that governing parties tend to disintegrate because of the responsibilities of power. A party in opposition needs only to attack; a party in power must produce policy, which means making choices. Choices inevitably cause disagreements, which often become hardened into factions. Not only do party militants become disaffected, but supporters also become disillusioned when their party fails to deliver on the facile promises it once made before assuming office.[15] On the other hand, Duverger fails to appreciate the strengthening effects of being able to distribute government patronage, and the debilitating effects that being out of power have on opposition parties in Third World countries like Paraguay, where a government job is one of the very few avenues to the middle class.[16]

Party fortunes rise and fall also because the world changes. If in the nature of things societies must choose between two broad alternatives, as Duverger says, then two-party systems are likely to be composed of a dominant party supported by a majority, and an opposition party that appeals to all those who disagree with that majority. The dominant, or majority, party is the one that addresses itself to the main issues of the day in such a way as to appeal to most of society's relevant political groups. In Everett Ladd's terminology, the demographic and economic makeup of the time and the relationship of groups (both friendly and unfriendly) to each other constitute what he calls a "sociological period," while the main issues that arise from that situation are the "political agenda." So long as the dominant party deals with the political agenda in such a way as to satisfy the most important social groups, there is little hope that the opposition will dislodge it from power, however fiercely it launches its attacks.[17]

There is more than a little resemblance between Ladd's theory about parties and Marx's historical materialism. Just as antagonistic classes are, according to Marx, inextricably linked by the "mode of production," so in Ladd they arise from a "sociological period" and range themselves on opposite sides of a "political agenda." Only when one sociological period gives way to another, forcing a change in the political agenda, can parties change their respective roles.

Aside from a certain determinism, which leaves out chance or charisma, such theories do help to understand how long periods of rule by a dominant party eventually reach their end, as in 1904 or 1936. But it is not just the external society that changes; the parties themselves undergo change as new generations enter and make their way up the ranks. This also has a volatile effect, because generational cleavage is not uncommon in political parties.[18] Although Panebianco does not expressly make this point, it seems logical to suppose that "strongly institutionalized" parties, with their bureaucracies and control from the top, would be more resistant to "elite circulation" than the loose, "weakly organized" parties. Panebianco does observe, however, that weakly institutionalized parties are highly permeable and allow people to "enter . . . at high levels from the outside environments in which they already occupy elite positions."[19] Since dynamic new elements are better able to capture top positions in those parties, they are more likely to reorient them to take advantage of changes in the environment, or "political agenda."

Panebianco, like Ladd, sees realignment as stemming from "environmental pressure," but he is more concerned about how such pressures translate themselves into changes of party leadership. He sees party elite circulation as being enhanced by two closely related factors.[20] First, an incumbent elite's hold on the organization may be shaken by a defeat in the political arena. Defeat shakes the members' confidence in their leaders and stimulates criticism. Even if an elite survives a challenge by purging its critics, it may do so at the cost of hollowing out the party or demoralizing the rank and file.

Defeat, which may be the result of bad luck as well as a bad response to the issues, tends to speed up a second factor, which is always present to challenge an elite: the continuous pressure of generational change. In normal times party elites may be able to minimize this by coopting "safe" elements from below, while isolating or eliminating "unstable radicals." In defeat, however, the old leaders may find that the bulk of party activists have turned to those "unstable radicals" who have long been preaching change. The "old guard" is now perceived as being too rigid and out of touch. Different ideas and new blood are now thought to be needed to keep up with the times. This leads us to studying the problem of generations.

An individual's role in society changes as he moves from childhood to youth, from youth to young adulthood, from there to middle age, and finally to old age. He does so, furthermore, as part of a generation, or age cohort, that springs from a common social environment and shares similar attitudes and behavior patterns. It is this relationship of "generation" to the life cycle that has caused some writers to view it as a fundamental concept for explaining social change, in the same way that economic, ethnic, or class factors are.

José Ortega y Gasset is perhaps the earliest modern writer to take this approach. In *The Modern Theme*, published in 1923, he argued that it is ideas that produce political and economic change, not the reverse; and while innovative ideas are always the product of individual genius, their diffusion throughout society depends on there being a sympathetic "vital sensibility," defined as a prevailing, comprehensive feeling about life or existence. That, in turn, is the product of a particular generation whose members share a common outlook that differentiates them from other generations. While it may be true that individual members of a given generation may be radicals or reactionaries, beneath their most violent conflicts there is agreement about *which* questions, issues, and aspects of life are important.[21]

Karl Mannheim is another pioneer in the development of the concept of social generations. For him, a generation only consists of the actively involved members of an age cohort. It is the political and intellectual elites who give a generation its distinctive expression, so only they are the proper subject of analysis. What they do is to engage in the creative process of absorbing the accumulated experience of their elders while also reinterpreting it in the light of new situations.

Members of a generational elite, or "generational unit," to use Mannheim's vocabulary, must be born in the same culture and in the same historical period. More important, they must share common social and intellectual experiences. It is these latter, affecting the generation at an early, impressionable age, that form its outlook and style ("entelechy"); and although individuals within the "generational unit" may vary in their opinions, their disagreements will be expressed by a distinctive vocabulary and with new concepts. Just how sharply a given generation departs from the previous one will depend on the nature of its formative experiences. Wars, revolutions, mass unemployment—the radical undermining of an established way of life—are likely to produce "generation gaps" whereas stable conditions are more likely to result in a "silent generation" whose attitudes are only moderately different.[22]

Some writers criticize the concept of generation as being difficult to operationalize. Although it is easy to point to generations within a single family, the fact that people are being born every minute in a society makes it impossible to draw the exact boundaries of a generation. Nonetheless, it is no harder to draw generational boundaries than it is to mark off boundaries for social classes, income groups, attitudinal groups, or a host of other categories commonly used in the social sciences. All such boundaries are arbitrary, to a degree, but that does not lessen their usefulness.

With respect to how wide a generation's boundaries should be, Ortega's use of fifteen-year periods has much intuitive appeal. His argument starts with the assertion that the active years in a man's life are generally between the ages of thirty and sixty. However, he adds, this span should be divided into two periods. The first, from thirty to forty-five, is that in which "a man normally finds all his ideas, the first principles, at least, of that ideology which he is to make his own." In other words, it is then that the experiences and impressions of youth are formulated into a working doctrine about life. For a generation, this is its creative period. "After forty-five he devotes himself to the full development of the inspiration he has had between thirty and forty-five." Thus, "from thirty to forty-five is the period of gestation, or creation and conflict; from forty-five to sixty, the stage of dominance and command."[23]

At either end of these active periods lie the beginning and end of the life cycle, for the individual as well as for the generation. The first fifteen years is the time of childhood, in which one learns about the world as a passive recipient of information. Participation begins during the second fifteen, when youth both receives the experience of its elders and reacts against the world it finds. The last fifteen years are a time of withdrawal from active participation as old age sets in.[24]

In sum, a historic generation is composed of people from the same society, and mostly from the same social class, who have been conditioned by shared events of their youth to have a common Zeitgeist. Whenever this is the product of dramatic experiences, the generational challenge to the received order will be more radical; and wherever such experiences are missing, the result is likely to be a "silent generation" that accepts more of the traditional values—though still modifying them to some degree.[25] Each generation takes its turn at the top of society, though not always without resistance from its elders, and attempts to modify thought and behavior to suit its particular values. The kinds of values involved in a given Zeitgeist and the amount of generational conflict they provoke help to explain how societies change from periods of tranquility to those of agitation. Although certainly not a precise instrument, generational analysis suggests that the events of today that impress adolescents should begin to produce discernible effects on the nature of public debate in fifteen to twenty years; and, if the rising generation is successful, a change in dominant attitudes and public policy in thirty years.

The march of generations naturally was reflected in the composition of Paraguay's party and government leadership. To chart this, I compiled a list of over 950 names. These were men who had been presidents, vice-presidents, cabinet ministers, Supreme Court justices, or chiefs of police in the government between 1869 and 1940. The list also included all the members of political clubs from 1858 on, the founding members of both the Centro Democrático (Liberal Party) and the National Republican Association (Colorado Party), the executive committee members of the Liberal and Colorado parties down to 1940, the executive committee of the Chaco War Veterans' Association (ANEC), and the executive committee of the Unión Nacional Revolucionaria. For each name the following information was noted, whenever possible: (1) date and place of birth; (2) level of education and where the instruction was received; (3) profession; (4) membership in political organizations; (5) executive positions held in clubs or parties, with dates; (6) government positions held, with dates;

(7) membership in party factions, if relevant; and (8) any other available data, such as in-law relations, foreign travel, business associations, or authorship of books and articles that might be helpful in understanding the individual's place in Paraguayan politics. This kind of information would indicate a number of important things about Paraguayan politics. Were there regular turnovers in the top leadership, or did the party and government elites tend to be monopolized by a gerontocracy? What kinds of people got to the top? Did this change in different time periods, and was there a difference between the two parties in this respect? To what extent were changes in the society reflected in the kinds of men being recruited to party leadership roles? The answers to these questions were expected to shed light on the parties' development, their internal quarrels, and their alternations in power.

In order to chart trends, the parties' development down to 1940 was divided into ten periods, of unequal length, whose boundaries were delimited by what I considered to be key events that influenced that development. The first period ran from the founding of Paraguay's first modern political club, the Sociedad Libertadora, in August 1858, to the installation of the first postwar government, in August 1869, after Paraguay's defeat in the War of the Triple Alliance. The second period covers the time of familial and *caudillo* rivalry, from the Triumvirate until General Caballero installed himself in power by a coup in September 1880. The third period is characterized by Caballero's political monopoly, which nevertheless gives rise to the Liberal and Colorado parties, a process that terminates in September 1887. The fourth period is also dominated by the Caballero political machine, but this is ended by the presidency of a rival Colorado leader, General Juan Bautista Egusquiza, in November 1894. Under Egusquiza and his designated successor, Emilio Aceval, moderate (*civilista*) Colorados attempt to reduce military influence and achieve a political compromise with moderate Liberals. This is the fifth period, which comes to an end with Aceval's ouster by a military coup in January 1902. During the sixth period the *caballerista* Colorados pull off a brief counterrevolution, which provokes an exodus of *civilista* Colorados into the Liberal Party and leads to the revolution of 1904. Most historians probably would use that revolution, which replaced the Colorados in power with the Liberals, as a natural cutoff date, but I have extended the sixth period to July 1908, when General Benigno Ferreira was overthrown as president. My reason for doing so is that General Ferreira and his followers in the Liberal Party represented for the most part an older generation, which included the *civilista* Colorados. As such, they reflected the politics of the past, whereas the Radical Liberals that took power in 1908 were mostly a new group of men.

The seventh period, from July 1908 to March 1912, revolves around the controversial Colonel Albino Jara, military chief of the coup that ousted Ferreira. His ambitions split the Radical Liberals and led to a civil war that ended only with his death. In the confusion various governments, including a brief Colorado restoration, took turns in power. The Radical Liberals returned to power in March 1912 and imposed peace of a sort. Eventually, however, fresh quarrels arose that split them and led to a second civil war. Order was restored at last in July 1923. Thus, the eighth period is from March 1912 to July 1923. The ninth period, which runs until February 1936, was as turbulent as its predecessors. Although the majority faction of the Radical Liberals consolidated its hold on the government, among the educated population at large (the only politically important public at that time) the whole ideology of liberalism was giving way to xenophobic nationalism. The source of this was Bolivia's encroachment on what Paraguayans considered to be their rightful claim to the Chaco Territory. This led to the Chaco War (1932–35), which ended in a Paraguayan victory. Despite this, nationalistic opinion was dissatisfied both with the Liberals' prewar diplomacy and their conduct of the war. On 17 February 1936 a military coup brought to power a nationalistic revolutionary government. The tenth period starts with the February Revolution, continues through the counterrevolution of August 1937, and includes the Liberals' partial restoration under the governments of Félix Paíva and General José Félix Estigarribia. It ends, as does this study, with General Estigarribia's death in September 1940 and the coming to power of a nationalistic military regime headed by General Higinio Morínigo.

As might be expected, background information was easier to get on men who entered politics during the later periods. It was not always easy to establish the age of those whose careers were confined to the mid-nineteenth century, especially if they did not occupy the very topmost positions. Another measure of elite turnover, and (indirectly) of generational change, besides age was to classify individuals as to when they first entered politics in a major way. A "major way" could be interpreted so broadly as to include serving in a government post, joining a club or party, writing editorials for a newspaper, or running for office. Those who entered politics at more or less the same time have been designated in this study as a "promotion," following the Spanish usage of the word *promoción* to designate cohorts. There are ten "promotions," corresponding to the ten periods into which this seventy-year period was divided for analytical purposes. Strictly speaking, of course, a promotion is not the same thing as a generation because people of widely different ages may become politically active at the same time. Still, in the passage of time promotions succeed each other as generations do. There is a tendency for the average age of each promotion to be younger than the preceding ones as new people come in and old age does the work of attrition. Consequently, there is a large overlap between promotions and generations; and in any case it is the handiest device for overcoming shortcomings in the available data on age.

Taken altogether, the use of "periods," "promotions," "age sets," and other personal data allowed this study to go behind the parade of historical events to analyze the human dynamics of political change and party development. Though only a small, remote republic, Paraguay's experience nevertheless fits easily within the general literature on political institutionalization. In turn, the evolution of its parties, charted by the methods used here, may add useful knowledge to that literature.

one

THE FAMILY ORIGINS

On New Year's Day, 1869, Brazilian, Argentine, and Uruguayan troops occupied Paraguay's capital city, Asunción, after four years of bitter, bloody fighting. The triumphant soldiers rampaged through the almost deserted city, searching for booty and women but found very little on which to wreak their vengeance. Most of the inhabitants had abandoned the capital at the command of their leader, Marshal Francisco Solano López. After the fashion of the Russians retreating before Napoleon's armies, they followed him northeastward, into the forests, leaving in their wake burned fields and abandoned farms. Fighting would continue for another fifteen months until finally, on 1 March 1870, López was cornered and killed at Cerro Corá, near the Brazilian border. His grand scheme to make Paraguay the region's paramount military power had died long before.

For Paraguay, the costs of the war were devastating. The victors claimed vast tracts of territory and saddled the country with huge war debts. A formerly modest but self-sufficient nation of farmers was ruined by the pillaging of marauding soldiers and the forcible uprooting by López of the population Most appalling of all was the cost in human lives: a great many people had perished from fighting, hunger, and disease. Rather than surrender when he knew his cause to be hopeless, López had continued to hurl his loyal followers at the superior enemy forces. By the war's end the thinning ranks of his bedraggled army were being filled by young boys between the ages of ten and fourteen. All along the path of his retreat the horrified Allies found thousands of people wandering homeless, literally dying in heaps along the roads from starvation and exhaustion.[1]

This war, the War of the Triple Alliance (in reference to the alliance of Brazil, Argentina, and Uruguay against Paraguay), proved to be a watershed in Paraguay's history. Prewar and postwar Paraguay were radically different; indeed, one can say that the war's consequences were revolutionary. During most of its existence after independence, prewar Paraguay was governed as a strong, centralized dictatorship under three men: José Gaspar Rodríguez de Francia (1813–40), Carlos Antonio López (1844–62), and Francisco Solano López (1862–70). Its guarantee of continued independence rested upon a strong army, and since Paraguay's resources for sustaining its military were only modest the state took a leading role in directing the economy. Most of the country's simple industries and much of its land were publicly owned; everything else, including trade, was closely regulated by the state. All this changed after the war. Paraguay's army was destroyed, leaving the country open to interference by its larger neighbors, Argentina and Brazil. Instead of the stability provided by Francia and the Lópezes, factions and parties struggled for power, often aided by foreign interests. Debt-ridden and starved for revenue, the state sold off its property to private, often foreign, investors.

In brief, Paraguay passed from an autocratic, state-directed pattern of development, which we may call the era of the indigenous Socialist State, to one in which the role of government was deemphasized in favor of private initiative, while individuals were accorded constitutional rights and liberties against state power. This I have called the period of the Liberal State, or the Liberal Era.

The Liberal Era began in the last year of the war, after Marshal López abandoned Asunción. More specifically, it may be said to have begun on 15 August 1869, when the Allies allowed a provisional government, formed of anti-López Paraguayans, to take office. This government, in the form of a Triumvirate, declared the marshal to be an outlaw and confiscated all his property. The provisional government lasted for just over a year, until a constitutional convention completed its work and elections could be held. The Constitution of 1870 was a classic liberal document, patterned after both the United States and Argentine constitutions. It provided for a popularly elected democratic republic with three branches of government, including a bicameral legislature. To prevent a recurrence of dictatorship, no president was allowed to serve two consecutive terms. Slavery and other forms of servitude were abolished; all citizens were declared to be equal. The usual liberal freedoms—press, speech, and association—were guaranteed; private property was to be inviolate. The Constitution of 1870 remained in effect until 15 August 1940, when it was replaced by another, which many critics have called "totalitarian" because it facilitated the suspension of constitutional liberties, strengthened the executive power at the expense of the legislative and judicial, and restricted property rights. The Liberal Era therefore covers seven decades, bounded by the establishment of the Triumvirate on one end and the promulgation of the Constitution of 1940 on the other.

Many patriotic Paraguayans consider the Liberal Era to be an "Age of Brass," in contrast to the "Golden Age" of Francia and the Lópezes. Certainly it is true that with the passing of the absolutist state there arose the anarchy of *caudillismo*. Presidents often failed to finish their terms and revolts sometimes took on the proportions of a civil war, the most notable being in 1873–74, 1904, 1911–12, and 1922–23. Distracted by its internal troubles, Paraguay remained backward and poor. Susceptible to foreign pressure, it was practically an economic satellite of Argentina. Finally, the Liberal Era was discredited and brought to a close by the second great war in Paraguay's history, the Chaco War (1932–35), for which a series of weak governments left it unprepared.

On the other hand, it is well to remember that the stability of the Socialist State was purchased at the cost of liberty. There was no rule of law or right of appeal from the dictator's whims. The regime was accepted by the great mass of peasants, who were allowed to lease small plots from the state and did not mind its paternalistic controls; but the educated and wealthier citizens chafed as trade dwindled and the school system was reduced to only the primary grades. To speak out, however prominent the critic, meant jail or exile, along with the confiscation of one's property. This total suppression of dissent proved to be the regime's fatal flaw. Under a cautious, conservative dictator like Francia or Carlos Antonio López, the state kept to a more or less steady course; but a megalomaniac like Francisco Solano López had no check upon him to prevent his leading the country into disaster.

It is probably most accurate to view the Liberal Era, with all its shortcomings, as the seedtime of modern Paraguayan politics. Besides laying down the fundamental social and economic structures that persist right to the present, it gave rise to the two traditional parties, the National Republican Association (better known as the Colorado Party) and the Liberal Party. Both were founded in 1887, the Liberals (known at the time as the Centro Democrático) in July and the Colorados in August. Since then they have always dominated Paraguay's essentially two-party system, overcoming every attempt by third-party movements to supplant them. In this respect, Paraguay is different from most Latin American countries. The age and durability of its party organizations is unusual in a region better known for its personalistic and ephemeral parties, and for its lack of enduring political loyalties.

Paraguayans tend to explain the persistence of their two old parties as being the products of opposing political traditions whose rivalry goes back to the founding of the Republic, in 1811. Justo Prieto, whose *Manual del ciudadano liberal paraguayo* (1953) was for many years the Liberal Party's official "bible," saw a direct connection between the men who founded the Liberal State in 1869–70 and those members of the first postindependence junta who opposed Francia's bid for political supremacy in 1813. Nothing in official Paraguay from Francia up to the Triumvirate was considered by Prieto to be in the Liberal tradition. Colorados would agree. For example, Epifanio Méndez Fleitas, in *Lo histórico y lo antihistorico en el Paraguay* (1976), saw the roots of his party growing out of the era of Francia and the Lópezes. The Colorados' first great postwar leader, General Bernardino Caballero, fought loyally beside Marshal Solano López to the end. Thus, Colorados like Méndez argue that their party is the continuation of *lopismo*, which in the sloganeering of modern Paraguayan politics is the equivalent of nationalism. This is in contrast to the Liberals, who, by condemning López, are forever painted as being "antinational."[2] As we shall see, both of these attitudes are based on myths that do not stand the test of close analysis; yet the myths are important factors influencing the nature of political debate in Paraguay.

To separate myth from reality it is necessary to trace the origins of the modern party system, which takes us much further back in time than the parties' formal appearance in 1887. The Colorado and Liberal organizations grew out of several political clubs that began appearing in 1869 with the objective of controlling the new Liberal state. Formed around strong personalities and families, these clubs frequently broke up and re-formed in different combinations, much like a kaleidoscope. Ideology had little or no role in all of this because most of the leading political figures of the early Liberal Era emerged from a common background: the controversial Paraguayan Legion.

The Paraguayan Legion was started in April 1865 by a group of exiles who offered their services as soldiers to Argentina and Brazil at the beginning of the War of the Triple Alliance. Subsequently, the Legion was attached to the Argentine army and fought against López. Out of its ranks came the first political clubs and most of the personnel that governed Paraguay in the 1870s. The Paraguayan Legion, in turn, was created by a self-proclaimed government in exile called the Asociación Paraguaya, which was formed in December 1864. The first Legionnaires were recruited from the Asociación's younger members. But many of the Asociación's leaders had belonged to a still earlier club known as the Sociedad Libertadora, which appeared in August 1858 to rally Paraguayan exiles against the dictatorship of Carlos Antonio López. Thus the seedbed of the political parties that sprouted during the Liberal Era lies far back in the time of the Socialist State. To understand the nature and outlook of those parties we must begin there, with the men who made up the Sociedad Libertadora, the Asociación Paraguaya, and the Paraguayan Legion.

THE EXILE ORGANIZATIONS

Many of Paraguay's leading families had chosen the path to exile ever since Francia claimed absolute power in 1813 and began to create an isolated, self-sufficient autocracy. As merchants with commercial ties to Buenos Aires, some had opposed independence in favor of federation with Argentina. Another wave of exiles began descending upon Buenos Aires after Carlos Antonio López got a handpicked Congress to make him dictator in 1844. The bitterness at being ruined economically and uprooted from their homeland drove some of the exiles to extreme positions, as when Carlos Loizaga and Fernando Iturburu—both future leaders of the Sociedad Libertadora, Asociación Paraguaya, and Paraguayan Legion— wrote to the notorious Argentine tyrant, Juan Manuel Rosas, in September 1851, urging him to invade Paraguay and incorporate it into the Argentine Confederation.[3]

The approach to Rosas was both a mistake and a dead end. A few months later Rosas himself was on his way to exile and Argentina was in the hands of a new generation of reformers whose outlook was shaped by British, French, and American liberal ideas: men such as Juan Bautista Alberdi, Bartolomé Mitre, and Domingo Sarmiento. Buenos Aires soon became a refuge for liberals from other lands, among whom was Francisco Bilbao, a Chilean political exile. Bilbao seems to have circulated widely in the Paraguayan exile community, for when the Sociedad Libertadora was founded, on 2 August 1858, he was appointed to be the chief editor of its newspaper, *El Grito Paraguayo*. The Sociedad's statutes reflected the liberal environment in which it was born, for they promised to devote the club to fighting for a democratic Paraguay in which constitutional government would guarantee the rights of liberty, equality, and property.

Among the founders of the Sociedad were Loizaga and Iturburu. There were other members of the Loizaga and Iturburu families on the executive committee as well, along with a rather large contingent from the aristocratic Machaín family and a couple of members of the Guanes family. In effect, the club was a coalition of prominent Paraguayan families, with a sprinkling of young, up-and-coming individuals like Pío Otoniel Peña. Peña, in turn, was related by marriage to another large and powerful family, the Decouds. There was only one of them (Angel Decoud) represented on the Sociedad's executive committee, but the Decouds would weigh heavily in most subsequent exile organizations.

The Sociedad Libertadora achieved relatively little beyond issuing a manifesto calling for the overthrow of Carlos Antonio López and publishing a few editions of its newspaper. Little is known about it after the first few months of its existence. Then, on 19 December 1864, a new club, the Asociación Paraguaya was founded. This was in response to a new wave of exiles from Paraguay, following the seizure of power there by Francisco Solano López in September 1862, after his father's death. Attempts by a handful of Paraguayan liberals to prevent the continuation of one-man rule had led to a brutal crackdown whose shock waves reached Buenos Aires. Like the Sociedad, the Asociación's declared purpose was to liberate Paraguay from the tyrant, López, and replace him with a democratically elected government. But the Asociación went even further: two days after its founding, the club issued a manifesto proclaiming itself to be a government in exile. Although it never was recognized as such by any other government, the Asociación's leaders did form the core of the provisional government installed in power by the Allies in 1869—in large part, no doubt, because they were the only organized alternative to López.

Fifteen men constituted the original Asociación Paraguaya, and from the very beginning they divided into two factions whose loyalties ran along family lines. The larger group of eight formed around the Iturburu family, which provided a core of four, headed by Fernando Iturburu. Aligned with them were the Loizagas, a representative of the Recalde family, and one of the Machaíns (Evaristo). The smaller, seven-man faction had the Decoud family, led by Juan Francisco Decoud, at its center. Gregorio Machaín was part of this group, as was another man who would figure prominently in the future, Jaime Sosa Escalada.

Over the next four months more were recruited, until by April 1865 there were thirty-six men in all. Seventeen supported the Iturburu faction, fourteen were behind the Decouds, and the remaining five seem to have been not only neutral but inactive. The Asociación's first executive committee had a *decouista*, Gregorio Machaín, as its president, but the other officers were *iturburistas*. Succeeding presidents, Carlos Loizaga and José Díaz de Bedoya, were from Iturburu's faction. Both were to serve also on the postwar Triumvirate.

Each of the factions had its share of talent and influence. Besides counting on the support of the Loizaga, Guanes, and Recalde families, the Iturburus enlisted two men who later would become president of Paraguay: Salvador Jovellanos and Juan Bautista Egusquiza. They also had the backing of Federico Guillermo Báez, who presided over the opening session of 1870 Constitutional Convention. The Decouds not only had the bulk of the Machaín family as allies, but also individuals of talent like Jaime Sosa Escalada, Pío Otoniel Peña, and Benigno Ferreira—the last of whom also became president of Paraguay. Moreover, the Decoud family itself produced two exceptional men: José Segundo Decoud and Juan José Decoud. José Segundo, whose career covered the last three decades of the century, was perhaps the greatest statesman his country produced in that period, besides being the founder of the Colorado Party. Juan José, a talented journalist, might have had an equally brilliant career, but it was cut short by his untimely death in 1871, at the age of twenty-two.

War broke out in November 1864, just a month before the Asociación was started. López seized a Brazilian vessel on the Paraguay River in retaliation for Brazil's invasion of Uruguay, with whom Paraguay had an alliance, and then proceeded to break relations with Brazil and the new Uruguayan puppet government. Argentina entered the war in March 1865 after López, having been refused permission to cross its territory in order to attack the Brazilian state of Rio Grande do Sul, sent his troops across anyway. One of the Asociación's first acts was to send Fernando Iturburu and Carlos Loizaga to Rio de Janeiro, in January 1865, to ask for Brazil's recognition of it as a government in exile in return for a pledge to raise an army of 2,000 Paraguayan exiles to help defeat López. The cautious Brazilians withheld diplomatic recognition but encouraged the Asociación to form its Paraguayan Legion. The Legion was duly launched on 22 April and immediately offered its services to the Brazilian army. By this time, however, the Brazilians had decided to do nothing to encourage any organization that might become the nucleus of an independent Paraguayan government after the war, and so rebuffed the offer. The Asociación next turned to Argentina, which had just declared war on López, and found President Bartolomé Mitre more receptive. In May 1865 he gave the Legion his approval to attach itself to the Argentine army.[4]

Far from being a shameful act, joining the Allies to fight against López was a noble thing, in the Legionnaires' eyes, for liberty was an ideal that transcended national boundaries. Héctor Decoud reminds us that they had before them the example of the 5,000 Brazilians and 2,000 Uruguayans who were part of the 23,000-man army that liberated Argentina from Juan Manuel Rosas. For Liberals, the "rights of man" were superior to reasons of state or national sovereignty, and despotism—even if cloaked in patriotism—could never be tolerated anywhere in the world by free men. In bringing their fellow countrymen freedom and enlightenment, the Legionnaires saw themselves as benefactors, not traitors.[5]

The Paraguayan Legion went through three phases of recruitment. The first Legionnaires joined in April 1865, recruited mainly from the Decoud, Iturburu, Loizaga, Machaín, and Recalde families. José Díaz de Bedoya, president of the Asociación Paraguaya, appointed Fernando Iturburu first in command, with the rank of colonel. Second in command was Juan Francisco Decoud, whose rank was lieutenant colonel. No sooner did the Legion set up its training camp, however, than Iturburu and Decoud fell to quarreling. The feud dragged on from June to October, with each side appealing to the Asociación's executive committee. When the latter finally backed Colonel Iturburu, on 3 October, the Decouds and Machaíns, together with their allies, withdrew from both the Legion and the Asociación.

Before that final break, however, there was a turn of events that would strongly influence the Legion's development—and, through it, the development of postwar Paraguay. A Paraguayan detachment of 12,000 men under Colonel Antonio de la Cruz Estigarribia, sent to attack Rio Grande do Sul, was surrounded by a superior Allied force at Uruguaiana in late August. Although the Paraguayans' position was hopeless, their fanatical bravery in previous battles convinced the Allied commanders that wiping them out would entail heavy casualties, so the Legion was asked to send a party to convince their countrymen to surrender. Three men, Jaime Sosa Escalada, José Segundo Decoud, and Benigno Ferreira—all decouistas—were chosen. They were successful, for on 18 September Colonel Estigarribia, his forces reduced by now to only 5,000, surrendered. The common soldiers were made prisoners of war, while the officers were free to reside anywhere outside of Paraguay. About 600 of the officers and men chose to join the Paraguayan Legion.[6]

The Legion's second phase began, therefore, with this sudden influx of new recruits, which happened almost simultaneously with the withdrawal of the decouistas. It managed to field a cavalry regiment and an infantry battalion, under Colonel Iturburu's leadership. Although it played no prominent role in the war, it entered Asunción in January 1869 with the Allied armies.

The third phase began in that same month, when Iturburu reorganized his forces for the final campaign against Marshal López. Many of his men left the service after returning to Paraguay, but he was urged by Mariano Varela, the Argentine foreign minister, to recruit their replacements in order to pursue López's retreating army. About 377 men signed up, some of them veterans of the old Legion and others new volunteers who escaped from López's control and now described themselves as "victims of a most cruel and destructive tyranny." During the next several months more desertions from López's army brought the new Legion's numbers up to around 500.[7]

THE PROVISIONAL GOVERNMENT

Immediately after taking Asunción, the Allies turned to the task of setting up a pliable government staffed by friendly Paraguayans. This was complicated by two factors. First, Argentina and Brazil, the principal allies, quickly turned into rivals as each sought to control Paraguay and exclude the other's influence. Second, the Paraguayan exiles, who would have to run the new government, were still divided between *iturburistas* and *decouistas*. Each of these factions organized a political club to enhance its ability to gain ascendancy in the postwar state.

The first to appear was the Club Unión Republicana, which was founded on 31 March 1869 at a meeting held in Colonel Fernando Iturburu's home. What was most remarkable about this meeting was that it not only brought together men from the Paraguayan Legion and Asociación Paraguaya, such as Salvador Jovellanos, Federico Guillermo Báez, Juan Bautista Egusquiza, and José Díaz de Bedoya, but there was an impressive contingent of young men who might be considered as residuals of the old López regime. Cándido Bareiro had been López's commercial agent in Europe. Unable to return to Paraguay because of the Allies' blockade, he had escaped the debacle, but now he was soon to become the leading spokesman of the surviving *lopistas*. Félix Egusquiza had been López's commercial agent in Buenos Aires. Cayo Miltos (who became the club's president), his brother, Fulgencio, and Juan Antonio Jara had been in Europe during the war, on scholarships granted by López. Adolfo Saguier had once held such a scholarship too, but he had returned in time to enlist in the Paraguayan army, only to fall prisoner at Uruguaiana.

Actually, the two groups composing the Club Unión Republicana were not so dissimilar in their background. Félix Egusquiza was Juan Bautista's elder brother; Díaz de Bedoya's elder brother had once been López's finance minister; and Jovellanos had studied in Paris on a scholarship from López but later became influenced against the regime by his Argentine wife. Saguier's sojourn in Argentina during the war brought him into friendly contact with many anti-López exiles, although he did not join the Legion.

According to the signatures affixed to the Club Unión Republicana's first manifesto, which stated its aims and principles, it had 338 members. Héctor Decoud claims that this was an exaggeration: that many of the signers were inactive and indifferent, and that quite a few names were taken from tombstones at the cemetery. Admittedly, Decoud is a hostile source, but F. Arturo Bordón, a later Liberal writer, agrees with him and sets the membership at closer to 100. Of those, 74 were Legionnaires who followed Colonel Iturburu's political lead.[8]

The Decouds responded by organizing the Club del Pueblo on 26 June 1869. Its membership was smaller, estimated at between fifty and sixty members, of whom nine were ex-Legionnaires. Only one Decoud appeared on the executive committee: José Segundo, who filled the post of secretary. But if the Decouds preferred to work quietly behind the scenes, they were ably represented by a number of talented allies such as Jaime Sosa Escalada, José Mateo Collar, and Juan G. González. The first two men would become cabinet ministers in future governments, while González was destined to be president of the Republic.

Two other Club del Pueblo members worth noting were Rufino Taboada, a member of the executive committee, and his younger brother, Antonio. Both had served in the Legion. This last statement raises a sensitive point, which may as well be dealt with at the beginning of this study. Liberal Party historians, who are naturally touchy on the subject, often claim that not a single founding member of the Centro Democrático—later renamed Liberal Party—had ever been in the Paraguayan Legion. Héctor Decoud, however, tells us that Antonio Taboada, who became the Centro Democrático's first president, joined the Paraguayan Legion, along with his brother, after being taken prisoner at Uruguaiana. Both he and Rufino were given the rank of alférez, which might best be translated as "second lieutenant."[9]

Once founded, the two clubs immediately began trying to enlist the support of Argentina and Brazil, who were trying to work out the details for establishing a provisional government. The politics involved were extremely opportunistic and byzantine, with no clear lines of influence. The Brazilian minister in Paraguay, José Maria Silva Paranhos, originally put his support behind the Club Unión Republicana because he feared the Decouds were too pro-Argentine. Iturburu, meanwhile, was negotiating secretly with the Argentines to name General Juan Andrés Gelly y Obes, an Argentine officer who was Paraguayan by birth, as provisional president. The Brazilians quickly vetoed this project as soon as they learned of it, whereupon the Allies agreed upon the cumbersome compromise of setting up a triumvirate to govern Paraguay.[10]

But who would form the triumvirate? And how would it be chosen? Colonel Iturburu proposed himself and two friends from the Club Unión Republicana: José Díaz de Bedoya and Félix Egusquiza. Lieutenant Colonel Decoud was able to sow doubt in Paranhos's mind, however, that this would result in a decidedly pro-Argentine government—although he, Decoud, was himself very pro-Argentine. Indeed, Decoud might have supplanted Iturburu as the Brazilians' candidate but for the fact that his son, Juan José, kept turning out anti-Brazilian polemics in an exile newspaper published in Corrientes, Argentina. Decoud tried to counter this by drawing up a more conciliatory list that included himself, Carlos Loizaga, and Cirilo Antonio Rivarola. Or, as an alternative to any of the three, Decoud proposed Serapio Machaín.

Decoud's proposal of Loizaga and Machaín was significant, for it reflected a gradual shift in the balance of power toward the *decouista* side. Loizaga, a former ally of Iturburu, had switched camps; and the Macháin family, which originally had held aloof from the Club del Pueblo, now reestablished its former alliance with the Decouds. This apparently split the club, however, with its vice-president, José Maria Mazó, and the Taboada brothers going over to the *iturburistas*.[11]

The inclusion of Cirilo A. Rivarola on Decoud's list was significant too, for he was a favorite of Paranhos. His father, an army captain in the fight for independence, had opposed granting absolute power to both Francia and Carlos Antonio López, and spent years under house arrest for his bravery. Cirilo inherited his father's temperament. Having trained for the law, he too was jailed, because of a quarrel with one of Solano López's district commanders. Released in 1868, he was drafted as a common soldier. He fought bravely, was taken prisoner, and escaped. He eventually rose to be a sergeant, but when some wounded soldiers he was in charge of drowned during a torrential downpour he was whipped and sent to the front lines. Taken prisoner again, this time he freely gave the Brazilians much information about the Paraguayan positions and expressed such hatred of López that he rose to high favor with his captors.[12]

After much negotiation, the Allies and the rival Paraguayan clubs devised a complicated method of choosing the governing triumvirate. On 22 July 1869 some 130 leading Paraguayans met in the National Theater to select twenty-one delegates. Those would then confer separately and pick five of their number to be electors; finally, the five electors would name the triumvirate. This time Decoud's group won a majority of the twenty-one delegates. They, in turn, chose Ignacio Sosa, José Segundo Decoud, and Mateo Collar—all of the Club del Pueblo—as electors, along with Bernardino Valiente of the Club Unión Republicana and Miguel Palacios, an independent.

Despite Colonel Decoud's diplomacy, Paranhos still favored the Club Unión Republicana, so these results displeased him. In a high-handed fashion he sought to impose his own five electors, all *iturburistas*: Félix Egusquiza, Cándido Bareiro, Colonel Iturburu, Carlos Saguier, and José Díaz de Bedoya. With that, the *decouistas* threatened to walk out. Passions rose on the floor of the convention, reaching a peak when Benigno Ferreira, a *decouista*, threatened to kill Félix Egusquiza for his scheming. The latter took this threat seriously and left both the meeting and the country, never to return. Eventually Paranhos and the Decouds reached a compromise. The five originally chosen electors were allowed to name their triumvirate, which consisted of Colonel Decoud, José Díaz de Bedoya (an *iturburista*), and Carlos Loizaga. When Paranhos continued to demur,

Colonel Decoud, seeing that he was the stumbling block, withdrew in favor of Cirilo A. Rivarola. Paranhos accepted this, and Paraguay had its first postwar government.[13]

From the very beginning Rivarola dominated the Triumvirate, installing himself in the old Government Palace and issuing orders without bothering to consult the other triumvirs. In return for the *decouistas'* support, he placed their leading men in key positions. Colonel Decoud became head of the police, Juan José Decoud was made the attorney general, and José Segundo Decoud was named Rivarola's private secretary. Benigno Ferreira took over as captain general of the ports, with a militia under his command; Facundo Machaín was placed in charge of organizing a system of courts, and his chief assistant, Juansilvano Godoi, became head of the civil courts; Serapio Machaín assumed the post of Loizaga's secretary; Sinforiano Alcorta was named intendant of Asunción; and Jaime Sosa Escalada headed the capital's financial, educational, and public works departments. The only non-*decouista* at the second level was the "independent" Miguel Palacios, who served Díaz de Bedoya as his secretary.

Installed in office, the Triumvirate faced a disheartening situation. Much of the city had been destroyed by fire, and of those buildings still standing most were requisitioned by the occupation forces. There were terrible shortages of food, clothing, and medical supplies. Paraguayans who straggled back to the town, most of them women and children, often had only the trees for shelter and were forced to go from house to house begging for something to eat. To its credit, the provisional government did what it could by way of emergency aid, but it had no real power and no money. Work camps were set up on abandoned farms in order to grow crops; orphans and invalids were taken in; and a school building program was started in order to provide jobs. To pay for these projects, the government levied taxes on stamped paper, license fees, and customs duties. It got little or no help from the Allies, who after four years of bitter war were in a punitive frame of mind. Beyond these relief measures, the provisional government took steps to create necessary political institutions: a police force, courts, a post office, schools, a customshouse. Slavery and other forms of servitude were abolished. López and his Irish mistress, Eliza Lynch, were declared outlaws and their property was confiscated. And, as an indication of their determination to make Paraguay a progressive, liberal state, the Guaraní Indian language was banned from the schools.[14]

In the meantime, the Triumvirate was becoming a one-man operation. Cirilo Rivarola completely dominated Carlos Loizaga, an elderly, bookish man with little taste for practical politics. José Díaz de Bedoya, meanwhile, had left the scene on a mission to raise money in Argentina by selling all the silver ornaments the Legion had collected from the various Catholic churches. He simply pocketed the proceeds and never returned. With his departure, the *decouistas* were firmly in control of the government—but only of a provisional government. To solidify their control would require the calling of elections and the holding of a constitutional convention. This they proceeded to do.

ELECTORAL RIVALRIES

It is axiomatic in Paraguayan politics that, failing a miracle, the government's party always wins. After all, it supervises the polls, counts the votes, and decides all appeals. Nevertheless, the Decouds, Machaíns, and their allies were put on notice that the electoral campaign would be bitter when, on 3 April 1870, the opposition brought to an angry close a meeting held at the National Theater to explore the possibility of a single, compromise list of candidates. Led by Cándido Bareiro, those outside the governing circle walked out of the meeting, calling upon the Allied occupation forces to exert greater supervision over the electoral process. Another meeting, scheduled for 5 May, never took place because Bareiro and several heavily armed men, seconded by some Argentine soldiers, occupied the National Theater and refused entrance to anyone else. After that, both sides went their separate ways, determined to win at any cost the elections, which were now set for 3 July.[15]

In the meantime, the original political clubs had disappeared to make way for new factional alignments. As we saw, the incorporation of the Machaín family into the Decouds' Club del Pueblo had created tensions that led some of the original members to go over to the Club Unión Republicana. Over the next few months the Club del Pueblo's president, Ignacio Sosa, together with three other executive committee members, dropped out of politics, for reasons that remain obscure. A reorganization followed, leading to the formation, on 23 March 1870, of the new Gran Club del Pueblo, with Facundo Machaín as president.

If the purpose of the Club del Pueblo was to influence the composition of the provisional government, that of the Gran Club was to organize mass support in the forthcoming elections. As before, the core membership was the Decoud and Machaín families, joined now by the Guanes, Recalde, and Fleitas families. José Segundo Decoud served as the organization's secretary and his brother, Juan José, sat on the executive committee as a *vocal* (simple member). Of the fifty-two founding members, twenty-four had been previously active: ten as members of the Asociación

Paraguaya or Sociedad Libertadora, fourteen as Legionnaires, nine as members of the ex-Club del Pueblo, and ten as switchovers from the Club Unión Republicana. This last group, the switchovers, was significant because it included the Guanes and Recalde families, Zacarías Jara, Salvador Jovellanos, and Federico Guillermo Báez, all of whom had been followers of Iturburu. Bernardo Recalde became vice-president of the Gran Club, while Báez and Jovellanos served on the executive committee as *vocales*. Finally, the Gran Club's leadership included the long-time *decouista* loyalists, men like Jaime Sosa Escalada, Juansilvano Godoi, and Benigno Ferreira. Ferreira, the "hard man" of the bunch, headed up the Gran Club's security forces, which were organized in the face of growing violence on the part of the opposition. But if Ferreira represented the club's "muscle," its "brains" were reflected in its newspaper, *La Regeneración*, financed by Colonel Juan Francisco Decoud and ably edited by his sons, Juan José and José Segundo. Polemical but highly literate, it stood for the advanced liberal causes of the time: separation of church and state, civil marriage, abolition of standing armies, full political rights for women, free immigration, and honest, democratic government. It excoriated Solano López and all he symbolized.[16]

The opposition also had regrouped, abandoning the old Club Unión Republicana and adopting the name of Club del Pueblo. Whether or not this was a ploy to confuse the public (the name change occurred a day after the Gran Club del Pueblo was founded), the new group was far stronger in talent, despite the desertions noted previously. It too had a party newspaper, *La Voz del Pueblo*, edited by an Argentine physician, Miguel Gallegos. Colonel Fernando Iturburu was its president, but he was surrounded by even stronger personalities. Chief among these, perhaps, was Cándido Bareiro, a proud, intelligent, but ruthless man who became the leader of the remnants of the old López regime. He had a particular talent for organization and strategy, but he was disinclined to compromise. Politically isolated at first, his star would rise as more war veterans and war prisoners returned to the capital.

Another faction formed around Cayo and Fulgencio Miltos, two brilliant brothers who had been educated in France. Their importance to the Club del Pueblo derived from the fact that they were the intellectual equals of the Decouds. Besides their old friend and business partner, Juan Antonio Jara, they drew to their circle ambitious men like the Taboada brothers and Juan G. González. Yet a third faction followed the leadership of Juan Bautista Gill, who had studied medicine in Buenos Aires but returned to Paraguay before receiving his degree in order to enlist in the army as a medic. By the time he was taken prisoner by the Brazilians in 1869, he had lost all enthusiasm for López and joined the Paraguayan

Legion for the final campaign. After the war he cultivated his Brazilian connections with an eye to achieving the presidency. Wily and unscrupulous, he was at least Bareiro's equal as a political strategist. Chief among his followers was his cousin, Higinio Uriarte, who also had been in the Legion.

One of the impressive aspects of Paraguay's politics at this time was the extreme youth of its principal figures. Facundo Machaín, the Gran Club's president, was only twenty-three years old in 1870. Juan José Decoud also was twenty-three, and José Segundo was twenty-two. Jaime Sosa Escalada was twenty-four, as was Benigno Ferreira, while Juansilvano Godoi was a mere twenty. At the other extreme, Cirilo Rivarola was all of twenty-nine. On the whole, the opposition Club del Pueblo was a little older. Rufino Taboada was twenty-six, Cayo Miltos twenty-seven, Juan B. Gill thirty, and Cándido Bareiro was a practically ancient thirty-six! The collapse of the old Socialist State had thus opened up a wide field for talent and ambition, making it possible for young men to rise much faster than would have been the case under stabler conditions. But at the same time, it brought to the fore men who were inexperienced and, with the vigor and impatience of youth, often went to extremes.

The election campaign for the Constitutional Convention deepened the division between the two clubs. On 29 June, just four days before the voting, Bareiro's faction attempted to take over the militia's barracks and stage a coup, but was foiled. And on election day Rufino Taboada seized the polling station in the Asunción city parish of Encarnación, beat up Facundo Machaín, and tore up the registration list. But he was arrested and jailed by Colonel Decoud; and in any case these tactics failed to help the Club del Pueblo, which elected only twelve delegates in comparison with forty-two for the Gran Club del Pueblo.[17]

THE CONSTITUTIONAL CONVENTION

The Constitutional Convention opened its sessions on 15 August 1870, with Colonel Federico Guillermo Báez (Asociación Paraguaya, Paraguayan Legion, Gran Club del Pueblo) acting as temporary chairman. The first meetings were devoted to choosing a permanent chair for the sessions, which turned out to be José Segundo Decoud, and appointing committees to draft different parts of the constitution.

While all this ordinary business was going on, Facundo Machaín and Juansilvano Godoi were hatching a plot that amounted to a coup against the provisional government, for the purpose of making Machaín president of the Republic. The idea was to convert the Constitutional Convention into a kind of parliament that would install a new executive. To facilitate this, Machaín and Godoi convinced Carlos Loizaga to resign his position as triumvir. Since José Díaz de Bedoya already had abandoned his post, that left Cirilo Rivarola as the sole executive. On 31 August a majority of the convention delegates declared the existing provisional government to be dissolved and named Machaín to succeed Rivarola, with the title of president.[18]

What is surprising about this series of maneuvers is that Machaín and Godoi even succeeded in getting Cayo Miltos and Colonel Iturburu to go along with it. In fact, it was Miltos who went to Rivarola to inform him that he was being replaced for his "incompetence." On the other hand, neither José Segundo Decoud nor Benigno Ferreira approved of these procedures, which not only exceeded the convention's authority but also threatened to split the Gran Club del Pueblo by driving Rivarola and his supporters into the arms of Bareiro and the hard-line opposition.

Bareiro, meanwhile, had been kept in the dark about the coup, but now he went into action. Hurriedly calling Miltos and Iturburu into a conference, he browbeat them back into line. Then he and Rivarola went to Miguel Gallegos, who besides editing the *Voz del Pueblo* also headed the Argentine military hospital and had excellent contacts in the Brazilian army as well. The following morning, 1 September, Brazilian troops surrounded the old Cabildo, where the convention was meeting. Machaín was deposed and he and five other ringleaders were expelled from the convention. Despite the objections of Bareiro, who wanted to eliminate all of his enemies, those in the Gran Club, like Decoud, who did not back the coup scheme kept their seats—although Ferreira and Sosa Escalada were subsequently purged. One of the survivors, José del Rosario Miranda, was made chairman in Decoud's place and elections were held to replace all those who had been purged. Only Bareiro's Club del Pueblo could offer candidates, however. Among the newly seated were Juan Bautista Gill, his brother, Emilio, Adolfo Saguier, and Rufino Taboada (who was released from jail and made chief of police in Colonel Decoud's place). After that the convention went about its affairs. However, the Decouds' newspaper, *La Regeneración*, was sacked by a mob and put out of business.

These events made little difference in the final form of the Constitution. The two clubs were separated by personalities and by family loyalties, not by ideology. Both were liberal in orientation and were largely composed of former Legionnaires. Some writers have claimed to perceive subtle differences in the type of liberalism each club professed. Manuel Pesoa believes that José Segundo Decoud and Benigno Ferreira, having been raised in Buenos Aires, were under the influence of British thought as expressed through John Locke and Adam Smith. Facundo Machaín, who studied in Chile, came to the same laissez-faire doctrines through his famous teacher, Andrés Bello. By contrast, Cayo Miltos and Cándido Bareiro, having studied in Paris, were influenced by Rousseau.[19] In any case, the Constitution of 1870 followed the classic separation of powers and included guarantees of the usual liberties, much like the U.S. Constitution. There were two important differences, however: the prohibition on the president's immediate reelection; and a greater centralization of power in the national government, relative to the local communities. This latter feature, perhaps, reflects French influence.

The greatest fallout from Machaín's misguided grab for power was in the realignment of factions. As José Segundo Decoud predicted, the Gran Club fell apart. Of a total of eighty-one men who became members between March and September 1870, fifty-eight dropped permanently out of active politics. Their names never appear again on the roster of any political club. The remaining twenty-three broke into squabbling factions, with Rivarola going over to the Bareiro-Miltos-Gill side. The Decouds and the Machaíns also went their separate ways, blaming each other for the failure of the 31 August coup. Still another faction formed, with Benigno Ferreira as its *caudillo*.

For the moment, Cirilo Rivarola continued to lead the government, enjoying as he did the backing of the Brazilian occupation forces. General elections, held on 25 November, installed him in office as Paraguay's first constitutional president of the postwar era. Like many of his successors, he was fated not to last the full term.

two

FROM FAMILIAL POLITICS TO

PERSONALISMO

The previous chapter located the origins of Paraguay's political party system in the Sociedad Libertadora, Asociación Paraguaya, and Paraguayan Legion, all exile organizations dominated by a few prominent families, including the Iturburus, Decouds, Machaíns, and Recaldes, and all professing liberal values. Those same families formed the core of the Club Unión Republicana and the original version of the Club del Pueblo, Paraguay's first postwar factions. In this chapter we shall see how the contest for power caused politics to go beyond the narrow boundaries of family-led factions. For a short time the Iturburus, Decouds, and Machaíns will play leading roles, but more and more it will be only a certain few individuals from those families who continue to do battle. By the end of the 1870s only José Segundo Decoud will remain a central figure; all the others will have been shouldered out of politics by hard men whose loyalty is chiefly to themselves. *Caudillos* like Cándido Bareiro, Benigno Ferreira, Juan Bautista Gill, and General Bernardino Caballero will then occupy center stage.

Paraguay's *caudillo* politics differs from that of other Latin American countries in one respect: it is focused entirely on controlling the national government. In the Wolf and Hansen model, *caudillos* usually start their careers as local or regional chieftains; only when their plundering exhausts the immediate resources do they begin to raid beyond their home bases. The encroachment upon one another's territories then raises the struggle to a general free-for-all to control the national treasury and the customshouse as the ultimate, renewable sources of patronage. In Paraguay, however, the population in the latter half of the nineteenth century was highly concentrated. Two-thirds lived either in Asunción or within a sixty-mile radius of the capital. Beyond that radius, another 20 percent lived in small regional centers that were hardly more than villages: Villarrica, in the central highlands; Concepción, on the northern end of the Paraguay River; Pilar, on the southern end; and Encarnación, the southernmost port, on the Upper Paraná. Each of these had its local political boss, or *jefe político*, but the county's economic and political life were so concentrated in Asunción that only control of the capital really mattered. Local *caudillos,* or *jefes políticos,* might be important building blocks in creating an alliance, but from the very beginning the overriding goal of all ambitions was to control the national government.

There is another aspect of Paraguay's politics after 1870 that deserves mention: the existence of a mass electorate created by the Constitution of 1870. Articles 38 and 39 provided for universal manhood suffrage by enfranchising all males over eighteen, regardless of race, property, or literacy.[1] As a consequence, political battles in Paraguay might at times involve large numbers of people. Given the ignorance and poverty of the great majority of the people, however, political leaders were drawn from a relatively small portion of the public: mostly educated civilians and high army officers. It is that elite stratum that constituted the only effective "public opinion."

As Huntington's theory predicts, factional politics presents a confusing series of brief alliances whose composition constantly changes, often for obscure reasons. We shall trace the making and unmaking of these various Paraguayan alliances in this chapter, but we also shall see the confusion gradually die down because of two tendencies at work. First, there is the inner dynamic of *caudillo* politics, which eliminates the main contestants until only one dominant figure (or political machine) is left. Second, as politics become more violent, hatreds build up that have a polarizing effect. Men with common enemies group together, their alliances have a more emotional basis, and the shared dangers of battle encourage personal loyalties that give the grouping more permanence. By the end of the chapter we shall see the anarchy of the early 1870s giving way to a national dictatorship. First, however, it is important to bring the *caudillos* to the fore and describe their type of factional politics. We will begin with the subtle jockeying for power under President Rivarola, which culminates with his being outwitted and eased from office; then we will see a raw struggle for power that climaxes in a series of bloody revolutions and assassinations. Only when most of the combatants are either dead or in exile will *caudillo* rule disappear.

THE RIVAROLA PRESIDENCY

Cirilo Antonio Rivarola was a mediocre man who had risen far above the level deserved by his talents. He had virtues, to be sure: he was brave, and he had a common touch that made him popular with the humbler classes. (While in office he made several trips to the countryside, sometimes bringing with him a band of musicians.) But he let power go to his head, began taking for his personal use state property that once belonged to the Lópezes, and acquired an increasingly pompous and despotic manner.[2] Lacking insight into the human character, he eventually was outmaneuvered by smarter, subtler politicians who first used him and then destroyed him.

Rivarola was heavily dependent on the Brazilians, a situation that gave them a large say in the makeup of his cabinet. Having broken with the Gran Club, he was forced to draw exclusively upon the Club del Pueblo, and accordingly offered the vice-presidency to Cándido Bareiro. Bareiro, however, had counted on getting the presidency himself and, when foiled by the Brazilians, would take nothing less. Besides, he despised Rivarola as a vain fool. In that judgment he was joined by most of his contemporaries; nevertheless he was censured by his fellow members of the Club del Pueblo, especially Rufino Taboada and Juan B. Gill, for passing up a position of potential power. In reply, Bareiro lost his temper and withdrew from the club. Meanwhile, Rivarola offered the vice-presidency to Cayo Miltos, who accepted.

Rivarola's main concern, in composing his cabinet, was to maintain a balance of power so as not to allow any one of his nominal servants to become too independent. The key figures, besides Miltos, were Taboada and Gill, each of whom had his own personal following, including thugs to break up opponents' meetings and stuff ballot boxes. Each was ambitious to succeed Rivarola in the presidency as soon as possible. Gill's prospects were especially good, for the Brazilians were turning more to him as they came to recognize Rivarola's limitations. Accordingly, Gill got the important Finance Ministry, which would allow him to control government spending and siphon off funds for his own political following. To balance that, Taboada was made minister of interior, which put him in charge of the police. Rivarola's men in the cabinet were Salvador Jovellanos, the war minister, and José Mateo Collar, who headed the Ministry of Justice and Public Instruction. The Foreign Affairs portfolio was assigned to Miguel Palacios, a political independent acceptable to both the Brazilians and the Argentines.

Luck eluded Rivarola from the very beginning. In January 1871 Vice-President Cayo Miltos died of yellow fever, depriving the Club del Pueblo of its most respected leader and the government of an important moderating influence. Both Taboada and Gill had their eye on the vice-presidency, but Rivarola forestalled them by naming Salvador Jovellanos to fill the vacancy. Even so, the struggle between Taboada and Gill became hotter as each tried to get Rivarola to drop the other from the cabinet. It was clear that he could not keep them both, so in April Rivarola sacrificed Taboada because he could not dismiss Gill without angering the Brazilians.[3] Once outside the government, Taboada might have become a threat, but he died in June—like Miltos, a victim of yellow fever. Miguel Palacios also stepped down in April because of poor health.

With Taboada and Miltos gone, the Club del Pueblo was left with only Juan B. Gill as a major figure. But Gill was a man about whom few were neutral, and within the club he had many enemies. Among them were Antonio Taboada, Fulgencio Miltos, and Juan Antonio Jara. To prevent Gill from gaining control they encouraged Cándido Bareiro to rejoin and take the leadership. This turn of events posed new problems for Rivarola. On the one hand, it made Gill more dependent on him in order to block Bareiro's renewed influence; on the other hand, Bareiro was a dangerous opponent too. The president's first move was to put more power in the hands of Jovellanos by making him both interior and war minister, as well as vice-president. But that could be only temporary: eventually the solution would have to be a dispersal of power among several factions, and that meant approaching certain elements in the Gran Club del Pueblo. Accordingly, Palacios's place at Foreign Affairs was given, *ad interim*, to Carlos Loizaga, until José Segundo Decoud could be induced to take it over in May. Then, in July, Rivarola made a truly bold appointment by giving the War Ministry to General Bernardino Caballero, a popular officer who had fought at Solano López's side to the very end and had just returned to Paraguay from Brazil. Rivarola's immediate concern was the head of the militia, Colonel Pedro Recalde, whom he suspected of plotting a coup with Bareiro. Caballero took care of that threat by dismissing Recalde and running the militia himself.[4]

Nevertheless, Bareiro continued to gain ground, working busily among the López army officers returning from prisoner-of-war camps and recruiting them for the Club del Pueblo. Of all the prominent political figures, he alone could rightfully claim to be a true *lopista*, having never fought against or betrayed the fallen marshal. Consequently, he was successful in bringing a number of war veterans into his club—among them, colonels Patricio Escobar, Germán Serrano, and Juan Antonio Meza. Unfortunately for Rivarola, General Caballero swung over too, thus undermining the plan to use him against Bareiro. The opening to the Decouds failed to work either, despite the fact that Rivarola sacrificed justice minister José Mateo Collar in July in order to give José Segundo Decoud a second portfolio. Instead of supporting Rivarola, the Decouds were so anti-Gill—and so afraid that the Brazilians would make him president—that they rediscovered a common ground with the Machaíns and were ready even to go so far as making an alliance with Bareiro. Once again Rivarola found himself having to choose between dismissing Gill and angering the Brazilians, or shuffling his cabinet. In desperation he reached out to another *caudillo* whom he hardly dared to trust, Colonel Benigno Ferreira, who agreed to support him.

RIVAROLA'S FALL

With most of the Club del Pueblo and the Gran Club ranged against him, Rivarola faced a hostile Congress. Already the Chamber of Deputies had begun a debate on a bill to impeach Juan Bautista Gill on charges of misappropriation of Treasury funds. In the meantime, by-elections were held on 1 October to fill some vacant seats in the Chamber of Deputies, the lower house of Congress. Instead of a contest between the Club del Pueblo and Gran Club del Pueblo, the new factional alignments presented themselves as parties. The Rivarola-Gill-Ferreira coalition called itself the Partido Liberal, while the opposition Bareiro-Decoud-Machaín-Taboada coalition ran as the Partido Nacional. Although the two groupings could not really classify as parties, because of their lack of structure, their appearance indicates a gradual polarizing process that eventually would result in party formation. As expected, the government's side won. Finance Minister Gill spent lavishly to buy votes by sending in carts laden with liquor and food for the impoverished citizens. Opposition protests were squelched.

The violence and chicanery of the October elections deepened Paraguay's divisions, generating resentments that proved to be permanent. The alliance of Bareiro, Caballero, and Decoud would hold together, despite its leaders' dissimilar backgrounds, and become the main current leading eventually to the National Republican Association, or Colorado Party. Meanwhile, the Machaíns and Decouds never forgave Benigno Ferreira for siding with the infamous Gill. For the next three years they would work tirelessly with Bareiro to get him out of politics. As for Gill, his enemies redoubled their efforts to get him impeached. Although the government now controlled the Chamber of Deputies, the impeachment charges already had been sent to the Senate, which had not been affected by the elections. On 12 October the opposition-controlled Senate voted to impeach Gill. On the following day Rivarola insisted that the Senate reconsider, and when it refused to do so he declared Congress to be dissolved, setting 19 November as the date for new elections to both houses.

Rivarola's actions were a clear violation of the Constitution, which included no provision for a presidential power of dissolution. He was following a plan by Gill, which, the latter assured him, would strengthen his hand. According to the plan, Gill would resign, "to show his respect for the Constitution," but would mount a massive campaign to win control of Congress. After that, the legislators would give Rivarola an overwhelming vote of confidence. Meanwhile, Decoud and Caballero resigned in protest over Rivarola's high-handedness, leaving vacant three cabinet posts—which were promptly filled by Benigno Ferreira. Gill's departure from the cabinet soon afterward left Ferreira as the new "strongman" in the government.

The November elections proved to be as violent as the ones a month before. One of the major casualties was Fulgencio Miltos, murdered by the so-called Guarará Battalion, the name for Gill's armed thugs. When, on 25 November, the government published the vote and proclaimed its own victory, the Partido Nacional revolted. The militia, now under Ferreira, stayed loyal, however, and the rebels were scattered. In Asunción the Guarará Battalion instituted a reign of terror by breaking into the homes of suspected opponents, beating up the inhabitants, and vandalizing their property.[5]

On 18 December the "refurbished" Congress reconvened, with Gill as president of the Senate and his cousin, Higinio Uriarte, president of the Chamber of Deputies. Rivarola addressed the joint opening session, defended all his actions, and offered to resign, as he had promised to do on the day of the dissolution. While the legislators deliberated, Rivarola, confident in his own mastery of the situation, retired to his *estancia* outside of town to await the call to return. Great were his surprise and dismay when he learned that he had been tricked. The summons never came because the wily Gill had gotten Congress to accept the resignation and appoint Vice-President Salvador Jovellanos to succeed him.

BENIGNO FERREIRA

Salvador Jovellanos, the provisional president, was a good-natured man, but weak. Now he found himself caught between two strongminded *caudillos*, Benigno Ferreira and Juan Bautista Gill, each of whom had his eye on the presidency. His cabinet reflected the division of power. Ferreira held the powerful Interior Ministry and his close friend, Francisco Soteras, was minister of finance and interim minister of justice and public instruction. The ministries of War and Foreign Affairs still lay beyond Ferreira's reach, however. The Baron de Cotegipe, Brazil's new diplomatic representative, saw to it that they went to Pedro Recalde and José Falcón, respectively. Recalde, whose political base was the town of Paraguarí, had been an ally of Bareiro and one of the principal antagonists of the pro-Machaín liberals at the 1870 convention. Therefore, he was known to oppose Ferreira. Falcón was an old *lopista* who had served as Carlos

Antonio López's foreign minister and as interior minister under both Carlos Antonio and Francisco Solano López.

Cotegipe's concern was to prevent any increase in Argentina's influence inside Paraguay, for he feared that this would lead to the signing of a separate peace by which the puppet government would surrender the Chaco territory. That would put Argentina right on Brazil's western flank. Since Ferreira had served in the Argentine army, Cotegipe assumed that any government in which he took the lead would necessarily be pro-Argentine.

On the surface, Cotegipe's suspicions of Ferreira were not ill-founded. Born in 1846 in the village of Isla Aveiro, Ferreira was raised in the Argentine province of Entre Ríos because his parents, though humble, got on the wrong side of the López family. After finishing high school in Entre Ríos, he studied for a law degree in Buenos Aires but dropped out to join the Paraguayan Legion when the war broke out. His closest friends were Facundo Machaín, Juansilvano Godoi, and Jaime Sosa Escalada, so he became a member of Colonel Decoud's faction. When the *decouistas* quit the Legion, Ferreira joined the Argentine army and rose to the rank of captain. Under the Triumvirate he served as captain of the ports, and in the convention of 1870 he supported Machaín's bid for the presidency. Afterward, he was deprived of his post and broke with the Decoud family for its refusal to back Machaín. A year later, however, a rift opened between himself and Machaín when he accepted Rivarola's offer to reenter the government as minister of interior. Machaín, a brilliant and dedicated liberal, but also somewhat doctrinaire and impractical, never forgave Ferreira.[6]

Ferreira was too clever a politician for Cotegipe to box in. He quickly dominated President Jovellanos and got him to drop Falcón from the Ministry of Foreign Affairs and replace him with Gregorio Benítes. Although Benítes also was a former López agent in Paris, he proved to be a malleable tool. He was sent to London in 1871 to negotiate a foreign loan, the proceeds of which would allow Ferreira to grease the wheels of the political organization he was building. In fact, two loans were made, both from the Baring Brothers' banking firm, at extortionate terms. The total amount borrowed came to 3 million pounds, of which over half was drained away by upfront bankers' fees, "expenses," and interest discounts before ever leaving England. Only 403,000 pounds ever reached Paraguay. Of that, 125,000 pounds in gold was stolen right off the ship as it lay anchored in the harbor, and the rest was squandered in political payoffs. Although there is no hard proof as to who took the money, most writers assume that Jovellanos, Ferreira, and their friends were the principal beneficiaries. Pedro Recalde presumably received his share too, because he became a very close ally of Ferreira.[7]

With the control of such a slush fund, Ferreira was ready to forge a political machine that would insure his control of the government. He revived the old Partido Liberal as a counterbalance to Gill's Guarará Battalion, and placed friends like Carlos Loizaga, Jaime Sosa Escalada, and Francisco Soteras in charge of it. Nor did he neglect to pass out high offices to members of the party. Loizaga served briefly as justice minister and Soteras continued to handle the Finance portfolio. Other Partido Liberal supporters who occupied top posts were Gregorio Benítes, who remained at the Foreign Ministry, and both Eduardo Aramburu and José del Rosario Miranda, who took turns being war minister. Colonel Antonio Luís González, a former Legionnaire, held the key post of police chief. Despite its name, however, the Partido Liberal was not a true party. As Warren notes, accurately: "At this stage what were to become the principal parties had not emerged with unmistakable clarity. . . . Convenience, not conviction, and selfish interest, not patriotism, determined party [i.e., factional] affiliation."[8]

Meanwhile, Gill was not idle. He too had been working on President Jovellanos, reminding him that he not only controlled a majority of both houses of Congress but that he had Cotegipe's backing. On 8 March 1871 he delivered an ultimatum to Jovellanos: either dismiss Ferreira from the cabinet or face impeachment!

Dismayed and uncertain, Jovellanos went to Ferreira, who wasted no time in dealing with the matter. First, he drew up a formal bill of charges against Gill for threatening the president and using undue influence, and got Jovellanos to sign it. Next, he ordered Colonel González to arrest Gill immediately. Finally, two hours after the police took Gill into custody, Ferreira appeared before the Senate with President Jovellanos's formal complaint in his hand and informed the members of what had happened. Although most of the senators were Gill's partisans they caved in before Ferreira's audacity and voted, as he demanded, that they expel their fallen leader from the Chamber. His seat was declared vacant. Cotegipe and his generals were caught by surprise too. The most that they could think of to do was to intercede for Gill's release, on the understanding that he would leave the country. The next day he was put aboard a riverboat and sent to Uruguay.[9]

Had Ferreira been the Argentine puppet his enemies accused him of being, he might have held on to power, but in fact he lost Argentine support by refusing to sign any peace treaty granting territorial concessions in the Chaco.[10] Instead, the Argentines turned to Cándido Bareiro and

Bernardino Caballero, who put together a coalition consisting of the Decoud, Machaín, and Iturburu families, as well as politically influential
individuals like Antonio Taboada, who had become the political leader of
Villarrica, Paraguay's second city; Juan B. Egusquiza, the *jefe político* of
Encarnación; and Juansilvano Godoi. Other followers who would later
play important political roles were: Ildefonso Benegas, who helped found
the Liberal Party and played a key part in the 1904 revolution that brought
it to power; Major Eduardo Vera, who would come to head the Liberal
Party and die during a revolt in 1891; and Major José A. Dolores Molas,
whose base was the strategic town of Paraguarí.

In March 1873 this Argentine-backed opposition revolted against Jovellanos and Ferreira. The uprising's center was at Paraguarí, about fifty
miles away, where General Caballero set up his headquarters. With him
were Cándido Bareiro, Colonel Juan Francisco Decoud, José Segundo Decoud, and Juansilvano Godoi. Another contingent of rebels gathered at
Villarrica, under the command of Caballero's two close army comrades,
Colonels Patricio Escobar and Germán Serrano. Just before they began to
march on Asunción, General Caballero issued a strange manifesto in
which he excoriated the memory of the old Francia-López regime. Paraguay's backwardness, its lack of liberty or public spirit, he claimed, was
due to the "three tyrants, of whom there is no parallel throughout cen-
turies of history." Paraguay's "hecatomb," the result of the "iron will of
a despot," should teach the people to rise up and claim their rights."[11]
Whether these were really the general's own sentiments, or whether they
were ghostwritten for him for Argentine consumption, they have long
been an embarrassment for those who want to draw a straight connecting
line from Marshal López to the Colorado Party by way of Caballero.

In any case, Caballero's personal popularity enabled him to assemble
a force of around 4,000 poorly armed and mostly untrained men. Against
these, Ferreira had about 1,500 which he divided into two, unequal contingents, the larger one under himself and other commanded by Colonel
Antonio Luís Gonzalez, whom he sent to Villarrica. The government
routed the rebels on both fronts. At Paraguarí, Colonel Decoud and one
of his sons, Adolfo, fell prisoner. Also among the prisoners was an adolescent named Albino Jara, of whom we will hear much more later.[12]

A grateful Congress promoted Ferreira from the rank of major to lieutenant colonel and made him supreme commander of the government
forces. The revolt was by no means over, however. In their pursuit of the
enemy, the government forces were ambushed in May by new recruits
crossing the border from Argentina at the village of Yabebyry. That gave
Caballero a chance to regroup. At the same time, the rebels recognized
that their hopes of winning hinged on getting Brazilian support. Accord-

ingly, they sent emissaries to Uruguay to enlist Gill in their cause. He agreed to join, and soon thereafter fresh arms and recruits swelled their ranks. Ferreira, meanwhile, set up his military headquarters in Paraguarí, from which he could intercept any rebel marches from the south or the central highlands, and ordered defense works to be built in the capital. All opposition newspapers were closed and Higinio Uriarte was removed as president of the Chamber and put under arrest for criticizing the government.

The rebel army had rebuilt itself to a force of around 3,000, twice the size of Ferreira's. Confident of victory, they marched on the capital on 15 June. Four days later the two armies met on the outskirts and once again Ferreira inflicted a severe defeat on Caballero and dispersed his forces. This time Congress made him a full colonel.

But time was running against Ferreira. By now Brazilian financial aid, funneled through Gill, was filling the opposition's treasury, allowing the Partido Nacional to rearm. A new revolt broke out in January, centered in the southern port of Pilar. On 12 February 1874 the rebels defeated the government forces under Colonel Francisco Lino Cabriza and started to march on the capital. This turn of events crushed the government's morale, which already had been lowered by the knowledge that the new Brazilian ambassador, José Duarte de Araujo Gondim, was actively encouraging the rebels. As Caballero's men closed in on the city, Jovellanos accepted Gondim's offer to mediate. The terms were that (1) Ferreira would resign and go into exile, his place as interior minister to be taken by General Caballero; (2) Juan Bautista Gill would resume his old post as finance minister; (3) Colonel Serrano would become war minister and Colonel Escobar would be chief of police; (4) Cándido Bareiro would take the Foreign Affairs portfolio; (5) Jovellanos would schedule elections for 1 June, with the new president to be inaugurated on 25 November; and (6) Gill would be the official candidate.[13]

ARGENTINISTAS VERSUS BRASILERISTAS

Because I have been using the terms Partido Liberal and Partido Nacional, I think it is useful to remind the reader that these were not true political parties. Each of them was nothing more than a cluster of personalist factions. There was no structure, no organization, no ideology or binding sentiment, no recognized chain of command. The Liberal Party was Benigno Ferreira's personal vehicle and it evaporated as soon as he was out of power. Four of its most prominent men, Jaime Sosa Escalada, José Tomás Sosa, Colonel Francisco Lino Cabriza, and Carlos Loizaga, even showed up on the executive board of Juan B. Gill's electoral committee in June![14] The explanation is simple: in those times there was very little hope of economic salvation for those outside the government. The country was still devastated from the war, which had ended only four years before. Thus, nine of the thirty-one men who appeared on Gill's electoral committee had opposed him in the past, either as members of the Partido Liberal or the Gran Club del Pueblo. The list contained fine old names like Macháin, Decoud, and Guanes. They had no choice.

As for Gill, he accepted help from any quarter. He had no choice, either, because his own Partido Nacional was a bag of squabbling cats. Immediately after taking power, the rebel forces split into two factions, according to whether they had Brazilian or Argentine support. Gill's faction were the *brasileristas*, among whom he counted Colonel Serrano. Caballero, Bareiro, and Escobar were the *argentinistas*, simply because they had no hope of getting Brazil to switch its backing of Gill.

Aware that Bareiro and Caballero were courting Argentina, Gill and Gondim got President Jovellanos to dismiss them, along with Colonel Escobar, from the government on 29 March. This time, however, the Brazilians were dealing with *caudillos* who enjoyed real popularity among the soldiers. Caballero and Escobar called out the troops, forcing Jovellanos and Gill to take refuge in the Brazilian embassy. Only the intervention of the Brazilian occupation forces prevented them from taking over the government. It was clear that a compromise was necessary. The cabinet was shuffled. Gill stayed on at Finance and Bareiro returned to the Foreign Ministry, but Escobar took over the War Ministry and Serrano was moved to Interior, while Gill's brother, General Emilio Gill, became police chief.[15]

General Caballero was the chief concern, however. There was no way to exclude him from the cabinet, but he was relegated to the fairly innocuous position of minister of justice and public instruction. Also, to balance off his authority inside the army, Serrano and Escobar were raised to the rank of general—with the idea, perhaps, of gradually turning Escobar into a rival. Finally, the Brazilians insisted that Caballero disband those forces that followed him personally, as being illegitimate rivals of the regular army. This he did, though reluctantly; but his troops departed with their arms and baggage. They soon presented themselves in Paraguarí, whose *jefe político* was Major José Dolores Molas, a friend of Caballero and an enemy of Gill.

Greatly augmented in his strength by the inclusion of Caballero's men, Molas declared himself against the government in April, demanding that Jovellanos, Gill, and Serrano resign. Ex-president Rivarola pledged his support to the revolt and raised a small contingent as well. On 24 April General Serrano, commanding a much larger force than the rebels', met

Molas outside Paraguarí and was utterly defeated. Once again the physical intervention of Brazilian troops was required to save the government. The rebels were beaten and dispersed. Molas and his chief officer, Captain Matias Goiburu, fled into exile, while Rivarola disappeared into the central highlands to carry on a desultory guerrilla warfare.[16]

With order temporarily restored, Gill's path to the presidency was clear. On 21 June he and his running mate, Uriarte, were elected without opposition. But to make sure there was no more trouble, the Brazilians got Jovellanos to send Caballero and Bareiro out of the country, on "diplomatic missions."

GILL IN POWER

Juan Bautista Gill was a complex character. He was ruthless and dishonest, yet in his own way he proved to be something of a patriot. Once in power he concentrated his tremendous energy and intelligence on solving two main tasks: getting the foreigners out of Paraguay and reviving the shattered economy.

Concerning the first goal, a boundary treaty (the Loizaga-Cotegipe Treaty) had already been signed by the Jovellanos administration in 1872, granting Brazil all of its territorial claims. This had been in violation of the Allies' agreement not to negotiate separately with Paraguay. Thus, Brazil was a satisfied power, while Argentina felt cheated. But Brazil kept its troops in Paraguay to prevent the government from making any generous concessions to Argentina, while the latter, being distracted by internal troubles, was unable to match the Brazilian presence there. Consequently, it was not able to bring as much pressure to bear on Paraguay, although it had a small occupation army based in the Chaco port of Villa Occidental, just upriver from Asunción.

The key to ending Paraguay's occupation was to sign an agreement with Argentina that both the major powers would accept. The Argentines wanted all of the Misiones territory in southern Paraguay and also claimed the vast Chaco wilderness to the west of the Paraguay River. Satisfaction of those claims would place Argentina on Brazil's border in two places, an event that the latter was determined to oppose. Gill's first diplomatic attempt was to send Jaime Sosa Escalada to treat with the Argentines. Sosa, whose dislike of Brazil was matched only by his admiration for Argentina, went far beyond his instructions and ceded Misiones, much of the Chaco, and Villa Occidental. The Sosa-Tejedor Treaty of 20 May 1875 hit the Gill administration like a bombshell. On hearing of it, the Brazilians lodged an angry protest with Gill and sent more troops to

Asunción. The Argentines, for their part, reinforced their garrison at Villa Occidental and encouraged rumors that they might attack the capital if the treaty were not approved.[17]

Gill acted quickly to diffuse the crisis. He repudiated the Sosa-Tejedor Treaty and got his docile Congress to do the same. Sosa Escalada was arrested and sent as an exile to his beloved Argentina. Then Facundo Machaín, the minister of foreign affairs, was assigned the task of negotiating another treaty. Although the Argentines protested, they were not ready to take extreme measures. The two sides returned to the bargaining table and in February 1876 produced a new treaty somewhat more favorable to Paraguay. Misiones was ceded to Argentina, but Paraguay kept more of the Chaco. A broad zone in the Chaco that included Villa Occidental would be submitted to arbitration (which was decided in Paraguay's favor in 1878). Argentina agreed to withdraw its troops upon Paraguay's ratification.

While Machaín and the Argentine minister, Bernardo de Irigoyen, were working out their terms, the Brazilians made one last attempt to upset the negotiations and assert their hegemony over Paraguay. Having grown cool toward Gill, whose attitude was becoming too independent, they turned to General Serrano as their new front man. Informed of this, Gill dismissed Serrano in October and placed him under house arrest. However, on 8 December Serrano slipped away from his guards during a religious fiesta and raised a revolt. It was was quickly crushed by an expedition under the command of General Escobar, after which Serrano and several of his officers were executed. A curious aspect of this incident, which shows how easily the *caudillos* switched alliances, was that Major José Dolores Molas lent his support to Serrano. He managed to escape the bloody aftermath, however, and lived to participate in even grimmer events.

The failure of Serrano's revolt ended Brazil's hopes of blocking the Machaín-Irigoyen Treaty, which was signed in February 1876. Three months later Brazil began withdrawing its troops from Paraguay, having found that its occupation was increasingly costly and fruitless. By June the Brazilians were gone, and in August the Argentines withdrew their small contingent from Villa Occidental. Paraguay was at last free of foreign troops, though certainly not of foreign influence.

That left Gill with a free hand to pursue his other major goal, the revival of the economy. Here he had a truly daunting task. Paraguay was still devastated by the effects of the war. Outside of Asunción there was little productive activity. The vast majority of the population eked out an existence from subsistence agriculture; here and there a few large landowners were beginning to revive export crops like *yerba mate* (a bitter green tea), tobacco, cattle, cotton, and timber, but they had little capital to work with. In addition, the country's internal communications had not recovered from the damage inflicted by the fighting. Roads were little more than mud tracks that wound through swamp, forest, and savannah. When it rained, they became impassable. There were few bridges or ferries. The railroad was in a dilapidated state and in any case extended only a short distance beyond Asunción. Land transport consisted mainly of men on horseback or mule, or oxcart. Few ships plied the rivers. Most goods were hauled on small boats and barges. Thus, most trade was confined to the capital, and it was in decline. Paraguayans had little to sell and were too poor to buy.[18]

Worse still, the country was deeply in debt. The British loans of 1871–72, though squandered and stolen, still had to be repaid. Every government from Rivarola on had exceeded its budget and borrowed from one or another of the Allies, who were willing to lend in order to strengthen their influence on Paraguay. The upheavals of 1873–74 were particularly costly in that respect.

To straighten out the mess, Gill proposed to float public bonds that would be backed by new taxes on consumer goods. There were few takers. Not only did most investors shun Paraguay, but the country's general poverty made it impossible to raise much money. Next, Gill resorted to inflation as an economic stimulus, issuing over a million *pesos* in inconvertible (and worthless) bank notes. That only made matters worse, because now inflation was added to stagnation. Then Gill attempted a mercantilist approach by establishing state monopolies on the import and sale of tobacco, salt, and soap. Merchants could gain exemption from those restrictions, however, by paying a tax. That scheme failed too because the government lacked an administrative apparatus to apply the law and stop evasion. Eventually Cándido Bareiro was sent to London to offer the foreign bondholders a deal by which they could establish a corporation and take over the government's railroad, *yerba mate* plantations, and other public lands in return for establishing a bank in Paraguay, of which the government would be coowner, to regulate the currency and funnel in much-needed investment.[19]

No matter which way he turned, Gill found himself blocked or under attack. The Brazilians objected to Bareiro's offer to the London bondholders, and they in turn rejected the scheme. Meanwhile, the evacuation of foreign troops gave another downward push to the economy, for the soldiers had been the main purchasers of Paraguay's few domestic products. The state monopolies came under attack by the local merchants and the large landowners' Agricultural Society, of which José Segundo Decoud was the head. As Gill lost popularity, he began to attack opposition papers such as *El Agrónomo* and *La Reforma* by sending his goons around to intimidate the editors. Meanwhile, he found himself increasingly overshadowed in the government by his new minister of interior, José Urdapilleta. Urdapilleta, a descendant of an old and prestigious family, was winning popularity by taking a different approach to the economic problem. Instead of extending state power, he began to attack the problem of corruption and trim back the number of jobholders. This austerity program was highly popular with the merchants and landholders—the only real "public opinion" at the time, except for the soldiers and politicians.

By early 1877 Urdapilleta was being discussed as a probable presidential candidate for next year's elections. He was not alone, however. Cándido Bareiro had his eye on the job and had the important backing of generals Caballero and Escobar. Finally, Facundo Machaín had resigned from the cabinet in November 1876 and was building up a coterie of supporters from the old Gran Club del Pueblo.

Any hopes for a clean election were set back by Gill's use of blatant force to steal the congressional elections held in January 1877. From that point on, many of Machaín's backers were convinced that their man's belief in an electoral solution was utopian and that only more violent methods would get Gill out of power. A plot formed around Juansilvano Godoi and Major José Dolores Molas to assassinate the president. On the morning of 12 April, Gill was accosted by a group of armed men and shot dead as he walked from his home to his office in the Cabildo. The assassins then fled to the countryside where they joined with Cirilo Rivarola to raise a revolt. General Escobar, following in hot pursuit, routed them. Rivarola escaped to the hills but most of the other plotters, including Major Molas, were taken captive and lodged in the public prison to await trial.[20]

THE CLIMAX OF *CAUDILLO* POLITICS

Vice-President Higinio Uriarte succeeded Gill at the head of the government, but he was little more than a figurehead. The real struggle for power centered on two main contenders: Cándido Bareiro and Facundo Machaín. Bareiro had the immediate advantage because he and his cohorts were already in the government. Bareiro was minister of finance, General Caballero was minister of justice, and General Escobar was war minister. Machaín had left the cabinet the previous November, to be replaced by Benjamín Aceval, another orthodox liberal. A cabinet shake-up in August strengthened the Bareiro faction's hold on power. General Caballero moved to the Interior Ministry, replacing José Urdapilleta, whose presidential hopes were dimmed considerably by the change. Aceval was replaced by Juan Antonio Jara, a *bareirista,* and Caballero's place at Justice was taken by Adolfo Saguier, a large landowner who was thought to be friendly to Bareiro.

Despite this, Bareiro was faced by a formidable opposition that was beginning to gather in a new club called Sociabilidad Paraguaya. Formed in May 1877, just after Gill's assassination, its leading figures were Machaín and José Segundo Decoud. In addition, Sociabilidad Paraguaya's membership list included other members of the Decoud family; their in-laws, the Peñas; the Guanes family; and—most interesting of all—several Iturburus. Indeed, many in the club, besides the Iturburus, were former *bareiristas*: José Tomás Sosa, who had switched from Bareiro's Club del Pueblo to the Gran Club, and then had backed Ferreira; Salvador Rivarola; Juan G. González; and Juan León Corvalán. Even Adolfo Saguier's name appeared on the list. Other notables were Hilario Amarilla, who was serving in the government as a criminal court judge; Juan José Alvarenga, another ex-Ferreira supporter; José G. Granados, who had served on Gill's electoral committee; and Manuel I. Frutos, a former López officer who had served in the 1870 Constitutional Convention as a representative of the Gran Club. In brief, this was a broad coalition of liberal-minded men, many of whom had become repelled by Bareiro's ruthless tactics and his increasing reliance on former *lopista* military men. By supporting Machaín for the presidency, they hoped to bring enlightenment to Paraguay's politics.[21]

It was a challenge that Bareiro and Caballero could not ignore. Fortunately for them, Machaín's virtues as an idealistic, civic-spirited liberal also were his vices, for he was completely impractical and impervious to sound political advice. Ignoring all warnings from his friend, José Segundo Decoud, he played into the hands of Bareiro and Caballero by becoming defense attorney for Gill's assassins. Immediately it was recalled that Machaín and Juansilvano Godoi had been close friends. The suspicion was thus raised that Machaín had been a silent partner in the plot, and despite the lack of any evidence to substantiate it, on 5 September 1877 Caballero had him arrested and jailed.[22]

Machaín now became the hero of a life and death struggle between the two factions contending for power. A writ of habeas corpus came before criminal court judge Hilario Amarilla, a member of Sociabilidad Paraguaya, who ordered Machaín's release. Caballero, as interior minister, got the case transferred to another court. This time the judge was Juan Gualberto González, another Sociabilidad Paraguaya member. After a hearing

at which Carlos Loizaga, Juan Guanes, and José Toribio Iturburu (*sic*) tes-
tified in his favor, Macha\u00edn's release was again ordered on 13 September.
This time Caballero complied.

Macha\u00edn's release set off an outburst of popular enthusiasm that
alarmed Bareiro, Caballero, and Escobar. As for Macha\u00edn, he was now
convinced that his enemies were on the run, and so he began an ag-
gressive public campaign to free Gill's murderers and portray them as
heroes. The trial, if held, promised to be a devastating condemnation of
the government, not the assassins, and a great boost to Macha\u00edn's presidential campaign. What Macha\u00edn did not realize in his naiveté, however,
was that the Bareiro clique was planning his destruction and redoubling
its efforts to get him back in prison and at their mercy. They did not have
long to wait. At the beginning of October, Caballero and his police chief,
General Ignacio Genes, uncovered another plot involving some of Ma-
cha\u00edn's friends who were in touch with the fugitive ex-president Rivarola.
According to Freire Esteves, Macha\u00edn knew about this latter conspiracy
but had not taken an active part in it.[23] Nevertheless, on 15 October Ma-
cha\u00edn was arrested with the other plotters and returned to jail. This time
not even the exertions of Adolfo Saguier, the justice minister, were able
to get him freed. Two weeks later General Genes and Colonel Juan A.
Meza, head of the Presidential Security Battalion (and Caballero's brother-
in-law) purposely left the prison doors unlocked overnight while they
waited outside in ambush. After allowing a couple of prisoners to escape,
they rushed the building on the pretext of stopping a breakout and murdered the rest in cold blood—including Macha\u00edn, who was sitting quietly
in his cell when he met his death.[24]

This bloodbath naturally had a chilling effect on the opposition. Sociabilidad Paraguaya, the last attempt by this generation of liberals from all
different factions to stop the Bareiro-Caballero *lopistas*, quickly evaporated. A few remnants, led by José Segundo Decoud, attempted to rally
behind Adolfo Saguier for president. Saguier, like Macha\u00edn, apparently
assumed that his wealth and social connections would make him immune
from official violence; but as the time for the 1878 elections approached
Decoud became frightened for his friend's safety. Accordingly, the two
men went to Bareiro and struck a deal: Saguier would withdraw and accept the vice-presidential nomination on the official ticket. On 15 August,
therefore, Bareiro won the presidency in yet another of Paraguay's uncontested elections.

With that, the age of anarchistic *caudillismo* came to an end and the age
of machine politics began. All of the prominent factional leaders of the
1870s had been eliminated except for Cándido Bareiro. Facundo Macha\u00edn,
Cayo Miltos, Rufino Taboada, and Juan B. Gill were dead. Benigno Fe-

rreira was in exile, where he wisely preferred the safety of Argentine soil to an offer of a job in Bareiro's government.[25] Cirilo A. Rivarola, much less wise than Ferreira, accepted an amnesty offer from Bareiro a month after the new regime took power. He was stabbed to death on a street in downtown Asunción by a band of thugs on the night of 31 December 1878, only a few steps from the police station.[26]

Of all those who had competed with Bareiro, only José Segundo De-coud was left, and he had become disillusioned by the incompetence of his liberal compatriots. "After the civil hecatomb of '77," writes Freire Esteves, "while accompanying Dr. Facundo Machaín's remains to Asunción's docks, where a ship would carry them to a distant foreign land, Dr. Decoud noted that there were only three people besides himself following the illustrious martyr. It occurred to him then, with certainty, that the entire Republic remained petrified before that spectacle."[27] Convinced that any further opposition was hopeless—and, moreover, that law and order were preferable to more anarchy—men like Decoud and Saguier made their peace with the new order and even tried to work inside it to "civilize" it. Their fate was to be condemned forever by their former friends as unscrupulous, while their new allies never trusted them.

three

THE EMERGENCE OF

A TWO-PARTY SYSTEM

By 1878 the violent struggles between *caudillos* had given way to a sort of peace by exhaustion, which would last for almost a decade until a new generation of political aspirants arose to challenge the incumbents. Meanwhile, the composition of Cándido Bareiro's electoral committee, called the Club Libertad, indicates by its diversity of background the compromises that all sides were willing to make to secure peace. Of the eleven men who composed it, two had been members of the Gran Club del Pueblo, Bareiro's old nemesis. Two others had served on Gill's electoral committee, and thus were former enemies too. One of them, José González Granados, now became president of the Club Libertad. Two men, González Granados and Juan Gualberto González, had been in Sociabilidad Paraguaya, as had Bareiro's running mate, Adolfo Saguier. Only three of the eleven-man committee had sided with Bareiro in the past by joining his Club del Pueblo.[1]

The Club Libertad was another ephemeral organization, hastily thrown together to attract the broadest support possible for Bareiro's candidacy. Nor can it be considered as a direct link in a chain that might connect it to the Colorado Party, because only three of the eleven (González Granados, Agustín Cañete, and Juan G. González) went on to become Colorados. By contrast, five of the men helped to create the Centro Democrático a decade later, which became the Liberal Party. Four of those started their political careers in Bareiro's Club Libertad.[2] Indeed, the Club Libertad's relative unimportance is shown by the failure of its executive committee members to secure any representation at all in the new cabinet, although González Granados and Cañete were named to the Supreme Court.

The key posts in the new government went to Bareiro's military backers: General Caballero, who became minister of interior, and General Escobar, who was named war minister. The Finance Ministry, which also had power potential, went to a long-time civilian ally, Juan Antonio Jara, who had been with Bareiro in both the Club Unión and the Club del Pueblo. At the same time, an olive branch was held out to Saguier's friends in Sociabilidad Paraguaya by appointing Benjamín Aceval as minister of foreign affairs and José Segundo Decoud as minister of justice. Also, two members of the three-man Supreme Court were from Sociabilidad Paraguaya (González Granados and José DeLeón).

Not everyone was placated, of course. There were still many political exiles. Some of them, led by Juansilvano and Nicanor Godoi, outfitted a riverboat called *El Galileo* and descended without warning, at the beginning of June 1879, upon the towns of Pilar and Humaitá. The revolt was cut short, however, when Argentina impounded *El Galileo* as it crossed the river to pick up supplies. Those rebels who remained in Paraguay were quickly dislodged when Bareiro ordered loyal army units to counterattack.

Other opposition, emerging from inside the governing faction, made itself heard the following year. As the new congressional session opened in April, Senator Cirilo Solalinde caused a certain consternation in official circles by questioning the accuracy of the government's budget.[3] Although he was easily outvoted, Solalinde's breach of discipline presaged more serious quarrels in the future.

The main achievements of Bareiro's administration were in the area of diplomacy. In November 1878 President Rutherford B. Hayes of the United States, who had been chosen as arbiter in the case of Argentina's and Paraguay's conflicting claims in the Chaco, handed down a decision wholly favorable to the latter. A year later the Decoud-Quijaro Treaty attempted to fix the boundaries of Bolivia and Paraguay by dividing the Chaco between them at just below the twenty-second parallel. If the treaty had been approved by Paraguay's Congress—which unfortunately it was not—a bloody war might have been avoided in the future.

During the night of 3 September 1880 Bareiro suffered a fatal stroke. Colonel Pedro Duarte, who had succeeded General Escobar as war minister the year before, was summoned to the presidential residence, where the dying president urged him to take control of the situation. At eight o'clock the following morning Duarte called a cabinet meeting but excluded Vice-President Saguier. There he informed the ministers of the grim turn of events and urged that General Caballero, not Saguier, be named provisional president. Within an hour after the meeting adjourned Bareiro died, whereupon Duarte, having gotten the support he sought, summoned Saguier to the Cabildo. Believing that he was about to be president, Saguier was persuaded to make a tour of the barracks to receive the military's oath of allegiance, but once inside he was made a prisoner and forced to sign a letter of resignation. Later that day Congress convened, accepted Saguier's note, and proceeded to approve Caballero's taking over the government.[4]

There was no outcry at the time against this coup; the opposition was too enfeebled. It was to have long-term effects on the evolution of the party system, however, because Adolfo Saguier had important connections. His father had been a French army officer and diplomat; his mother was a descendant of Fernando de la Mora, one of the Republic's founding fathers. Both sides of the family were wealthy. Saguier himself had fought bravely in the Paraguayan army as an artillery officer but had joined the reorganized Paraguayan Legion in March 1869. A member of Bareiro's Club Unión and also its successor, the Club del Pueblo, he had been elected to the 1870 Constitutional Convention. More liberal in outlook than Bareiro, he had become an ally of José Segundo Decoud in the Partido Nacional coalition that fought Ferreira and Gill. Saguier and Decoud personified what would be called the *civilista* wing of the Colorado Party, in opposition to General Caballero's military cronies.

In 1880 Saguier already had the backing of reform-minded men who would later figure prominently in the Liberal Party: senators Cirilo Solalinde, Francisco Soteras, and Antonio Zayas; deputies Francisco Fernández and Felipe Torrents; and *jefes políticos* like Antonio Taboada of Villarrica and Eduardo Vera of Itá.[5] Unlike his friend Decoud, who stayed in politics, Saguier turned to business after the coup. In 1886 he became one of the founders of La Industrial Paraguaya, a company that owned vast plantations and became the largest producer of *yerba mate*. Although La Industrial Paraguaya found it politically expedient to include General Caballero on its board of directors, its principal shareholders would contribute heavily to the 1904 revolution that ousted Caballero and his machine from power and ushered in the era of Liberal Party dominance.

THE CABALLERO "MACHINE"

General Caballero finished out Bareiro's term, making no changes in the cabinet other than to appoint Colonel Duarte to take over the Ministry of Interior in addition to the Ministry of War. Since he served *ad interim*, the constitutional prohibition of an immediate second term did not apply in his case, and so in September 1881 he declared his candidacy for the presidency. Caballero at this time was still a young, vigorous, blond-bearded, blue-eyed man who carried himself with the dignity of a soldier. For the average, simple Paraguayan he seemed like a benevolent father figure. Yet, according to Warren, he lacked the political acumen to be an effective president, was often drunk, and survived only because he recognized his limitations and surrounded himself with wise counselors. "Caballero," he insists, "was a simple, barely literate man whose mental processes could easily encompass a tactical situation on the battlefield;

but in the whirlpool and crosscurrents of Paraguayan politics he would have drowned quickly, as did Rivarola, had he not clung to Decoud as a lifesaver."[6]

Such a judgment may well underestimate Caballero, however. It is true that he had been content to follow Bareiro's lead, but he was not merely a follower. As minister of justice in Higinio Uriarte's cabinet, he was almost surely behind the massacre at the Public Prison that took the lives of Facundo Machaín, José Dolores Molas, and others. Colonel Juan A. Meza, who did the actual killing, was married to Caballero's sister. The assassination of Cirilo Rivarola, also carried out by Colonel Meza, was apparently done without President Bareiro's knowledge; but Warren himself quotes Caballero as exclaiming "Now we've got you for certain, you black bastard!" upon hearing that Rivarola had accepted an amnesty and was coming to Asunción.[7] In brief, Caballero was quite capable of acting on his own.

Furthermore, Caballero had a loyal personal following, both in the barracks and in the countryside, among the *jefes políticos* who dominated the villages and small towns of the interior. It was these latter who constituted the basic parts of Caballero's political machine as it began to take shape after 1874. *Jefes políticos* came from many different backgrounds, but they were often soldiers, landowners, or merchants who had settled in those communities after the war and had grown to the point where they had attained, as Juan Carlos Herken Krauer describes it, "a certain local hegemony" based on their relative wealth and their ability to provide jobs.[8] Thus, they had personal retainers, including—like feudal lords—fighting men who made up the local militia. Some *jefes políticos* operated only on a very small, very local scale; others, however, were regional bosses who controlled sizable followings, by Paraguayan standards. These latter might even pose a challenge to the national authorities, whose army, after all, was still poorly trained and equipped. Nominally under the authority of the Ministry of Interior, and acting as its legal agents, it was they who really controlled their local districts and organized the voting at election time.[9] Since 1874, when the "Partido Nacional" finally triumphed over Ferreira's "Partido Liberal," they had gradually swung behind Caballero.

Faced with this, liberal-minded civilians like José Segundo Decoud, Benjamín Aceval, José Urdapilleta, Juan G. González, Cirilo Solalinde, and others felt they had little choice but to work with the regime and try to civilize it from within. Once they learned that Caballero intended to run for president, they launched another Club Libertad in his support, hoping thereby to gain some posts in the future government and counteract, to some extent at least, the influence of the general's military cronies.[10]

Some 47 men were present at the club's founding, of whom twenty-seven had previous political experience. Eight of the activists, including the club's president, Juan G. González, had been in the Paraguayan Legion. Two (José Segundo Decoud and Juan B. Egusquiza) even went back as far as the Asociación Paraguaya. On the other hand, the largest number (nine) came from Bareiro's old Club del Pueblo, and only two of those—Juan G. González and Antonio Taboada—overlapped with the Legion. Another large contingent (seven) had been in Bareiro's Club Libertad. Curiously enough, though, the two *bareirista* groups did not overlap, except for one man: Miguel Haedo, who had been president of the first club and an executive committee member of the second. This suggests the frequency with which loyalties shifted in the period of *caudillo* politics. Indeed, four men had even followed Benigno Ferreira, General Caballero's hated rival, but were now ready to fall into line. Six had once followed Decoud's lead, although most later switched to Bareiro and Caballero as it became clearer that their faction's star was on the rise. Finally, taking all forty-seven Club Libertad members into account, thirteen had served in the army under López. Eight were on the fifteen-man executive committee and one, Ignacio Ibarra, was the club's secretary.[11] Ibarra, a civic-minded war veteran, had recently launched a newspaper, *La Democracia*, which was to become influential—and a thorn in Caballero's side—for its promotion of liberal causes and its attacks on government corruption.

As its reward for serving the *caballerista* cause, the Club Libertad got one of its members, Juan Antonio Jara, on the ticket as vice-president. Also, when the cabinet was formed it received three of the five portfolios. José Segundo Decoud was retained as foreign minister; Juan G. González was named minister of justice; and Juan de la Cruz Giménez, another ex-Legionnaire, was placed in charge of finances. The real "power positions" were reserved for trusted military colleagues, however. Colonel Duarte stayed on at the War Ministry and Caballero's brother-in-law, Colonel Meza, the country's most notorious assassin, became the minister of interior! It fell to his lot, too, to deal with the *jefes políticos*, keeping them satisfied and loyal, so that the Caballero machine could consolidate its grip on power.

FEEDING THE MACHINE

The liberals who wrote the Constitution of 1870 had a vision of Paraguay becoming a kind of Jeffersonian democracy of independent farmers. The tough-minded army men who formed General Caballero's intimate *camarilla* were more concerned with buying votes and rewarding themselves and their friends. Given the social and economic conditions prevailing in 1882, both groups were bound to be frustrated. A dozen years of endemic political anarchy had prevented any real recovery from the war's devastation.

To begin with, the government administration was poorly organized and short of funds. Educated men were in short supply, which was one reason why those in power were often forced to employ people whose political loyalties they suspected. Revenues never matched expenditures because of the limited ability to levy or collect taxes. There were, for example, no taxes on incomes, property, or inheritances. Official fees, stamps, and customs receipts were the only sources of revenues—and so far as customs duties were concerned, there was so much smuggling across Paraguay's extensive and sparsely populated borders that income from this source was very limited.[12]

Even if more taxes had been introduced and the means for collecting them had existed, the country's revenue potential was small. The vast bulk of the population lived from subsistence farming, which was carried on with the crudest of tools. The typical farmer might own a wooden hoe, a machete, and perhaps a wooden plow—which, however, he or his wife would have to pull by themselves. The definition of a well-off farmer was someone who owned an ox. Such crude production methods naturally resulted in very low output—barely enough to feed the farmer's own family. There was little left over to send to the towns, and the means to do so were often lacking. Roads had been abandoned instead of being put back into service. Bridges had not been rebuilt. Thus, there was little incentive to produce a surplus.[13]

Worse still, there was actually less land under cultivation than before the war. Farms abandoned during the fighting had not been reclaimed. The owners were either dead or had moved away, and in any case there was a shortage of men to work the soil. Those who remained in the countryside often had no title to the land they tilled and therefore no incentive to improve it. As squatters they would simply move on when the yield began to fall. The social conditions produced by such a shrunken economy can easily be imagined. Life expectancy at birth was only twenty-four years. As of 1887, there were only fourteen physicians in the entire nation.[14]

Low agricultural output meant that food had to be imported to feed the capital. It was estimated that approximately a fourth of Paraguay's imports consisted of foodstuffs that could have been produced locally. To pay for these, Paraguay exported cattle, hides, logs, tobacco, a little cotton and sugar, a tanning extract taken from the *quebracho* tree, and—most important—*yerba mate*. Most export crops were grown by large commercial companies like La Industrial Paraguaya and Domingo Barthe, Inc., which transported them by river, the latter using its own ships. Of industry there was next to nothing. A few primitive artisan establishments produced leather goods, simple furniture, paper, ink, and cloth. Beyond that, there were blacksmith shops and meat-salting plants to round out the picture of a crude, backward economy.

There were no banks. The Finance Ministry printed its own paper money. This currency was worthless; nevertheless it was turned out in large quantities to pay local creditors, with the result that inflation was endemic, despite the depressed economy. As for foreign creditors, Paraguay's inability to repay its debts, undertaken so blithely in the previous decade, meant that it was unable to borrow.

The restoration of political order under Caballero, however high-handed his methods, offered the first real possibility to tackle these problems. For José Segundo Decoud, who became the architect of economic recovery, it was clear that the goal of small-farmer democracy would have to be abandoned in favor of large-scale, export-oriented agriculture. To promote growth, the government would have to concentrate its efforts simultaneously in three main areas. It would have to encourage foreign investment, promote immigration, and create a stable, effective administration that would put the *jefes políticos* firmly under the rule of law.[15]

Like his Argentine counterpart, Juan Bautista Alberdi, Decoud considered immigration to be the master key to development. It was obvious to him, from the rapid progress being made in neighboring Argentina and Uruguay, that European immigrants were better educated, better skilled, and more hardworking than the native Creole population. Utterly aristocratic in his outlook, he was convinced that Paraguayans, with their Indian antecedents, were racially inferior and quite incapable of rationally exploiting the nation's abundant, fertile land. Only by inundating them with a massive influx of Europeans would Paraguay be able to tap its true potential. To attract them, however, it was necessary to provide a stable political order and to sell off the state lands taken over from the López family, so as to encourage foreigners to buy and settle in the country. The parcels sold off would have to be fairly large, so that only immigrants with some capital would be able to take advantage. As for the native Paraguayans, some uplifting might be possible through compulsory education and compulsory work laws. To prevent them from falling into peonage under the Europeans, the government might set up cooperatives, or "agricultural colonies," to resettle them. But in that case they should not be allowed to alienate any part of the common land, so as to avoid speculation.[16]

Beyond those policies, Decoud offered little more than the usual, sensible liberal recipes. He favored free trade and urged the government to eliminate import duties because they kept the price of food too high. Also, somewhat naively, he recommended trimming government expenditures by reducing the public payroll. Firing more government employees would, he pointed out, free up money to spend on schools and roads.

The Land Sales Law of October 1883 put into practice the basic financial core of Decoud's scheme, although with much different consequences than those he had imagined would follow. Public lands were classified according to their quality and put up for sale at very low prices, the only restriction being that investors had to purchase at least one square league (about 2,000 acres). Huge tracts were sold off, mainly to foreign buyers. At the same time, the land sales enriched the ruling clique because they were able to acquire the parcels first, at even lower prices, and resell them to foreign interests. In the end, much of Paraguay's territory was alienated to Argentine, British, and American companies while Caballero and his friends also acquired estates. Many of the properties sold came replete with agricultural tenants, who were forced to choose between paying higher rents or moving. Since most of them had nowhere else to go, yet could not afford to pay more, they agreed to make up the difference by offering their personal labor. Thus began a process by which poor but independent leaseholders were turned into indebted peons. From the ideal of a yeoman farmer society, Paraguay turned to the reality of a hierarchical system, half-feudal and half-capitalist, in which the rulers lived like barons while the rural poor became like serfs.

Other land sales followed in the next few years. By 1890 over 16 million acres were sold off to seventy-nine different foreign purchasers. Much of that was in the almost empty Chaco region, but even in eastern Paraguay eleven big investors acquired over a quarter of a million acres apiece. In some cases, whole villages were bought up.[17]

The bad effects of this wholesale alienation of public lands were not felt right away. Only a few individuals foresaw the coming foreign economic domination, the degradation of the peasants, and the *latifundio* system. They were dismissed as naysayers because in the short term the land sales seemed to be the tonic that Paraguay's economy needed. Suddenly the country had plenty of hard currency in circulation, which stimulated economic activity. Families that had been land-poor suddenly were prosperous as speculation drove up the value of their property. Those in the administration, plus the *jefes políticos,* and all their relatives and friends rode the crest of the "boom." Enough trickled down, too, to those who provided them with services to make the government truly popular.

As an example of the heightened economic activity, banks now made their appearance for the first time since the war. A public National Bank was set up to control currency exchanges, and a private Banco del Paraguay was chartered for the purpose of receiving deposits and making business loans. With the growth of the local business class came the establishment of a Chamber of Commerce. Many of the new entrepreneurs were immigrants. As Paraguay began to attract more immigrants, the government set up an Immigration Department and also established the first Civil Register. The general prosperity also increased the state's revenues, making it possible to undertake some important public works, such as the rehabilitation of the telegraph lines that had been destroyed in the war and the building of several primary schools. Indeed, education made a comeback during the 1880s. Already in 1878 an elite public high school, the Colegio Nacional, had opened its doors. Now, in 1882, the government authorized the creation of the National University, with the first step being the establishment of a law school. Within a few years a medical school would be added. Finally, flushed with success, the government even repurchased the old railroad, which had been sold off in the 1870s to a local private capitalist to gain ready cash. More symbolic than practical, the railroad proved too costly to run and was quickly resold to a British company.[18]

As might be expected, the new prosperity also had its critics. The manner in which the land sales were carried out, enriching the ruling *caballerista* machine, excited the moral indignation of Ignacio Ibarra, who attacked growing governmental corruption from the pages of *La Democracia*. He was seconded by a fiery young journalist named José de la Cruz Ayala, who wrote under the pseudonym of "Alón" for Héctor Decoud's paper, *El Heraldo*. In addition to corruption, these men protested the long-term consequences they foresaw from the land sales. In doing so they were swimming against the main current of public opinion, but their protests eventually gained effect by touching the sensibilities of a younger generation of educated men who had just graduated from the Colegio Nacional and were entering the newly created university.

Ibarra and "Alón" also found a receptive audience among a minority of congressmen. Opposition to the ruling clique first appeared in Congress on 25 October 1883, when the finance minister, Juan de la Cruz Giménez, found himself under attack for irregularities in the government accounts he presented. The interpellation was begun by José Maria Fretes, who then found sturdy backing from the even more forceful Antonio Taboada. The discomfited finance minister was extricated temporarily from his plight by the appointment of a commission to study the matter. A week later the commission reported its findings to a crowded Chamber of Deputies. This time Giménez was flanked by José Segundo

Decoud, the foreign affairs minister, and Juan G. González, the justice and education minister, to put more authority behind the government's case. Taboada, Fretes, and Ignacio Ibarra (who was also a deputy) were not cowed, however. A tumultuous debate followed, ending with the cabinet ministers walking out of the Chamber. When the vote was taken on the budget the government still managed to get its way, but subsequently Giménez was replaced at Finance by Agustín Cañete, a Supreme Court judge who was close to both Caballero and Decoud.

As Freire Esteves observes, this "parliamentary battle had immense repercussions unforeseen by anyone in Paraguayan politics at the time. From then on a quiet dissidence began to form in the ranks of officialdom which later, as circumstances allowed, would in turn give rise to the formation and organization of a true opposing party."[19] In Congress and in the press, a determined minority would solidify and become increasingly vocal in its opposition to the ruling machine; but it would not become effective until the regime's failings were more obvious. That would not happen so long as prosperity continued.

THE ESCOBAR NOMINATION

Prosperity was kept alive by a second land sale law, passed in 1885, which put another 14 million acres on the block. As before, the law required the sales to be in parcels of not less than 2,000 acres. Some seventy investors, both individuals and companies, took advantage of the opportunity. Most of the land sold belonged to the state, but some of it was taken from private owners who could not show clear title to their property. Also, some of it was timber and pastureland that previously had belonged in common to villages. Commonly held property was alien to orthodox liberalism so the state seized it and sold it to individuals. As a result, many villagers, who depended on the use of those lands, were now reduced to destitution. Along with these land sales went the sale of other valuable state properties, such as *yerba mate* fields, sawmills, and warehouses.[20]

As with the previous land sales, the chief beneficiaries were Caballero's friends and allies, together with the *jefes políticos*, who were allowed to acquire the properties first at cut-rate prices in order to resell them to foreign buyers. Nevertheless, the general effect was to encourage production. The involvement of new capital from abroad meant a rapid expansion of the livestock sector, which now was able to satisfy local needs and even export to neighboring countries. The same was true with other agricultural sectors, as well as with those simple industries that used local primary products. With industry, banking, and shipping progressing, urban property values rose along with those in the rural areas. Meanwhile, the government's popularity continued to climb as it financed even more public works: a national library, a national museum, a hospital for the poor, and—in conjunction with the British—an extension of the railroad line to the east.[21]

In brief, as the Caballero administration drew to a close those Paraguayans who mattered politically were much better off than they had been a decade earlier. The question was, would General Caballero change the Constitution and keep himself in office? He certainly was popular enough to do so, and there were rumors that he was considering such a step. On the other hand, if he stepped down, as he was supposed to do, who would he choose to succeed him? Might it be José Segundo Decoud, who had served Caballero loyally as the "brains" of his administration and was known to covet the presidency? Such questions spurred a group of concerned civilians to form a club, with the already much-used name of Club del Pueblo, on 27 July 1886.

The Club del Pueblo drew together various liberal figures who shared two main concerns: they wanted to see popular government institutionalized by having the Constitution respected, and they did not want José Segundo Decoud, whom they considered to be an unprincipled schemer, to succeed Caballero. Benjamín Aceval, who had been edged out of the cabinet by Decoud, was the club's president; its vice-president was Fernando Saguier, Adolfo's brother. There were two secretaries: José ("Alón") de la Cruz Ayala and Cecilio Báez. The latter recently had graduated first in his class from the Colegio Nacional and was now in the law school. Brilliant, intellectual, well spoken, and passionately interested in civic questions, Báez was rapidly becoming the chief spokesman for his generation. Besides these, there were other men in the club whose names were identified with political reform: Antonio Taboada, José Maria Fretes, Cirilo Solalinde, Ignacio Ibarra, to name just a few. Many of them later helped to start the Centro Democrático; others became leaders of the so-called *civilista*, or moderate, wing of the Colorado Party.[22]

Compared with the Club Libertad that nominated General Caballero in 1881, the Club del Pueblo attracted many political novices. Out of thirty-two names on the Club del Pueblo's roster, seventeen (53 percent) had never been involved before in politics, compared with twenty of the forty-seven men (43 percent) in the Club Libertad. Four others in the Club del Pueblo went back no further in politics than the Club Libertad. Nevertheless, the club showed political astuteness by picking General Patricio Escobar as its presidential candidate. Personally honest and upright, Escobar was second only to Caballero in popularity among military men.

He had a simple faith in the Constitution, which would make it difficult for him to accept Caballero's continuation in office; at the same time his long-time friendship with Caballero made it easy for the latter to accept him as his successor. The nomination also satisfied Caballero's military cronies' desire to have one of their own in office, thus effectively spiking José Segundo Decoud's chances.

General Escobar accepted the Club del Pueblo's nomination, but then he split the club by his vice-presidential choice. After first offering the job to Aceval, who turned it down, he passed over Fernando Saguier and picked José del Rosario Miranda as his running mate. Miranda was a former major in López's army but had been a member of the Gran Club. Elected to the 1870 convention as member of its slate, he took over as presiding officer after Facundo Machaín was expelled. Later he served as President Jovellanos's minister of foreign affairs and minister of justice, and twice sat on the Supreme Court. Despite these liberal credentials, Miranda was known to have participated, as the *jefe político* of Caraguatay, in the corruption that attended the land sales and was friendly with many in the Caballero administration. José de la Cruz Ayala and Héctor Decoud resigned from the Club del Pueblo rather than endorse a ticket with him on it.[23]

Although considered temperamental, Ayala and Decoud had the correct instincts. The pragmatists who swallowed Miranda's candidacy in order to get Escobar into power as the lesser evil eventually found that the price they had to pay was much greater than they ever had imagined. The dignified but simpleminded Escobar let Caballero and Decoud name his cabinet. As a result, the sinister Colonel Meza remained as interior minister, while Colonel Duarte, author of the coup that deprived Fernando Saguier's brother of the presidency, stayed on as war minister! Agustín Cañete, another member of Caballero's entourage, also kept the Finance Ministry. The Justice Ministry went to Colonel Manuel A. Maciel, who, though a member of the Club del Pueblo, was also a friend of Caballero's. Benjamín Aceval accepted the Foreign Affairs portfolio, the only real sop thrown to the club. He was replaced the following year by José Segundo Decoud, just as he had been under Bareiro.[24] In sum, the high-minded members of the Club del Pueblo found themselves completely outgeneraled by the *caballeristas*. Thoroughly disillusioned, the club dissolved itself, but new opposition groups quickly formed at the local level, with an eye toward getting reformers elected in the February 1887 congressional elections.[25]

THE TWO PARTIES ARE BORN

The reformers concentrated on five electoral districts where they could expect strong support from family, friends, and neighbors: the well-to-do Recoleta and Catedral *barrios* of Asunción; the northern town of Concepción, where the liberal Yegros family ruled; the Misiones district in the far south, where Juan Antonio Jara was *jefe político*; and Villarrica in the Central Highlands, where the *jefe político* was none other than Antonio Taboada. Meanwhile, the *caballeristas*, affronted by such challenges, decided to snuff out these dissidents. Using a combination of violence and fraud, they managed to steal enough votes in Misiones to elect Juan G. González over Jara. In Recoleta armed thugs prevented voters known to be sympathetic to the opposition from entering the polling station. On the other hand, similar tactics resulted in an opposition victory in Concepción, and Felipe Torrents won what appeared to be a clean race in the Catedral *barrio*. In a couple of other places the opposition won unexpected victories due to the laxity of the local *caballerista* machine.

The most violent confrontation came in Villarrica, where Taboada was running for the Chamber of Deputies and his good friend, Esteban Gorostiaga, for the Senate. Because Taboada was becoming the dissidents' chief spokesman, the government decided to concentrate its greatest efforts in this district. The *caballeristas* picked a man named Gorostiaga to run against Taboada, hoping that his name, which was the same as the senatorial candidate (though they were not related) would confuse the voters. For the senatorial race their candidate was General Caballero himself!

Because of his local popularity Taboada was able to field a sizable force of armed men, which prevented Caballero's followers from carrying off the ballot boxes. As the two miniarmies glowered at each other it became clear that the election was a standoff. The national authorities then decreed a postponement until 12 June. On that date Caballero returned with reinforcements and a bloody battle was fought, ending in the defeat of Taboada and his followers, who were arrested and sent aboard a train to Asunción. At every stop along the route, however, crowds gathered to cheer the prisoners and load the coaches with flowers. Startled by this spontaneous show of support for the reformers, the government soon released them.[26]

These incidents only encouraged the opposition. When their attempts to censure the government in the Chamber of Deputies were voted down by the majority bloc, they gave up any further hopes of reforming the system from within. On 2 July 1887 Taboada called a meeting of the leading dissidents at his Asunción residence, at which it was agreed to organize formally an opposition party. Eight days later a much larger assembly of 128 men met to found the Centro Democrático.[27]

Eighteen men formed the executive committee, with Taboada as their president and José de la Cruz Ayala as first secretary. I do not have birth dates for four of them, but it seems that the average age was around thirty-six. Their backgrounds were very dissimilar. Ayala and his friend, Cecilio Báez, were in their early twenties. They had studied together at the Colegio Nacional and had Facundo Machaín as their professor. Both had been profoundly affected by his murder. Also in their circle was Fabio Queirolo. Orphaned in the war, he had not been able to go to the Colegio, but supported himself through journalism. His friendship with Báez and "Alón" came as a result of his working for El Heraldo. Very different from these young liberals were the war veterans on the committee: Pedro V. Gill, the Centro's vice-president, once a gunboat captain and now a successful rancher; Cirilo Solalinde, now a successful businessman and banker; José Mateo Collar, minister of justice under Rivarola and currently a member of the Supreme Court; Ignacio Ibarra; Juan Ascenscio Aponte, Felipe Torrents, Antonio Zayas, and Juan Bernardo Dávalos (the Centro's treasurer), all of whom were congressmen. Other notables on the committee were José Z. Caminos, who recently had succeeded Benjamín Aceval as director of the Colegio Nacional; and Francisco Soteras, once a close friend of Benigno Ferreira (living comfortably now off the money he stole while serving as President Jovellanos's minister of finance). Besides these, there were some other young men who were just beginning their political careers, but who would figure prominently later: Victor M. Soler, Ildefonso Benegas, and Avelino Garcete. The final committee member, José J. Goiburu, soon left politics.

The cynical army men, such as Colonel Meza, who formed Caballero's inner circle were inclined to brush off the Centro Democrático as just another collection of ineffectual outsiders. If it became too troublesome, they would squash it. José Segundo Decoud, however, perceived that the Centro Democrático was different from any of the previous clubs. Not only were its leaders popular and much-respected but many were rich and in partnership with the country's leading capitalists. Solalinde, for example, was a director of the Banco Territorial, which had strong financial connections with the largest ranchers, plantation owners, and shippers.[28] Ayala, Queirolo, Báez, Ibarra, and Caminos were prominent in journalistic and intellectual circles. Half of the Centro Democrático's executive committee had served in López's army and another two were children of war veterans. Cracking down on them would have repercussions that would reach into Caballero's own entourage. You could hardly lash out against a man like Pedro Gill who not only had fought bravely in the war but had once been Carlos Antonio López's foreign affairs minister and had served on Francisco Solano López's Supreme Court. Besides, public opinion was clearly beginning to cool toward the regime as the ephemeral prosperity from the land sales gradually spent itself. Impatience was growing toward blatant corruption and electoral fraud. The opposition might not have majority support yet, but the trends pointed in that direction for the future. Moreover, the Centro Democrático was not organized merely to contest the next election; its aim was the replacement, whether sooner or later, of the regime in power.

For Decoud, the Centro Democrático posed both a challenge and an opportunity. Instead of turning to repression, the government needed to make a fresh start by casting off unsavory connections with the past and forming its own party, staffed by high-minded citizens dedicated to continuing the work of national recuperation. Fortunately, he was able to enlist the backing of Colonel Juan Crisóstomo Centurión, who, despite his checkered past, was an educated man with a sophisticated outlook. Because of his influence, Caballero was brought around to the idea of an official party. The actual founding of the Colorado Party—or National Republican Association, as it was called officially—took place at Caballero's home on 25 August 1887.[29]

Some 106 men took part in the founding of the Colorado Party.[30] Its 20-man executive committee was headed by General Caballero, with José Segundo Decoud as first vice-president. Its second vice-president was Higinio Uriarte and its first secretary was Juan G. González. Other notables included José González Granados, Juan Crisóstomo Centurión, and the formerly disgraced finance minister, Juan de la Cruz Giménez. With the completion of this event, Paraguay had the second of the two great political parties that have dominated its politics right down to the present day.

Any serious examination of the political background of the 234 men who founded the Colorado Party and the Centro Democrático (later, the Liberal Party) not only explodes the myth of the latter's "Legionnaire" origins but will acquaint the researcher with what must be accounted as a peculiarly ironic paradox. Once in possession of these names, it is possible to trace the political careers of most of those men. The trail leads through the various political clubs that formed, broke up, and realigned throughout the hectic period from 1869 to 1886. In some cases it ends in the Paraguayan Legion, the Asociación Paraguaya, or the Sociedad Libertadora. In other cases it identifies some men as having served in López's army, government, or diplomatic corps, or as having been studying abroad during the war as recipients of state scholarships. These latter, unless they also served in the Legion, can be considered *lopistas*.

TABLE I. PROMOTIONS AS AN INDICATION OF ACTIVISTS' PRIOR POLITICAL
PARTICIPATION

Promotion	Centro Democrático (n = 34)	Colorado (n = 44)
First	2.9% (1)	72.7% (32)
Second	47.1 (16)	13.6 (6)
Third	50.0 (17)	13.6 (6)
	100.0 (34)	99.9 (44)

Under each of these names was recorded, wherever possible, the date of birth, membership in previous political clubs, government positions held, and participation (if any) in the López regime or army. With respect to all previous political activity, whether in the government or in clubs, people were further classified as belonging to cohorts—or, to use the Spanish term, "promotions" (*promociones*). Thus, those who had been active in the Sociedad Libertadora, Asociación Paraguaya, or Paraguayan Legion were classified as the First Promotion. The Second Promotion began with the establishment of the Triumvirate in 1869 and ended with General Caballero's seizure of power in 1880—a date that accords with the Colorados' own definition of "the Colorado Era" as beginning with that event. The Third Promotion was defined, for analytical purposes, as beginning in September 1880 and ending with the establishment of the Colorado Party in August 1887. With respect to these and future "promotions," it should be emphasized that they refer to when a person entered politics, and not to one's age, so they are not the same as "generations." Thus, the Centro Democrático's president, Taboada, was thirteen years younger than its vice-president, Gill; yet Taboada belonged to the First Promotion, whereas Gill, who had not been active previously in politics, belonged to the Third Promotion.

The comparative results are as follows. First, a much higher proportion of the Centro Democrático's membership had never participated before in politics: 73.4 percent to 58.5 percent. That was not the case with the executive committees, though. Some 83.3 percent of the Centro Democrático's leaders had previously been active in politics, as compared with only 65 percent of the Colorados. But how far back did their previous activities extend? If one takes only the "activists" in the general membership into account, the use of "promotions" as an analytical tool yields the truly startling finding presented in Table 1.

Similar results occur when just the executive committees are examined. Forty percent (eight men) of the Colorado executive committee was from the First Promotion: that is to say, had been members of the Sociedad Libertadora, Asociación Paraguaya, or Paraguayan Legion, as compared with only 5.5 percent (one man) in the Centro Democrático. Thus, not only are Colorado accusations about the "Legionnaire" origins of the Liberal Party inaccurate, but just the reverse is the case! Practically all the Legionnaires still active in politics in 1887 were in the Colorado Party and were prevalent among its leadership.

There are still other findings that run counter to the accepted wisdom in Paraguay. Not only were Legionnaires practically absent from the Centro Democrático, but, as we have seen, nine of the eighteen executive committee members had served in López's army during the war and two others were direct descendants of *lopista* war veterans. By contrast, only two of the twenty Colorado leaders were López soldiers: General Caballero, the party's president, and Colonel Juan Crisóstomo Centurión.

SUMMARY AND CONCLUSIONS

Should we conclude that the truth is just the reverse of commonly accepted generalizations about Paraguay's traditional parties: that the Colorados were really liberals and the Liberals were really nationalists? There is a grain of truth to that line of thought. The Colorados were indeed liberals. Under the presidencies of General Caballero (1882–86) and his ally, General Patricio Escobar (1886–90), most of the properties accumulated under the old Socialist State were sold off to wealthy private buyers. Most of the men who were instrumental in organizing the National Republican Association, such as José Segundo Decoud and Juan Gualberto González, were Legionnaires and still believed in classical liberalism. For them, the party was the only feasible way to organize liberal civilian elements to take power away from the crude military chiefs who were then running the country. They were *civilista* Colorados. Rejecting outright rebellion as suicidal, based on their experiences in the 1870s, they hoped to civilize the regime from within.

The Centro Democrático's membership might be said to fall into three general categories. First, there were those who were getting into politics for the first time, inspired by a desire for reform. Many of those in the *caballerista* machine, which dominated the government in 1887, had been in power since 1874. Their rule had been marred by corruption and violence, even assassination. Although it had brought a measure of peace and prosperity to Paraguay, the machine had alienated a large part of the educated, politically active citizenry, especially a younger generation typified by men like Cecilio Báez, Fabio Queirolo, and "Alón."

Something similar might be said for the *lopistas* who joined the Centro Democrático. Their national pride was offended by the wholesale alienation of Paraguay's lands and the creation of vast, foreign-owned *latifundia*. They were as disgusted as the young intellectuals by the speculation and corruption that attended those sales. Men like Pedro V. Gill, Juan Bernardo Dávalos, and Juan A. Aponte, all ex-López officers, had stayed out of politics for most of the postwar period, but now they got involved out of a sense of crisis.

The last group, the men with political experience, were mostly veterans of the various political clubs that flourished between 1869 and 1874. Most of them had been early followers of Caballero and his more intellectual predecessor, Cándido Bareiro. When Bareiro and Caballero came to dominate the scene after 1874, some of these men acted as their *jefes políticos* in the various towns and villages, or served the regime as congressmen or judges. Like the other Centro Democrático components, they eventually turned against the system because of its rampant corruption. Taboada's break with the regime, for example, came because as a deputy in Congress he dared to question Caballero's finance minister on his handling of government funds. His daring soon encouraged others, and when the government attempted to purge these maverick congressmen, the rift was made permanent.

In sum, Paraguay's two traditional parties arose not because of any great ideological differences but because of growing criticism of the existing regime. The *civilista* Colorados and the men of the Centro Democrático shared many of the same reforming values, but they could not work together because the former were considered to be too compromised. Thus, two battle lines formed: incumbents and reformers, ins versus outs. Intransigence on both sides inevitably led to violence, thus hardening those battle lines. This was the sort of durable polarization that Samuel Huntington had in mind as a prerequisite for party formation. Over the next decade both parties competed, in a process Huntington calls "expansion," to mobilize the citizenry as a whole. Not electoral strength but fighting capacity finally determined success, however. Despite the attempts by certain moderates on both sides to find a peaceful compromise, Paraguayan politics became locked in a perpetual cycle of repression and revolt that deepened the sense of partisanship and defeated the liberal democratic ideals that underlay the Constitution.

four

THE COLORADO ERA

The dominant political coalition that came to known as the National Republican Association, or Colorado Party, had taken over the government in 1874, after the Partido Nacional succeeded in getting Benigno Ferreira out of power. The main *caudillos* of that coalition—Juan Bautista Gill, Cándido Bareiro, Bernardino Caballero, Patricio Escobar, and José Segundo Decoud—had kept together afterward and provided Paraguay with a reasonably consistent set of policies. The "political agenda" of that time was simple: to settle all boundary questions and get the foreign troops off Paraguay's soil, to put an end to *caudillo* anarchy and establish an effective central government, and repair the war-torn economy. Although their methods included murder and corruption, these proto-Colorados did manage to achieve the first two goals rather better than might have been expected. Furthermore, they also brought about a temporary prosperity, at least for those who stood well with the government. It was Gill, after all, who initiated the policy of land sales, although the bulk of these were carried out during the presidencies of Caballero and Escobar. In brief, it is possible to trace a fairly direct line of personnel and policy from the old Partido Nacional coalition to the founding of the Colorado Party. Connecting links were even sealed, in some cases, by family ties. Colonel Juan A. Meza, head of the Presidential Escort under Gill, Uriarte, and Bareiro, and minister of interior under Caballero and Escobar, was Caballero's brother-in-law. Also related by marriage to Caballero was Juan Gualberto González, who succeeded Escobar to the presidency in 1890, and Marcos Morínigo, who became González's vice-president. Caballero, meanwhile, had married Juan Bautista Gill's widow.

Gradually, very gradually, the political agenda was beginning to change. The establishment of an official party in 1887 was at least a partial recognition that the rough-and-ready methods of the old military-based ruling clique were no longer suitable. It was an attempt to regularize the procedures for candidate selection and by so doing to recruit government talent from a broader pool. As such, the Colorado Party was the brainchild of liberal, civilian elements inside the regime—men like José Segundo Decoud, the leading spirit behind the project; Juan Gualberto González, who like Decoud had been a Legionnaire, and was related by marriage to Decoud as well as to Caballero; Miguel Alfaro, a relative of Decoud's who became the party's second vice-president; Esteban Rojas, the youthful president of the Banco Agrícola, who became the party's treasurer; and José González Granados and José Tomás Sosa, both veterans of various liberal clubs during the 1870s. Not only did they hope to rein in the old *lopista* officers, but they even thought it possible to work with their opponents in the Centro Democrático to establish a grand coalition of moderate, liberal civilians.

They did not have a clear, open field, however. The old *lopista* clique had an energetic leader in Colonel Juan A. Meza, who often claimed to know General Caballero's "real" wishes. Indeed, Caballero did share Meza's suspicion and contempt for the *civilistas,* although the general also recognized the need for the regime to present a more modern face to the public. As Escobar's minister of interior, however, Meza was in a position to continue the heavy-handed tactics that worked so well in the past. In December 1888 the two new parties contested elections for the Chamber of Deputies. To insure a Colorado victory, Meza sent mounted police to all the polling places in Asunción with orders to prevent any known Liberals from voting. There were clashes, but the Liberals were driven off. Four people were killed, thirty-seven wounded, and sixty-eight arrested.[1]

Nevertheless, the *civilistas* pressed ahead with their strategy and even succeeded in getting Meza replaced the following year by Colonel Manuel A. Maciel, a much more moderate officer. As the time for the 1890 general elections approached, José Segundo Decoud convinced General Caballero to allow him to ask Antonio Taboada, the Centro Democrático president, about forming a fusion ticket. Otoniel Peña, Decoud's brother-in-law, was deputized to represent the Colorados and Taboada brought with him José Zacarías Caminos, head of the Colegio Nacional, to help speak for the Liberals. After lengthy discussions, the two sides agreed to field a single ticket, with Juan Gualberto González as the presidential candidate and Victor M. Soler, from the Centro Democrático, as his running mate.[2]

Although it was approved by a majority of the Centro Democrático's executive committee, this pact split the new party. Cecilio Báez and José de la Cruz Ayala, two young firebrands, walked out of the meeting and promptly started a rebellion against Taboada, Caminos, and Ignacio Ibarra, accusing them of selling out to the government.[3] In reality, Taboada was neither naive nor cynical when it came to dealing with the Colorados. He was willing to deal with the *civilistas,* but at the same time he was in touch with Benigno Ferreira and Juansilvano Godoi, exiled in Argentina, to lay the groundwork for a revolt in case the government practiced treachery. On the Colorados' side, Colonel Meza was determined to wreck the truce and, if possible, even prevent the *civilistas* from getting their man, González, the party's nomination. In January 1889 he used his old ham-handed tactics to keep Liberals from registering to vote by sending policemen to the cathedral where the process was taking place. This time, however, he was foiled by the mayor, Colonel Juan Antonio Jara, who arrived with his own armed men to make sure that registration proceeded fairly.[4] It was not long after this that Colonel Meza was replaced in the cabinet.

Nevertheless, Meza's tactics had their effect. Cecilio Báez and José de la Cruz Ayala gained strength among Liberals, forcing Taboada and his followers to repudiate the electoral pact and accuse the Colorados of bad faith. The Centro Democrático announced that it would boycott the elections. Soler withdrew his candidacy and his place on the ticket was taken by Rosendo Carisimo, a Colorado senator. But Carisimo was forced to withdraw too when Colonel Meza threatened to split the party by declaring his own presidential candidacy. Meza finally abandoned that project, despite considerable support from hard-line *lopistas,* when neither Caballero nor Escobar would endorse him. The *civilistas* felt obliged to throw him a sop, however, by nominating Caballero's son-in-law, Marcos Morínigo, for vice-president.

The Colorados' choice of Juan Gualberto González as their presidential candidate in 1890 and his subsequent election marked the apex of José Segundo Decoud's influence in politics. González's cabinet appointments were highly favorable to the *civilistas.* Decoud became finance minister; Benjamín Aceval got the Justice and Education Ministry; José Tomás Sosa went to Interior; and the War Ministry went to an old Legionnaire, Colonel Juan B. Egusquiza, who for some time had quietly served as the *jefe político* of the southern border town of Encarnación. The *lopistas* had to be content with Venancio López, a young lawyer with no political experience, at Foreign Affairs and Colonel Juan A. Meza as police chief. González's Supreme Court appointments were further indicative of the new administration's liberal intentions: Colonel Fernando Iturburu, who declined to return from Buenos Aires to take up the post; César Gondra, a young liberal lawyer who had served as minister of justice and education near the end of President Escobar's term; and Emiliano González Navero, a twenty-nine-year-old member of the Centro Democrático.

The new administration had a sharply different character than its predecessor. Eleven men, including the president, vice-president, and the cabinet ministers, had held top posts in the Escobar government. Six of them had served as officers in López's army, and eight had been drawn from the Second Promotion. By contrast, eleven of the top twelve men in the González government were civilians, and only two were from the Second Promotion. Moreover, the lone military man, Colonel Egusquiza, had achieved his experience and rank in the Paraguayan Legion, not under López.[5] The Legionnaires from the First Promotion were more in evidence: there were four of them, including the president, as compared with only two in the preceding administration. But there were lots of new faces too. Five men were from the Fourth Promotion, the most recent, and one other was from the Third Promotion. In short, the *civilistas'* ascendancy shifted the political emphasis simultaneously toward liberalism and youth.[6]

THE 1891 REVOLT

Despite all the positive aspects the new administration possessed, it was threatened from the outset by intransigents from both parties. During the Escobar period, Colonel Meza, as minister of interior, had prodded the *jefes políticos* to set up local Colorado Party committees throughout the country. The organization's grass roots were firmly in *caballerista* hands, and eventually this began to reflect itself in the upper echelons. The original 1887 party executive committee was headed by General Caballero as president, with José Segundo Decoud as first vice-president doing the actual running of the party organization with the help of Juan Gualberto González as first secretary. The following year Colonel Juan Crisóstomo Centurión replaced Decoud while Remigio Mazó, a civilian *caballerista*, replaced González. Miguel Alfaro, a relative of Decoud's exercised some *civilista* influence as second vice-president, but not much. The post of second secretary, which Mazó held on the original executive committee, was abolished when he moved up. By 1891 *caballerismo* was in full control, with General Escobar replacing Centurión as first vice-president and Agustín Cañete, a *lopista* major, taking over the post of second vice-president. Héctor Carvallo, another civilian *caballerista* was now secretary. The only *civilista* among the top officers was Esteban Rojas, president of the Banco Agrícola, who was party treasurer. This hardening of the Colorado Party's organization was reflected in the renewed violence that marred the February 1891 congressional elections. Instigated by Colonel Meza, whom General Caballero had imposed on the government as police chief, Colorado thugs stole ballot boxes and fought battles to keep the opposition from voting. One particularly bloody clash forced the Liberals' chief publicist, José de la Cruz Ayala ("Alón") to go underground, from which he eventually made his way into exile. Also, Colorado goons kidnapped Ignacio Ibarra, the editor of *La Democracia*, and roughed him up. That caused César Gondra to resign from the Supreme Court in protest.

Understandably, the Liberals lost their patience. In August 1891 the Centro Democrático reorganized its executive committee so as to put the party on a fighting basis. Taboada stepped aside as president in favor of Major Eduardo Vera, one of many ex-*lopista* officers who were disgusted by the current regime. Vera, a career soldier who had been part of Francisco Solano López's personal guard, had a distinguished war record. Afterward he had devoted himself to ranching, performing his duties as a regional *jefe político* in the Colorado machine, and serving in Congress as deputy for Encarnación. But as he grew wealthy he began to travel to Europe, the result of which was a broadening of his outlook. Shocked by the brutal tactics of his party colleagues in the 1891 elections, he resigned and accepted the Centro Democrático's offer of the presidency. Like the Liberals, he was convinced that only a revolution could bring democratic government to Paraguay.

The ingredients for a revolt were beginning to blend. The social ambience was propitious too, because the ephemeral prosperity built on the land sales of the 1880s had worn off and now Paraguay was in the throes of a severe recession. Even before Escobar stepped down from the presidency, the government's treasury was empty. In addition, Paraguay was feeling the effects of a financial crisis in neighboring Argentina, its principal trading partner and source of most investment capital. As Argentina's economy contracted, so did Paraguay's. Exports to Argentina plunged, farmers faced ruin, and banks folded. The Escobar government tried to meet its obligations by selling bonds, but nobody would buy them. Then it resorted to turning out paper money in large quantities to pay its bills, with the result that the currency soon became worthless and inflation soared.

As finance minister, Decoud labored between twelve and fifteen hours a day trying to raise loans and find new sources of revenue. With the economy whipsawed between recession and inflation, he turned to austerity measures, starting with a lid on new currency emissions. This was extremely unpopular with businessmen and politicians. The former, already in financial straits, demanded easy credit while the latter protested the cutback in public works projects in their districts. Complaints mounted until finally an exhausted and frustrated Decoud admitted defeat and resigned in July 1891. As Caballero Aquino points out, this brief stint as González's finance minister was the high point of his political career. Decoud had distinguished himself earlier as a diplomat and political strategist, but it was in the less visible area of finance that, in trying to reform Paraguay's wayward practices, that he showed himself to be a true statesman. He continued to be a potential presidential candidate and returned to government service as foreign minister later in the decade, but after 1891 his political star was on the wane.[7]

Decoud's departure did little to restore the government's popularity, although his place was taken by the banker, Esteban Rojas, who represented the business community. Meanwhile, the Liberals pressed ahead with the plans for their revolt. The chief conspirators, besides Major Vera and Taboada, were Fabio Queirolo, a close friend of the exiled "Alón"; Alejandro Audivert, a former Supreme Court justice under Escobar who was impeached because he defended the freedom of the press against official censorship; Pedro P. Caballero, one of the Liberals' few congressmen and a fiery orator; Juan Pablo Machaín, another Liberal deputy who continued in the family's political tradition; and Juan Bautista Rivarola, who headed the Customs Bureau and so was able to supply the rebels with smuggled arms.

The conspirators' strategy was complicated.[8] One group was to seize the cavalry barracks in the heart of Asunción, a second contingent was to take the infantry barracks a few blocks away, and a third was to capture the Central Police Station. Smaller parties were to attack the telephone exchange, get control of the port, and go to General Caballero's home and take him prisoner (or kill him if he resisted). Sunday, 18 October, was set as the decisive day, because most army officers and government officials would be away from their posts.

The attack began at seven o'clock in the evening, as Major Vera led a raid by some thirty-six men that overpowered the sentinels at the cavalry barracks and captured the unit. Unfortunately, this was earlier than originally planned, so the soldiers at the nearby infantry barracks heard the shots and were alerted by the time Pedro P. Caballero showed up there with his men. Indeed, Colonel Egusquiza, the war minister, was already in touch with all military and police units in the region, organizing a counterattack. Not only were Caballero's men driven off but Taboada's failed to take the telephone exchange and Queirolo's were held at bay by a stiff police resistance. Only those, led by Rivarola, who attacked the docks were successful. In fact, they didn't have to fire a shot.

From that point on, things fell apart quickly. After being driven from the telephone exchange, Taboada's men retreated toward the cavalry barracks. On coming in sight of the place, they saw uniformed men milling in the entrance and, mistaking their own *compañeros* for government troops, fired in panic. Major Vera fell dead. Meanwhile, as some of the rebels at the docks left to back up Major Vera's forces, they encountered government troops proceeding in that direction. They quickly returned to the port and reported that the coup had failed, whereupon Rivarola and the rest commandeered a ship and fled across the river to Argentina. While this was going on Queirolo's men ran out of ammunition and had to abandon their attack on the police station. Perhaps the silliest debacle concerned the party sent out to arrest General Caballero. Led by Colonel José del Carmen Pérez, who undertook the mission unwillingly, they arrived at Caballero's home just as the general was sitting down to dinner with a couple of friends. Pérez refused to go any further with the scheme and stayed out on the sidewalk while the others forced their way into the house. Alarmed by the servants, Caballero and his friends blew out the candles on the table, grabbed rifles, and began blasting away at the intruders. The latter yelled out "Death to the tyrant Caballero!" and promptly fled, leaving behind one of their wounded.

As midnight approached the rebels in the cavalry barracks began to come under increasing fire from reinforced government troops. One of those killed was young Juan Pablo Machaín, who became the latest in this unfortunate family's political martyrs.[9] Taking advantage of the dark, most of the other rebels were able to make their escape. A triumphant Egusquiza quickly announced that the revolt was over and the government was saved. Over the next several weeks there was a roundup of all Liberals suspected of having had any part in planning the revolt. The period of repression did not last long, however. With order restored, the country soon settled back into normality. Or so at least it seemed, for beneath the surface things were no longer quite what they had been before.

THE CAMPAIGN OF 1894

Egusquiza's alertness and courage, along with the rebels' ineptitude, had decided the outcome of the October revolt. Despite his Legionnaire past, he now became the Colorados' new military hero. As his reward, he was promoted to general. That made him an equal of Caballero and Escobar, which had political consequences. A man of liberal convictions whose career extended back to the exile clubs of Buenos Aires, he was committed to furthering the *civilista* program of political reconciliation.

By the midpoint of 1892 the Liberals were also in a less belligerent mood. In the first months following the revolt, Antonio Taboada and Pedro P. Caballero continued to send bands of guerrillas across the border, but Egusquiza quickly snuffed them out. As it became clear that they had no hope of destabilizing the government, the Liberals abandoned their intransigence. Through the complicated network of family and friendship connections that permeates Paraguayan society, they let it be known that they were willing to cooperate. The government was receptive, both because the *civilistas* still hoped for a centrist coalition with the Liberals and for pragmatic reasons as well. There was, after all, a dearth of educated men in Paraguay—a fact that President González had referred to in his inaugural address to Congress when he noted that "the limited number of men capable of handling the various government departments requires us to use all the skill available without regard to political affiliation."[10]

On 21 August a new Centro Democrático directorate was elected from among those Liberals still in the country. This time the president was Manuel I. Frutos, a former *lopista* officer. Cecilio Báez was vice-president and Fernando Carreras, the most active in the party's rebuilding program, became secretary. Out of sixteen people on the directorate, four were entirely new. Very soon after reorganizing, the Liberals had to face congressional elections, scheduled for February 1893. Their leaders felt unprepared and preferred instead to support *civilista* Colorado candidates, who were facing a challenge from a rival list of *caballeristas*. With this support from the Liberals, the *civilistas* gained most of the seats.

In terms of the party system's development, this election was significant, for many reasons. First, it showed that General Caballero was no longer in control.[11] He could be successfully defied. Second, it showed that, by working together, the *civilista* Colorados and Liberals could claim the support of a majority of the active and articulate segments of the public—the only public that really mattered. Third, it encouraged further attempts to forge an alliance of moderate elements from both parties. Taken to its logical conclusion, that would have given Paraguay a three-party instead of a two-party system. The formation of a new Centro Democrático directorate did nothing to reverse this move toward the center. Although returning exiles like Taboada, Pedro P. Caballero, José Irala, and Avelino Garcete were elected to it, they had moderated their passions and were now ready to work within the system.

But just as the Centro Democrático was pulling itself together, the Colorados were splintering over who would be their presidential nominee in 1894. José Segundo Decoud, who had gone to Buenos Aires after resigning from the cabinet, returned to the country to pursue the prize that so long had eluded him. He had the backing of President González, his brother-in-law and a fellow Legionnaire. His candidacy became an international issue, however, because the Brazilians perceived him as being too pro-Argentine. "Brazil and Argentina were major political poles, magnets to attract Paraguayan politicians," Warren notes.

This polarity not only required Argentine and Brazilian leaders to be suspicious of one another but also prevented Paraguay from leading a truly independent political existence. During the Colorado era, Paraguay's two powerful neighbors generally refrained from overt involvement in Paraguayan politics. There were two notable exceptions: Brazil in 1894 planned and paid for a coup to prevent José Segundo Decoud from succeeding to the presidency, and Argentina in 1904 blatantly supported the Liberal revolt that ended Colorado dominance.[12]

Brazil preferred General Caballero, who was now constitutionally eligible to run again. The general was easily persuaded to throw his hat in the ring, supported, as the *Enciclopedia Republicana* puts it, by "the old guard of Cerro Corá."[13] Fired up at the prospect of regaining their old political monopoly, the *caballeristas* launched a newspaper, *La Libertad*, whose first issue directed a withering blast at Decoud. The article began moderately enough by admitting that Decoud might be an illustrious diplomat but insisted that he lacked the "sane ideas" or the "recognized patriotism" necessary to govern a republic. Warming to its theme, *La Libertad* then asserted that Paraguay would not allow anyone who had served in the Allied armies to become president of the nation. When this failed to achieve its aim of forcing Decoud to withdraw, the paper pressed its attack with more vigor in another article, entitled "Fuera Don Segundo!" ("Begone, Don Segundo!"). "Not only is he [Decoud] a traitor to the Nation," *La Libertad* claimed, "but to his party as well."

Decoud refused to bow out. Not until just before the party convention did he finally accept the defeat of his hopes. Then, on 22 November 1893, he announced that he would no longer seek the nomination, but neither would he endorse Caballero. Instead, he called on the *civilistas* to rally behind General Egusquiza, who had resigned as war minister in March in order to run for the presidency. For the *caballeristas* this was Decoud's crowning act of treachery. Still, they gave it little weight. The party machinery was in their grasp again and they had the support of the barracks, or so they thought. Five days after Decoud's announcement, the Colorado Party directorate informed the public that General Caballero would be their presidential choice and that Colonel Manuel A. Maciel would be his running mate.[14] On 17 December, a party assembly held at the home of Vice-President Marcos Morínigo, Caballero's son-in-law, ratified this.

In the meantime, on 1 December, a group of *civilistas* known as the Club Popular Egusquicista held a downtown rally in the Plaza Uruguaya and nominated Egusquiza for president. He, in turn, chose César Gondra as his running mate. The Club Popular attracted people from all walks of life. There were a few older men who had either been Legionnaires, *lopista* officers, or participants in the political clubs of the 1870s, but the great majority of members were new to politics. Quite a few were teachers and intellectuals: Manuel Domínguez was a respected literary figure who also had been director of the Colegio Nacional, head of the National Archives, and professor of constitutional law at the university; Benigno Riveros, a mathematics teacher, was editor of the *Revista de Instrucción Pública*; Aniceto Garcete, a primary school teacher, was editor of *El Normalista*; and Manuel Amarilla was currently the general superintendent of public instruction. Decoud's endorsement of Egusquiza brought the latter the support of Arsenio López Decoud, a famous writer and journalist, who also happened to be Carlos Antonio López's grandson. Pedro Miranda, another journal editor, had been picked by President González as a safe, anti-*caballerista* substitute for Egusquiza at the War Ministry.

Businessmen constituted, perhaps, the most interesting and revealing group of participants in the Club Popular. Some of the richest and most prominent were active in it. Emilio Aceval, the Club's vice-president, was the younger brother of Benjamín Aceval. He had been one of the young boys—*los niños heroes*-drafted to fight in López's army but had devoted himself after the war to getting an education. With his older brother's connections he was able to get into business and then into banking, becoming a director of the National Bank in 1892 and, later, president of the Banco Agrícola. Antonio Sosa, a close associate of Aceval's, was a lawyer who also figured prominently in business and banking circles. Federico Bogarín was a rancher from the northeastern border region who had gotten rich by smuggling cattle into Brazil. Rodolfo Saguier was the brother of Adolfo Saguier, the man who should have succeeded Cándido Bareiro to the presidency, instead of Caballero. Like his brother, he was a prosperous rancher and banker. What these men reflected, as a group, was the increasing concern of business interests to establish moderate, progressive government in Paraguay. What importers and exporters needed was order and stability—not imposed by the club and the gun, but institutionalized through constitutional practice as in that great liberal capitalist model, the United States. Having risen during the past decade to a position where they could challenge the old landowning elite for economic dominance, they now sought to consolidate their position through political alliances that would provide them with government backing.[15] Egusquiza offered them their best chance.

Egusquiza was, indeed, an attractive candidate. Handsome, courageous, resourceful, intelligent, and *simpático,* he was popular not only with intellectuals and businessmen but with military officers as well. The latter admired his decisiveness in the October 1891 revolt and they appreciated his efforts as war minister to modernize the army. Thus, when the *caballeristas* went knocking on the barracks doors, they were surprised to find that there was no support for any military action to force Egusquiza out of the race.

While the Colorados were dividing their ranks, the Liberals were being courted by all the factions. Shortly before he withdrew from the race, Decoud approached Taboada to enlist his support, but the Liberals were still unforgiving toward him. After Egusquiza got the formal endorsement of the Club Popular in December, Frutos, Báez, and Taboada held conversations with Rufino Mazó, the club's president, and Emilio Aceval, with a view toward uniting their forces. In that same month Frutos and Báez met with General Escobar and Agustín Cañete about supporting the *caballerista* ticket. There was also a suggestion that Caballero might withdraw in favor of Cañete if that were necessary to win over the Liberals. The *egusquicistas* were back in touch, through Adolfo Saguier, in January 1894. So were the *caballeristas*. Finally, on 24 May, the Liberals put an end to all the courtship by announcing that they would run their own slate, with Benjamín Aceval as their presidential candidate and Juan B. Gaona, a leading partner in La Industrial Paraguaya and the Banco Territorial, as his running mate.[16]

Two weeks later the country was startled by a coup that removed President Juan Gualberto González from power. It was the brainchild of Amaro Cavalcanti, the Brazilian ambassador, and had the approval of both General Caballero and General Egusquiza. It was not directed against the Liberals, who were still considered no threat to Colorado hegemony, but against José Segundo Decoud, who despite his withdrawal from the race was still plotting to get the presidency. According to the Brazilian ambassador, his sources reported that González, Decoud's brother-in-law and fellow Legionnaire, was planning a coup from above. Evidence to support this came from the proadministration newspaper, *La República*, which had suddenly dropped its campaign in favor of Egusquiza and began calling upon Colorados to unite and look for "a notable statesman" to lead the country. With suspicions raised in both the *egusquicista* and *caballerista* camps, it was an easy matter for Cavalcanti to bring their leaders together. In a statesmanlike gesture, Caballero agreed to stand aside for Egusquiza, in return for the latter replacing César Gondra with Facundo Ynsfrán on the ticket.[17] Ynsfrán was Caballero's nephew and a great favorite of his, besides being considered one of the most promising young men in the Colorado Party.

The pact having been made, Egusquiza lined up his support in the army and police and then demanded González's resignation. Just for good measure, he had three Brazilian gunboats in the harbor, ready to back him up. On 9 June the president was conducted to the cavalry barracks where generals Egusquiza, Caballero, and Escobar awaited him.

After signing his resignation he went to the docks, boarded a ship, and sailed for Buenos Aires. Vice-President Marcos Morínigo formed a provisional government, composed equally of *egusquicistas* and *caballeristas*.

Elections were held on 20 August, and the Egusquiza-Ynsfrán formula won unopposed. The Liberals, meanwhile, had fallen into such disarray that they were unable to field a ticket. Their split was deep and enduring, and it revolved around the controversial figure of Benigno Ferreira.

Ferreira, it will be recalled, was the Legionnaire liberal who, for a brief period in 1873–74, had been the brains and muscle of the Jovellanos administration. His tough-minded pragmatism about coalition building had alienated many of his former liberal friends and the strong suspicion that he stole most of the money from the British loans permanently tarnished his reputation. Nevertheless, the Centro Democrático leaders, convinced after the June coup that neither of the Colorado factions could be trusted, were again considering an armed revolt. Consequently, they felt the need of a skilled military leader and General Ferreira best fit that description, even though he had spent the years after 1874 studying and practicing law in Argentina. He was a business associate of Victor Soler, who was on the Centro Democrático directorate, and through him had kept in touch with the Paraguayan situation. On 13 July the party's president, Manuel Frutos, backed by other directors, proposed a complete reorganization, including the incorporation of Ferreira as the new chief. After a heated discussion, in which Cecilio Báez led the opposition, it was decided to present the idea to the general membership. Two days later the scheme was debated by a party assembly, which approved the formation of a new directorate under Ferreira's leadership, along with the adoption of the name "Liberal Party" in place of the Centro Democrático.

Ferreira, still in Buenos Aires, issued a statement after the August election offering Egusquiza the Liberals' cooperation. Although he did not return to Paraguay until the end of the year, the prospect of his leadership, together with his conciliatory policy, touched off a revolt in the ranks. Fernando Carreras, the party secretary, began receiving a stream of resignations. Others, led by Báez, set up an independent newspaper called *El Pueblo* which immediately began attacking Ferreira. Another assembly, called in February 1895 reiterated the party's support for him, but such support was "soft," at best. His secretary, Carreras, and his vice-president, Fabio Queirolo, were having their doubts, as were other notables like Antonio Taboada, who originally had supported the change. Unwilling to carry on under these circumstances, Ferreira resigned in March, although he continued to urge the Liberals to cooperate with the new Egusquiza administration.[18]

THE EGUSQUIZA INTERLUDE

Juan Bautista Egusquiza assumed the presidency on 25 November 1894. Most of his cabinet was composed of supporters from the Club Popular Egusquicista. Rufino Mazó, the club's president, was minister of justice; Emilio Aceval, the club's vice-president, took over the War Ministry, even though he was a civilian; Angel M. Martínez, the club's treasurer, became minister of interior. Héctor Velásquez, a young physician who was currently rector of the university, was made foreign affairs minister. The only *caballeristas* were Facundo Ynsfrán, the vice-president; and Agustín Cañete, the finance minister.

Egusquiza's main interest was to bring about a reconciliation between the Colorados and Liberals, with a view to marginalizing permanently "the old guard of Cerro Corá." A believer in civilian rule and honest government, he sought to recruit the "best," regardless of their party affiliations. His first step was to get Congress to grant an amnesty to all those who had been convicted of political crimes and allow political exiles to return. That cleared the slate for men like Ferreira and Juansilvano Godoi. Next, Egusquiza guaranteed honest elections and kept his word, with the result that Liberals increased their representation in Congress. Indeed, Liberals were even appointed to the cabinet. Benjamín Aceval replaced Cañete as finance minister in June 1895; and when Rufino Mazó took over from Martínez as interior minister in 1898, he was replaced at Justice and Education by José Mateo Collar. The Supreme Court became a Liberal stronghold. During the next four years Benigno Ferreira, Fabio Queirolo, Cecilio Báez, Alejandro Audivert, Emeterio González, and Manuel Gondra took turns serving as justices. Pedro P. Caballero became the government's chief prosecutor.[19]

As proof of his willingness to bring the brightest talent into his administration, regardless of past politics, Egusquiza appointed José Segundo Decoud as foreign minister after Héctor Velásquez was moved over to chair the National Board of Health. And it was a measure of his own statesmanship that Decoud accepted the appointment from the man who had snatched the presidency away from him. Egusquiza also continued to cultivate the rising new business class. After Benjamín Aceval stepped down as finance minister to take over the important new Foreign Exchange Board (Caja de Conversión), Agustín Cañete returned to the post briefly, but was then replaced by Guillermo de los Ríos, a very wealthy banker.

The average age of eleven men who held top office in this reform government was about forty-seven. They represented all the promotions from the First to the Fifth (1894–1902). Egusquiza and Decoud were the two Legionnaires from the First Promotion; Cañete, Collor, and Benjamín Aceval began their careers in the Second Promotion; Emilio Aceval, a founding member of the Colorado Party, was from the Third; Ynsfrán, Martínez, and Mazó became active in the Fourth; and Velásquez and de los Ríos were completely new to politics. Only two of the eleven, Egusquiza and Cañete, had military backgrounds. Cañete had long been out of the service and had prospered in business, while Egusquiza was a champion of civilian rule. In brief, this was a government suited to the emergent capitalist society that Paraguay was becoming.

SOCIAL AND ECONOMIC CONDITIONS

Egusquiza had the good fortune to enter office at a time of expanding trade with Europe. The industrial revolution there created a growing demand for food, much of which was supplied by Latin America. An increase in agricultural production in Paraguay meant more revenue for the government, which in turn used this to fund public works. Egusquiza benefited greatly from this return of prosperity.

Agriculture was divided into two broad sectors. The modern sector consisted of large capitalist enterprises that produced meat, *yerba mate*, timber, or quebracho extract for export. It was dominated by large companies like La Industrial, Carlos Casado, Inc., and Domingo Barthe & Co. The traditional sector was characterized by small farmers, often squatters or sharecroppers who rented their land from one of the big estates in return for a portion of the crop. They lacked capital and their tools were primitive—often no more than sharpened wooden sticks. Such farmers had no access to credit from the Banco Agrícola, which was set up to finance the big exporters. Nor was it easy for them to get their goods to market, for the road system was still very backward. Those who lived near the railway line were more fortunate. Indeed, every extension of the railroad boosted domestic production by opening up formerly inaccessible land and facilitating the shipment of goods. For this reason Egusquiza was willing to grant easy terms to the foreign concessionaires to extend the line all the way to the southern port of Encarnación, even though his opponents in Congress criticized the railroad contracts as "selling out" the nation. Egusquiza could reply to his critics that the inability to get produce from the farms to the capital meant that every year about a third or more of Paraguay's imports consisted of food that could otherwise be supplied domestically.[20]

It was the modern agricultural sector that provided the basis of the new business class that came into prominence during the 1890s. The great land sales of the previous decade together with the backward, corrupt administrative structure of the old *caballerista* governments originally permitted the accumulation of great fortunes. Companies like La Industrial reflected the tight personal networks that permitted government favoritism and tax evasion: its board of directors included General Caballero and the finance minister, Agustín Cañete. Also on the board, however, were real businessmen, such as Luigi Patri, an Italian immigrant who had gotten rich after the War of the Triple Alliance by supplying the Brazilian occupation army; Adolfo Saguier; Guillermo de los Ríos; Juan B. Gaona; and Rodney B. Croskey, the representative in Paraguay of the British foreign bondholders.[21]

These big landowners went beyond the commercialization of cotton, cattle, and *yerba mate* and had begun setting up banks, shipping companies, and even some light manufacturing. Patri, who once owned the railway line and was still under contract to manage it, was a director of the Banco de Comércio and the Banco Territorial; Gaona was on the board of the Banco Territorial and the Banco Mercantil; de los Ríos had his own family bank, the Banco de los Ríos; Saguier's family owned sugar mills. Besides owning *yerba* plantations, La Industrial roasted the tea and shipped it in bags produced in its own factories.[22]

This expansion of economic activity created a change in attitude among the businessmen. The buccaneering spirit of the old *caballeristas* was no longer attractive to them; future prosperity depended on governmental stability, administrative competence, financial responsibility, and internal improvements. They approved when the government channeled money into school construction and the paving of Asunción's streets. They applauded the new Foreign Exchange Board set up to collect taxes and regulate the currency. They were proud of Paraguay's participation in the 1897 World's Fair in Brussels, the rise of immigration, and the government's success in renegotiating the foreign debt. Egusquiza's reform of judicial administration, his recruitment of moderate Liberals to office, and his sending of promising young military officers to Chile—then South America's most prestigious military power because of its recent victory over Peru and Bolivia in the War of the Pacific—for advanced professional training were taken as signs of a progressive, enlightened government.[23]

All in all, the Egusquiza years can be seen, in retrospect, as the apex of the Colorado era. Both the economy and the population finally had begun to recover from the effects of the war. If one allows for all the slippages in Paraguayan census taking, it seems clear nevertheless that by the end of the 1890s the population stood at somewhere around 635,000, up from around 232,000 at the end of the war, and compared with an estimated prewar population of about 400,000. A modest proportion of that increase was due to immigration, which peaked in the early 1890s. About 12,241 immigrants were registered between 1882 and 1907, about half of which were Germans and Italians, with Frenchmen, Spaniards, and Argentines following close behind.[24]

Not everything was rosy, of course. Paraguay still had trouble meeting the interest payments on its foreign debt, and despite his promises to keep a balanced budget and sound money, Egusquiza sometimes resorted to the printing presses just as his predecessors had. More disturbing still were the continuing rifts within the ranks of both the Liberal and Colorado parties. In 1898, as the time for the presidential succession drew near, factional and partisan feelings rose again, threatening the government's hard-won stability. From the landowners' and businessmen's viewpoint, Egusquiza was in line with the new "political agenda," but this was not shared by the *caballerista* Colorados or the young intransigents of the Liberal Party. Thus, the Paraguayan elites were split, with the economic interests mainly on the side of the moderate center and the political activists struggling either to pull the country back to simpler times or to yank it forward toward a radical revolution.

five

REALIGNMENT AND

REGIME CHANGE

Progress is never automatic and it cannot be taken for granted. As the 1898 elections approached, the "era of good feelings" over which Egusquiza had presided began to show alarming signs of coming apart. The *caballeristas* still controlled key positions in the Colorado Party and were preparing to nominate Egusquiza's successor. Egusquiza and his supporters were equally determined not to jeopardize the gains made so far by allowing them to do so. A bitter fight loomed ahead. The Liberals were even more sharply divided. Those who favored continuing the policy of cooperation with Egusquiza were confronted by intransigents who demanded a complete break with the Colorado regime and a redirection of the party's efforts toward revolution. The former, led by General Benigno Ferreira, called themselves Cívicos, after their newspaper, *El Cívico*, which was edited by Adolfo Soler and Carlos Luís Isasi. The latter, led by Cecilio Báez and Fernando Carreras, called themselves Radicals and published their own paper, called *El Pueblo*. The two factions were so far apart that they almost constituted separate parties.

On the surface, the Colorados continued to show a united front, basking in the popularity that came from the economy's general improvement. There were some young faces in the party's ranks that suggested it was seeking to renew itself. Facundo Ynsfrán, vice-president of the Republic, was only thirty-three; yet he already had been the principal founder of the university's new school of medicine and served as minister of justice in the González administration. Aside from his obvious personal abilities, he enjoyed the special favor of General Caballero, his uncle, who considered him future presidential timber. Fulgencio Moreno, a congressman and teacher at the Colegio Nacional, was only twenty-four years old but was already attracting attention as a writer and a fiery orator. He recently had been elected to the Colorado executive committee. Blas Garay, only a year older, was the founder and chief editor of *La Prensa*, which Carlos Centurión tells us was "the most serious, best informed, and most correctly edited Asunción daily of its time."[1] Garay also edited the party's official journal, *La Patria*. Slightly older (in his early thirties) was Senator

Eduardo Fleitas, the party's secretary and a tough political militant. All were *caballeristas,* although Garay was something of a maverick for that camp. He actually proposed the dissolution of both the existing parties and the formation of a single nationalist-socialist party. That, he argued, would be in keeping with Paraguay's authoritarian, communal traditions and its social realities.[2]

The topmost positions in the Colorado Party were still held by the old *lopista* generals. Generals Caballero and Escobar, both senators, were president and first vice-president, respectively. Colonel Manuel A. Maciel was second vice-president. The *egusquicistas* had two high positions. Guillermo de los Ríos, the finance minister, was party treasurer; and Antonio Sosa, a deputy and also publisher of the *egusquicista La Opinión,* was pro-secretary. On balance, the *caballeristas* had the upper hand in the party, but with General Egusquiza in control of the government and the barracks the *egusquicistas* were at least equal to them.

Generals Caballero and Escobar favored their old military comrade and political crony, Agustín Cañete, for the presidential nomination. Other *caballeristas* mentioned as possible candidates were Héctor Carvallo, a senator, and Colonel Maciel. There were several possible *egusquicista* nominees. Rufino Mazó, the justice minister who had headed the Club Popular Egusquicista in 1894 was a strong possibility. So was Guillermo de los Ríos, who would have the backing of the business community. Eventually, however, Egusquiza settled on his war minister, Emilio Aceval, who was also a well-known businessman. This outraged the *caballeristas,* who protested that Aceval had never formally registered as a Colorado Party member. The party directorate not only deadlocked: it began to fragment. Caballero and Escobar refused to budge in their support for Cañete, Egusquiza was equally adamant for Aceval, and a third faction tried to promote Angel Martínez, the interior minister, as a compromise. Martínez seemed delighted at the notion, but when he began lobbying for *caballerista* votes, Egusquiza removed him from the cabinet and sent him to Buenos Aires on a "diplomatic mission." Finally, on 27 March 1898, General Caballero withdrew his objection to Aceval after the latter made a formal statement endorsing the goals and principles of the Colorado Party. That paved the way for his nomination, although Escobar continued to back Cañete and three other party directors voted for Martínez. As part of the compromise, Egusquiza accepted Héctor Carvallo, the *caballerista* senator, as Aceval's running mate.[3]

The Liberals' divisions were not so easily papered over. Benigno Ferreira was a powerful figure, and at forty-nine he was in the prime of his political career. No one else in the party could match his combination of practical intelligence, strong will, and political shrewdness. Though possessing a law degree and acquainted with the highest political circles in both Paraguay and Argentina, he nevertheless had enough of the old rough-and-ready *caudillo* style about him to appeal to the rural *jefes políticos*. If it came to another bloody fight with the Colorados, he would be the Liberals' natural leader.

Cecilio Báez, the Radicals' leader, was a far different sort. He was much younger (thirty-three) and more bookish. By today's standards his historical and political writings seem shallow and polemical, but at the end of the nineteenth century in Paraguay he towered intellectually over any other figure. And he had courage. Even as a student, he had risked his future by getting actively involved in the Centro Democrático and had always been outspoken in his criticism of the government. He was, like Domingo Sarmiento in Argentina, the principal promoter in his country of education and Europeanization. Moreover, he was an uncompromising advocate of laissez-faire liberalism. In all of his writings he hammered away at two main themes: the need to respect the letter and spirit of the Constitution of 1870, and utter loathing of the old López regime and all that it stood for. Having traveled abroad a great deal and maintained a correspondence with various foreign intellectuals, Báez stirred the pride of his countrymen by representing Paraguay at international conferences. His youth, his rectitude, and his scholarly reputation combined to make him the idol of Paraguayan students in the 1890s.

An idealist like Báez had little patience for a man of the world like Ferreira, especially since the latter was suspected of having stolen huge sums of cash during his brief experience with power in 1873–74. Ferreira's willingness to work with the enemy further condemned him in the eyes of Báez and the Radicals. Tension between the moderate and intransigent Liberals had been growing ever since the 1890 elections, when Victor Soler had agreed to run for vice-president with Juan G. González. The current split occurred when Liberals in the Senate and Chamber divided over whether to approve the contract Egusquiza signed with the foreign owners of the railroad. In that agreement, the government would turn over its minority interest in the company in return for the latter's surrender of any claims to public lands bordering the right-of-way. The Cívicos were willing to go along but the Radicals attacked the government mercilessly for striking a bad bargain that would prejudice the national interest. They hinted darkly at the likelihood of corruption and suggested that the Cívicos were expecting to share in the payoffs. As tempers rose, the two factions became enmeshed in a sordid fight over which of them owned the party newspaper, *El Pueblo*. It was after the Radicals won out on this issue that the Cívicos started their own, *El Cívico*.[4]

Both factions claimed the support of well-known Liberals. Besides Ferreira, the Cívicos included such well-known names as Antonio Taboada, José Mateo Collar, José Zacarías Caminos, Pedro P. Caballero, Ignacio Ibarra, and Fabio Queirolo (who had succeeded Ferreira as party president). There were young men as well. Adolfo Soler (Victor Soler's younger brother), Carlos Luís Isasi, Manuel Benítez, José T. Legal (José Segundo Decoud's son-in-law), and Eduardo Amarilla were all in their twenties and were to play leading roles in future events. A list of twenty-seven leading Cívico politicians, drawn from studies by Carlos Centurión and Gómez Freire Esteves, reveals an average age of thirty-three, with slightly more than half (fourteen) being drawn from the Fourth and Fifth Promotions.[5] The Radicals were younger, with an average age of twenty-five. Seventy-three percent (sixteen out of twenty-two) were from the Fourth and Fifth Promotions. Their most "elderly" figures were Báez, Fernando Carreras, Manuel Frutos, Alejandro Audivert, and Emeterio González. All were in their thirties except Frutos, who was a war veteran in his late forties. Among the twenty-year-olds who would later become prominent were Manuel Gondra, Liberato Marcial Rojas, Tomás Airaldi, Eduardo Schaerer, Ramón Lara Castro, and Teodosio González. This last, however, would switch to the Cívicos. There were even two nineteen-year-olds, Adolfo Riquelme and Belisario Rivarola, who would rise to fame from this early start in politics.[6]

Perhaps because of the youth of these two factions, it was difficult for them to reach a compromise. At one point it seemed that the Liberals might cooperate to the extent of fielding a ticket composed of Alejandro Audivert (Radical) for president and Rosendo Carisimo (Cívico), a rancher-businessman from Concepción, for vice-president, but continued bickering made them give up the attempt. Emilio Aceval won unopposed.

THE *CABALLERISTA* RESTORATION

Aceval showed by the composition of his cabinet that he intended to carry on Egusquiza's policy of recruiting qualified men from both parties. Guillermo de los Ríos (Interior), José Segundo Decoud (Foreign Affairs), and José Urdapilleta (Finance) represented the best elements in the *civilista* Colorado camp. All three came from the country's leading families, and de los Ríos and Urdapilleta were wealthy bankers and businessmen. Urdapilleta had been interior minister under the grim governments of Gill and Uriarte, it is true, but he now threw himself into the task of trying to cement an alliance of moderates. As before, the Supeme Court was staffed exclusively by Liberals: Benigno Ferreira, Benjamín Aceval, and

Emeterio González. Another Liberal, José Zacarías Caminos, became minister of justice.

During the thirty-seven months that he held office, Aceval made thirteen cabinet appointments, of which six were Liberals. Fabio Queirolo replaced Decoud at Foreign Affairs in March 1900 and was succeeded a year later by Juan Cancio Flecha; Gerónimo Pereira Casal, José T. Legal, and Pedro Bobadilla all had turns at the Justice Ministry. All were Cívicos, of course. Caballero Aquino observes of Aceval's cabinets that:

> Aceval was the first representative of the urban bourgeoisie to reach the presidency and he recruited others of a similar background to his cabinet. For example, the bankers, Guillermo de los Ríos and José Urdapilleta were in charge of the key ministries of Interior and Finance, respectively. Generals Caballero and Escobar still enjoyed a certain popularity in the barracks, but they were no longer the only *caudillos* in Paraguayan politics at the *fin de siècle*.[7]

The new administration had ambitious plans. With government financial assistance, the Banco Agrícola opened up a mortgage section that made secured loans to farmers and ranchers. Industry was promoted by a combination of subsidies and tax incentives. Administrative councils were created to foster education and improved health services. Another agency was set up to regularize payments on the foreign debt, and more agents were hired to improve tax collection. The most controversial innovation was an attempt to balance the army's power by creating a National Guard, which was headed by General Egusquiza. Even Radicals like Cecilio Báez and Alejandro Audivert agreed to join it, but the National Guard never attained the size or cohesion of the regular army and became more of a part-time reserve.[8]

Unfortunately, Aceval was unable to win over the Radical Liberals or the *caballerista* Colorados, although he brought one of the latter, Fulgencio R. Moreno, to the Finance Ministry in August 1901. The *caballeristas*, sensing that he was a weaker man than Egusquiza, went on the attack from the very beginning. Blas Garay, from the columns of *La Prensa*, was his bitterest critic. Aceval was blamed for all the country's problems, even the outbreak of bubonic plague in 1899. Because of the plague, Argentina imposed a quarantine on Paraguayan goods, which in turn threw the country into a severe economic depression. With that, Aceval's popularity plunged. Cabinet ministers quarreled with each other, the government seemed to drift helplessly, and although there was little that Aceval or anyone could do about the situation, the impression began to spread that the president was indecisive. Cabinet shake-ups, designed to bring new energy to the government, only deepened that impression. At the same time, Egusquiza, on whom Aceval ultimately depended, fell sick—a fact that did not pass unnoticed in military circles.[9]

As the year 1900 began, the economic situation in Paraguay had deteriorated so far, and the government's floundering had become so pronounced, that there were rumors of an impending coup. The entire cabinet offered its resignation in January and Aceval even considered taking asylum in the Brazilian embassy. Instead, however, he decided to struggle on rather than plunge the nation into anarchy. With the ailing Egusquiza's help, he got his ministers to withdraw their resignations. Another crisis erupted in March, resulting in the withdrawal of Decoud, Urdapilleta, and Caminos. Fabio Queirolo, then president of the Liberal Party, agreed to take Decoud's place; José Tomás Legal, Decoud's son-in-law and a rising Cívico, took over the Justice Ministry; and Francisco Campos, an elderly statesman who had been a delegate at the Constitutional Convention and was widely known for his honesty, became finance minister.[10]

The new government was respected but not loved. Nor was it possible to keep the Colorados and Liberals working in tandem. As the February 1901 congressional elections approached, the two parties signed a pact agreeing to support a certain percentage of each other's candidates. In the actual balloting, however, the *caballerista* and *civilista* Colorados closed ranks and bloc-voted against the Liberals, who were thus frozen out of most seats. Queirolo and Legal immediately resigned from the cabinet and Ferreira gave up his seat on the Supreme Court. Campos left the Finance Ministry a few months later.[11]

The long-awaited coup finally came on 9 January 1902. Egusquiza, gravely ill (he died on 25 August), no longer had a grip on the army. The war minister, Colonel Juan A. Escurra, was his protégé; but he was also an illiterate rustic who spoke Guaraní more fluently than Spanish. Although of decent inclinations, he became the cat's paw of generals Caballero and Escobar, who now saw their chance to regain power. They had been working on Escurra, convincing him that the policy of reconciliation between the parties had gone too far. The country was a mess for it, the president was fuzzy-minded, and the Liberals were busily sabotaging public order! The *civilistas* were preparing to turn the government over to another heartless businessmen, Guillermo de los Ríos, who had just resigned as interior minister to run. If elected, the generals argued, the country could expect the same ruinous, milk-and-water type of government. Far better to do the patriotic thing and turn the government back over to honest soldiers! Escurra listened and was convinced.

The *caballeristas* made their move when Aceval proceeded to fill de los

Ríos's place, along with the Justice and Education portfolio, which also happened to be vacant. The chief strategist behind the forthcoming confrontation was Fulgencio R. Moreno, the recently appointed finance minister. Prompted by him, Escurra demanded to be informed ahead of time about whom Aceval intended to appoint. A firm *civilista*, Aceval naturally ignored him and announced that Miguel Corvalán would be the new interior minister and Francisco Cháves would take over at Justice and Education. Both were Colorados, but this made no difference to Escurra and Moreno. After a stormy cabinet meeting on 7 January Moreno resigned, but Escurra delayed. Aceval, who considered the war minister too stupid to be dangerous was certain that he would resign in a few days, after which Egusquiza could be appointed to take his place. Instead, Escurra invited the *egusquicista* commanders of the cavalry and infantry garrisons to dinner "to discuss the crisis." During the meal soldiers entered the room and arrested them both. Then, early the next morning, Escurra invited the unsuspecting Aceval to breakfast "to discuss the matter of his [Escurra's] resignation." The president fell into the same trap. Once a prisoner, he was forced to sign his resignation. It was a classic *caballerista* coup, almost identical to the one that removed Saguier in favor of Caballero back in 1880. Egusquiza escaped arrest by taking refuge in the Argentine embassy, while the French provided asylum to Ferreira and de los Ríos. A few days later they were given permission to leave the country. Meanwhile, Vice-President Héctor Carvallo formed a provisional government; but it was really Caballero and Escobar who were in control.

THE REALIGNING COUP

Ever since V. O. Key published his pathbreaking article on "critical elections," political scientists have studied electoral results, past as well as present, to identify those which reveal a durable switch in voter allegiances. A critical election, for Key, was one in which voters were deeply concerned about something and came out in unusually large numbers to cast their ballots. Equally important, the issue had to be one that created a sharp, profound, and enduring shift in electoral groupings.[12]

Other students of voting behavior quickly added to Key's concept. The authors of *The American Voter* classified U.S. presidential elections into three categories: (1) realigning, which was essentially the same as Key's "critical election"; (2) maintaining, in which the usual pattern of partisan attachments prevailed; and (3) deviating, in which the basic pattern of partisan loyalties was not seriously disturbed but, because of personalities or events involved in the contest, the majority coalition lost.[13] To this schema, Gerald Pomper then added a fourth classification: the "converting election." Converting elections were similar to realigning elections, which they usually preceded, in that alienated groups left the majority coalition and adhered thereafter to the opposition. The difference was that in a converting election the incumbent majority party might still win, albeit with a different kind of coalition backing it, whereas in a realigning election changes in the distribution of party membership finally resulted in the incumbents being turned out of office.[14]

Walter Dean Burnham subsequently noted that there is a remarkable regularity in the appearance of realigning elections in the United States. They seem to occur every thirty years or so, or approximately once in a generation, and are often preceded by signs of breakdown in the party system. There tends to be a greater polarization between the parties and serious factional divisions within the parties that often lead to third-party revolts.[15]

Now it is true that elections do not matter very much in Paraguay because they are never fair, so such concepts are not applicable to our subject in their pristine state. Coups and revolts, on the other hand, do matter because they are the way in which changes in government really take place in Paraguay. Can concepts that were fashioned to study partisan attachments in elections be applied to violent, illegitimate acts that nevertheless affect the composition of a government and the groups that both support and oppose it? I shall argue that they can because coups are as natural a way of changing governments in some systems as elections are in others. What matters is the distribution of loyalties before and afterward.

First, we must understand something about coups. Not all coups are alike in their techniques. Some are aimed against the government but sometimes it is the president himself who violates constitutional procedure to keep himself in power, as in the case of President Rivarola in 1871. Mark Hagopian calls that type of coup an "executive coup."[16] Sometimes the coup comes from within the ruling clique and aims only at removing the president or a couple of his ministers, while keeping the rest of the regime intact. That is the essence of a "palace coup," such as the ones in 1880 and 1902 where a cabinet minister seized power. Coups that originate outside the palace differ as to the degree in which civilians are involved. The most common variety of coup is what Hagopian calls the "military coup." Other writers on the subject point out, however, that there are many subvarieties of this. A military coup, often called a "barracks revolt" (or *cuartelazo* in Latin America) may be carried out after a consensus among the senior officers determines that a government must go. In such cases there is likely to be little resistance or bloodshed. On the other hand, only a certain faction of the military may be involved. In that case, the ability to strike quickly and decisively at the center of state power usually lends special importance to infantry and cavalry garrisons located in or near the capital city.[17] Alternatively, a coup may start at some distant provincial garrison that has little hope of overthrowing the government by itself but gambles on holding out long enough to rally other forces to its cause. This tactic is often called a *pronunciamiento*. The last type of coup in Hagopian's classificatory scheme is the "paramilitary coup," which is staged by armed civilians, like the Liberals who followed Major Vera in October 1891.

It should be emphasized that a coup is not the same thing as a revolution, although in common speech the terms are used interchangeably. A coup may lead to a revolution by setting off a certain chain of events, but the two concepts are very different. Coups, unlike revolutions, do not try to involve large numbers of people and usually do not entail massive violence. A well-planned coup requires secrecy in the planning phase, which puts a premium on limiting the number of conspirators; and if it is executed properly it may be bloodless. Essentially, a coup is a matter of redistributing power among elite groups, whereas a revolution is an uprising of the nonelites that aims at fundamental social change. This does not mean, however, that coups may not have serious consequences for the political system. Among the elite groups struggling for control of the state a coup can result in a realignment of partisan loyalties, and I shall argue that this is what happened in Paraguay after the 1902 coup.

Applying the terms of critical election theory to coups, we may say that the palace coup of January 1902 was a "converting coup" because the majority party continued in power but basic changes occurred in the pattern of support. As we shall see, most of the moderate, business-oriented *civilistas* were alienated from the Colorado Party and passed over to the Liberal camp. From that point on, the bulk of public opinion, which in nineteenth-century Paraguay meant only elite opinion, was pro-Liberal. Two years later General Ferreira would lead an armed invasion—a realigning paramilitary coup—that would put a permanent end to Colorado hegemony.

In the narrative that follows all of the expected ingredients for a realigning coup will be present. Between 1902 and 1904 the two parties become more hostile toward each other. Factional divisions persist in both; but whereas the Liberals find it expedient to keep the party together, Egusquiza's followers desert the Colorado Party. Until 1906 they will constitute a third party, cooperating with the Liberals but not actually a part of them. Their break with the *caballeristas* will prove to be permanent, and when they do merge it will be with the Liberals. Thus, there is a true realignment of partisan loyalties. Moreover, the fall of the *caballeristas* in 1904 will put a definitive end to their kind of rule. Military *caudillos* might still disrupt the political order, but down to September 1940 civilian rule is the paramount value. Finally, the 1904 realigning coup comes almost exactly thirty years after Benigno Ferreira was overthrown by the National Party coalition, forerunner of the Colorado Party. It will usher in an era of Liberal Party hegemony that lasts thirty-two years, until the nationalistic February Revolution of 1936 brings it to an end. Like the United States, Paraguay seems to experience political watersheds about once every generation.

THE OVERTHROW OF THE COLORADOS

Late in the morning of 9 January 1902 Congress convened in joint session to receive the information that President Aceval had resigned and to recognize officially the provisional government headed by Vice-President Carvallo. Although the majority of senators present and most of the spectators in the gallery were *caballeristas*, there were a few brave *civilistas* present to protest. An angry shouting match quickly arose between Senator Eduardo Fleitas, who defended the coup, and Senator Federico Bogarín. Finally Fleitas drew a pistol and started toward Bogarín, at which point the latter's nephew, Vicente Rivarola, rushed from the gallery with his own pistol drawn and fired at Fleitas. A riot ensued. Shots were fired, knives drawn, and furniture hurled in every direction. By the time Colonel Escurra sent in troops to restore order, Bogarín, Fleitas, General Caballero, Miguel Corvalán, and Cayetano Carreras were wounded and bloody, and Facundo Ynsfrán, Caballero's favorite nephew, lay dead on the floor.[18] Under the glint of bayonets the resolution was passed that recognized Carvallo as provisional president, so the old guard had won—but at a price. It was to be their last hurrah.

The new government tried hard to appear conciliatory. The Foreign Affairs portfolio was given to the much-respected writer and historian, Manuel Domínguez. And when Domínguez stepped down on 2 June to be Colonel Escurra's running mate on the official ticket, his place was taken by another *civilista*, Cayetano Carreras. The Justice and Education Ministry went to José Irala, another moderate Colorado, who edited *La Democracia* and taught civil law at the university. The key positions in the cabinet were in the hands of trusted hard-liners, however: Eduardo Fleitas (Interior), Colonel Escurra (War), and Fulgencio R. Moreno (Finance).

With Facundo Ynsfrán's death, Fleitas became the Colorado Party's chief political strategist and, consequently, the cabinet's "strongman."

In the weeks and months following the coup, there were constant rumors of a counterrevolt, to be led by General Egusquiza. There is little doubt that most *civilista* Colorados looked to him to turn around the situation, and they were joined in this by most of the Liberals too. Furthermore, the Brazilian ambassador reported, Egusquiza had the moral and material support of Argentina. The danger appeared so grave that Escurra and Carvallo concentrated all available military forces around the capital in the expectation of a military coup at any moment.[19] Unfortunately for the would-be rebels, Egusquiza was a very sick man and unable to act. He died on 25 August, the day following the uncontested elections that made Escurra the new president.

Thus, the opposition's timetable was set back. But public opinion was running strongly in favor of a change of regime. One indication of this was the large crowd that greeted Cecilio Báez at the port when he returned on 21 May from Mexico City, where he had represented Paraguay at the Second Pan-American Congress.

Aware of its unpopularity, the Escurra administration sought to win back the public with an image of youthfulness and moderation. The vice-president, Manuel Domínguez, was thirty-five and a *civilista*. Cayetano Carreras, the justice minister, was about the same age and also a *civilista*. He had opposed bitterly the ouster of Aceval but, like Domínguez, preferred to work within the system to steer it back on a progressive course. Colonel Antonio Cáceres, the war minister, had been a friend of Egusquiza's and had served in Marcos Morínigo's provisional government as his stand-in. Other *civilistas* were recruited later to the cabinet: Antolín Irala, a lawyer and diplomat, was twenty-six when appointed foreign affairs minister in May 1903; Antonio Sosa was thirty-three when he took over the Finance Ministry the same month; and José Emilio Pérez, an *egusquicista*, was thirty-two when he came to the interior ministry in 1904.

Even the *caballeristas* were relatively young. Eduardo Fleitas, the first interior minister, was in his early thirties; Pedro Peña, the first foreign affairs minister, was thirty-eight at the time of his appointment; Fulgencio Moreno, the first finance minister, had just turned thirty; and Francisco Cháves, who replaced Carreras at Justice and Education in 1903, was only twenty-seven at the time. Colonel Escurra himself was only forty-three.

Outside the government, the *caballeristas* had the support of several brilliant young polemicists who were developing a new, chauvinistic nationalism that would eventually be adopted by the Colorados as the official ideology. This literary movement was what Warren has called "the López Apotheosis," for it consisted of a historical revisionism that sought to rehabilitate Marshal Francisco Solano López as a great national hero and the victim of foreign imperialism. Blas Garay, who might have led this school, was dead—killed three years earlier in a duel—but his paper, *La Patria*, had been bought by Enrique Solano López, the bastard son of the ex-dictator. Around him gathered writers like Fulgencio R. Moreno and Venancio López, bastard son of the ex-dictator's brother, Vicente. Arsenio López Decoud, another nephew of the dictator, also contributed to the movement through his own paper, *El Nacional*; but, unlike the others, he was a *civilista*.[20]

At the moment, however, the historical tide was running against the Colorados and no amount of historical revisionism or literary cleverness could reverse it. The successors of this generation of *lopista* intellectuals would see public opinion turn from liberalism to nationalism, but not before another thirty years passed. Meanwhile, the government's position kept eroding. Now that the *caballeristas* controlled the Foreign Exchange Board they plundered it instead using it to promote development. Gold, purchased with foreign exchange, was sold to friends of Caballero and Escobar at a discount. Also, the board was granted a monopoly over the export of hides and leather goods, and only businessmen who stood well with the ruling clique could get government loans through it. Similarly, in an effort to draw in more revenue the government levied export taxes on *yerba mate* and decreed that half of all the tobacco crop had to be turned over to the state, at a low fixed price, for the latter to resell abroad. It is hardly surprising, then, that merchants, bankers, and farmers turned against the regime, as did the lawyers, teachers, physicians, journalists, students, and others who made up the literate middle class.[21] The degree of public alienation went so far that it even affected the children of the *caballerista* elite. On 31 January 1903 Captain Patricio Alejandro Escobar, son of the ex-president, and Captain Albino Jara, son of the commander of the Northern Military District, were arrested for plotting. Both were tortured for information but later released when their parents intervened.[22]

To overthrow the government, it was necessary to bring together the Colorado *civilistas*, the Cívico Liberals, and the Radical Liberals. The momentum for doing so came from the leading bankers and businessmen: Guillermo de los Ríos, Emilio Aceval, Gualberto Cardús Huerta, Francisco Campos, Juan Bautista Gaona, and Emilio Saguier. Although they belonged to different parties and factions, they shared a common contempt for *caballerismo* and a belief in moderate, progressive civilian government. They also were willing to provide financial backing for an armed uprising. Because General Egusquiza was dead, their next preference went to General Benigno Ferreira. But it was necessary to involve the

Radicals too, because they had the most support among the younger generation. By the beginning of 1904 a revolutionary junta was formed consisting of Benigno Ferreira, Cecilio Báez, Emiliano González Navero, Emilio Aceval, Guillermo de los Ríos, Francisco Campos, and Emilio Saguier. This junta also had excellent contacts inside the Argentine government, which looked with concern on the pro-Brazilian orientation of General Caballero and his cronies. Two Paraguayan exiles, Lieutenant Manuel J. Duarte and Lieutenant Elías Ayala, both graduates of the Argentine Naval Academy and officers in the Argentine navy, provided the crucial entrée. Lieutenant Duarte, a friend and protégé of Major Eduardo Vera, had left Paraguay after the 1891 revolt. After arriving in Buenos Aires he had formed a close friendship with Benigno Ferreira. Now, having helped to effect a truce between the exiled Cívicos and Radicals, he agreed to be the nexus with the Argentine navy. As secretary of the Arsenal, he was well placed to do so.[23]

General Ferreira now formed a provisional government in exile, which included Adolfo Soler, Carlos Isasi, Antonio Taboada, and Manuel Benítez from the Cívico faction, and Cecilio Báez, Emiliano González Navero, Adolfo Riquelme, Eduardo Schaerer, and Manuel Gondra from the Radical side. Among this latter group, the last three were relatively new faces. Riquelme was a youthful militant of twenty-eight who recently had joined the Radical faction's central committee. Schaerer was a successful young businessman of thirty-one who recently started a newspaper, El Diario, that would become one of the most influential in the country. He helped pay for outfitting some of the rebel military units and even lent his estates out in the backlands as training bases. Gondra, thirty-three, was an extremely popular teacher of literature at the Colegio Nacional and also a professor at the university. He had come to fame in 1896 by publishing a ringing manifesto stating clearly the aims of the Liberal Party's Radical wing.

Of all these men Soler was the closest to General Ferreira, acting as his personal secretary. It was Soler, too, who held in his hands all the strands of the conspiracy that led up to the revolt. A relative of his, Pascual Velilla, was a director of the Banco Agrícola and negotiated the purchase in Buenos Aires of a merchant ship called the Sajonia, ostensibly to transport Paraguayan fruit. Ildefonso Benegas, one of the plotters, was then dispatched by the bank to go to Buenos Aires at the end of July, take command of the ship, and transport a load of fruit to Spain. Instead, Benegas loaded the Sajonia with seventy men, six cannons, and a sizable quantity of small arms provided by the Argentine navy. On 4 August the ship began to head upriver toward Paraguay with Lieutenant Duarte in command.[24]

The Paraguayan government, informed by telegraph of the *Sajonia*'s suspicious behavior, sent another gunboat, the *Villarrica*, under the command of Captain Eugénio Garay, to intercept it. The two ships met near the Paraguayan port of Pilar and exchanged heavy fire. The rebels won the day, capturing not only the *Villarrica* but also Captain Garay, one of the Colorados' best officers, and interior minister Eduardo Fleitas, who was caught trying to swim away from the scene. But the possibility of a surprise attack on Asunción was now out of the question, so General Ferreira decided to establish his headquarters in Pilar and gradually encircle the capital. Elías Ayala was sent upriver to Concepción in the *Villarrica* to disembark a party of one hundred men under Captain Albino Jara. Jara's father, Colonel Zacarías Jara, was the district commander. After a brief parley with his son, he surrendered the city. Meanwhile, Ferreira crossed the river and took the strategic Chaco port of Villa Hayes. Asunción was being squeezed in a pincers.

Apparently demoralized by its initial defeat, the government seemed unable to gather its forces. Escurra shuffled his cabinet. General Caballero came out of retirement to replace the captured Fleitas as interior minister. General Escobar took over the War Ministry from Colonel Cáceres, who had slipped out of town to join the rebels; but then it was learned that Escobar's son, Patricio Alejandro, was one of the rebel commanders, so General Caballero replaced him as well. It made little difference. In the weeks that followed the rebels' ranks were swollen with volunteers. At the end of September Vice-President Manuel Domínguez showed up at rebel headquarters, now relocated at Villeta, to pledge his support for the revolt. He soon was joined by all three members of the Supreme Court, the chief of police, the director of the Colegio Nacional, and several congressmen.

By the beginning of December, Escurra, having failed to get Brazilian military aid, was ready to surrender. General Caballero wanted to fight on, but the rest of the cabinet persuaded him that the cause was lost. After delicate negotiations carried on through the Argentine and Brazilian ambassadors, the two sides met aboard an Argentine gunboat. Colonel Escurra, accompanied by two *civilistas*, Cayetano Carreras and José Emilio Pérez, represented the government; the rebels were represented by General Ferreira, Lieutenant Duarte, and Adolfo Soler. It was agreed that the current Paraguayan government would resign and a new one, headed by Juan B. Gaona, one of the rebels' main financial backers, would form a new one. However, Cayetano Carreras and José Emilio Pérez would retain their cabinet posts (Justice and Interior, respectively), which would give the administration a bipartisan character. General Ferreira would become war minister and could name his police chief. There would be a complete reorganization of the armed forces, in which the Liberals would assume all the commands. Finally, elections would be called to renew half the congressional seats, and the Colorados would not contest them.[25]

Although this agreement gave the Liberals possession of the government, it did not please the Radicals. First, they were disgruntled because only Cívico Liberals had been present at the peace talks. Second, the more militant Radicals, led by Manuel Gondra and Captain Albino Jara, accused Ferreira of leaving too much in Colorado hands. The enemy would still have two cabinet posts and half of Congress. It was preferable, they argued, to continue fighting rather than accept such a compromise. But if the general terms were accepted anyway, then the Radicals deserved a lion's share of the posts in the provisional government, since they were backed by a majority of the Liberal Party. In reply, Ferreira pointed out that he, Duarte, and Soler, having planned, equipped, and led the invasion, had a right to determine the correct terms of peace. The agreement would avoid further bloodshed and destruction of property, which, when combined with a conciliatory attitude, would enable the new government to reestablish peace and order more quickly.[26]

Although a majority of the revolutionary junta sided with Ferreira, the Liberal Party's underlying divisions had surfaced again. The debate had been heated and at one point Captain Jara had even threatened to revolt against Ferreira and had to be restrained by Gondra. One minor outcome was that Cecilio Báez, more impressed by Ferreira's statesmanship than by the intransigence of Gondra and Jara, went over to the Cívicos' side. More important, though, the Liberal Party began its period in power deeply divided and weakened.

THE HEYDAY OF THE CÍVICOS

In keeping with the truce agreement, President Juan B. Gaona headed a bipartisan provisional government, with Carreras at Justice, Pérez at Interior, and Ferreira at War. The only Radical in the cabinet was Emiliano González Navero, the finance minister. Cecilio Báez, a Radical turned Cívico, rounded out the team at Foreign Affairs. The police chief was Elías C. García, an old military friend of Ferreira's from exile days. Lieutenant Duarte became the chief of staff of the armed forces.

The Cívicos also had a slight preponderance on the Liberal Party directorate. Antonio Taboada was the party's president. Together with the *egusquicista* Colorados, the Cívicos also controlled both houses of Congress. The *egusquicistas*, led by Emilio Aceval, Guillermo de los Ríos, and Francisco Campos, eventually would merge with the Cívicos, in April

1906. The Radicals, feeling cheated of their due, clustered sullenly around Eduardo Schaerer and his *El Diario,* from which they directed their criticisms at the government. Because their most admired leader, Gondra, had been shunted out of the country by an ambassadorial appointment to Rio de Janeiro, Schaerer came to the fore as their chief strategist. That earned him the government's baleful attention. Having been appointed director of the port, he now came under investigation. In September 1905 he was accused of misappropriating funds and forced to resign. *El Diario* accused Ferreira of persecuting him as the Radicals' spokesman.

Gaona lasted exactly a year in office. The cause of his fall, on 9 December 1905, is in dispute. Freire Esteves claims that he angered too many cabinet ministers and congressmen by vetoing a large state loan to build a hotel and social club in Asunción. Caballero Aquino notes, however, that Congress had sufficient votes to override the veto. He claims the real reason was the cabinet's refusal to approve a foreign loan negotiated by the Banco Mercantil—a bank owned by Gaona and his friends—at a usurious rate of interest, which the government would undertake to repay while the bank's directors collected fat commissions. Gaona sought to overcome the cabinet's resistance by waiting until General Ferreira was out of town and then dismissing three of the ministers: González Navero, Carreras, and Pérez.[27] On hearing of this, Police Chief García declared himself in revolt and telegraphed Ferreira in Concepción. The latter hurried back and, after consulting with congressional leaders, forced Gaona to resign. Cecilio Báez was then sworn in as the new provisional president. In all the confusion, the *El Diario* group tried to line up another coup, behind the leadership of the ever-restless Captain Albino Jara, but found little support in the barracks.

The Báez government made no changes in the cabinet except to fill the vacancy at Foreign Affairs with Adolfo Soler. General Ferreira continued to be the dominant force and, as expected, the Liberal Party nominated him as its presidential candidate in April 1906. The inclusion of Emiliano González Navero on the ticket as his running mate was intended to placate the Radicals, but it failed to do so. Alejandro Audivert, publisher of *La Ley,* went beyond all the bounds of discretion and launched a vitriolic personal attack on the general. *La Ley* was closed down by the police, but that only made a martyr of Audivert and confirmed other Radicals in their hatred of Ferreira. Captain Jara once again got busy, trying to foment a coup, but he was caught and disciplined. Scorn him though they might, the Radicals could not prevent Ferreira's election, on 1 October.

Perhaps the greatest loser in this whole process was Cecilio Báez, once the Radicals' unquestioned leader and hero of all progressive youth. His willingness to collaborate with General Ferreira cost him both those roles.

At bottom, Báez preferred the strong leadership of a Ferreira to the Radicals' moony faith in "the People." Indeed, it became increasingly clear that Báez had a certain contempt for the common man. Once, in a debate with Juan O'Leary, one of the new generation of revisionist *lopista* historians who pointed to the extraordinary loyalty that the Paraguayan masses had shown (and continued to express) toward *El Mariscal*, Báez sneered at what he termed "the cretinism of the Paraguayan people."[28] Obviously, he was not cut out for politics. Eventually he retired quietly to the post of rector of the National University.

The man who stole Báez's prestige and public, the "man of the future" at that period in Paraguay's politics, was Manuel Gondra. Austere, dignified, and scrupulous in all his actions, he possessed a mystique that attracted a fanatical following. He was an intellectual and, although he wrote very little, he was a compelling speaker and was considered to be the best-read Paraguayan of his generation. The brightest and best among the country's youth were behind him. In April 1906, the same month in which Ferreira captured the party's nomination, they formed an ostensibly nonpartisan club called the Liga de la Juventud Independiente (League of Independent Youth). Its central principle, as propounded in the columns of its newspaper, *Alón*, was respect for the Constitution of 1870. For the Liga, General Ferreira was the very personification of the old *caudillo* politics that undermined the constitution.[29]

Historically, the Liga's importance lies in the high quality of its membership, many of whom would later become presidents and cabinet ministers. The future presidents were Captain Albino Jara, Eligio Ayala, José P. Guggiari, all Liberals, and a Colorado, Juan Manuel Frutos. Among the Liberals who later rose to the cabinet were Narciso Méndez Benítez, J. Eliseo da Rosa, Mario Usher, Modesto Guggiari, Cipriano Ibañez, Adolfo Riquelme, Victor Abente Haedo, J. Manuel Balteiro, Rogelio Ibarra, Raúl Casal Ribeiro, and Lisandro Díaz León.

There were also young Colorados in the Liga. Some of those who became powerful leaders were Juan León Mallorquín, Salvador Fernández, and J. Isidro Ramírez. That was still far in the future, however. At the present, the Colorado Party was in disarray. Out of power for the first time in three decades, the exiled generals Caballero and Escobar seemed confused and ineffectual. José Segundo Decoud, whose political genius had served them so well in the past, was painfully ill and had retired from politics. He eventually committed suicide at his home in Asunción, on 3 March 1909. Caballero next turned to Emilio Aceval, hoping to entice the *egusquicistas* back into the party, but Aceval replied that he had disassociated himself from it from the moment that the 1902 coup took place, under the Colorado banner. Invited to participate in the 1906 general elections, the Colorados split. José Emilio Pérez, an *egusquicista* who stayed in the party rather than join the Cívicos, led a "participationist" faction. Many Colorados preferred to stay home from the polls, however. Led by Eduardo Fleitas, most of these "abstentionists" were old *caballeristas* who refused to accept the legitimacy of Liberal rule. Of these two wings, the "participationists" represented a majority of the Colorado activists.[30]

Ferreira's government showed signs of being vigorous, although it was too short-lived to bring any major project to fulfillment. He was the first president, save for Egusquiza, to recognize that Bolivia had designs on the Chaco and to begin preparing Paraguay for the coming fight. He upgraded the army's weaponry with purchases from Europe, modernized its command structure by creating a general staff, and took a strong diplomatic line with Bolivia, forcing it to recognize in the Pinilla-Soler Protocol (1907) Paraguay's claim to a major portion of the Chaco. Ferreira also tried to reform the nation's finances by establishing a Banco de la República to regulate currency emission; and it was during his administration, and with official encouragement, that the railway line finally reached Encarnación and linked Paraguay with the Argentine system. Ferreira's cabinet was composed entirely of Cívicos and *egusquicistas-*turned-Cívicos. All in all, they were an impressive group of men. Cecilio Báez stepped down from the presidency to take over the Foreign Ministry. Manuel Benítez, the interior minister, was a highly respected professor and judge who had graduated at the top of his law school class. Adolfo R. Soler, wealthy businessman, publisher of *El Cívico,* and chief political strategist of the 1904 rebellion, was finance minister. Carlos Isasi, at Justice and Education, was a doctor of law and well-known literary figure who helped found the Paraguayan Institute, the country's foremost cultural center, in 1895.

Captain Manuel Duarte, the hero of the 1904 rebellion, had been Ferreira's first choice for war minister; but Duarte declared himself to be weary of politics and declined the appointment, accepting instead a mission to Europe to purchase arms. Ferreira then offered the post to Guillermo de los Ríos. This selection of a civilian, and former *egusquicista* Colorado, may have been a mistake. In any case, Captain Duarte's refusal to join the government was certainly a setback because he had used his tremendous prestige as chief of staff to keep the armed forces out of politics. Captain Elías Ayala, the new army chief, was competent but he lacked Duarte's luster and would be unable to stop the intrigues that began to fester after the latter's departure. Even so, the new administration, headed by such a forceful figure as Ferreira and staffed by prestigious men in every department, looked ready to give Paraguay the peace and progress it had lacked for so many years.

Unfortunately, the Cívicos lacked a popular base. They were a party of notables, each individual being excellent in himself, but none enjoying a large following.[31] Worse still, they began to quarrel. The source of the trouble was Adolfo R. Soler, whom Carlos Centurión calls "the political soul" and "pilot" of Ferreira's cabinet. As finance minister he was able to control the budgets and poke into the affairs of the other ministries. "Nothing happened without consulting him first, and he had the time and the talent to be everywhere: cautious watchful, and timely."[32] In the process, he created enemies everywhere. He superseded Báez's authority as foreign minister by negotiating the Pinilla-Soler Protocol himself. A close friend of Police Chief Elías Garcia, he received private briefings on political matters before Manuel Benítez, the interior minister, did. Certain of his own talents as a political tactician, he ignored Antonio Taboada, the Liberal Party's president, and showed him little respect.

As is common in Paraguayan politics, tensions worsened as the time grew near to select Ferreira's successor. Naturally, Soler expected to be nominated, but his enemies now began to gang up against him. Benítez was their choice.

Taboada took on the task of leading the fight to stop Soler. Besides a majority of the cabinet, he had the backing of Captain Ayala, the chief of staff, but he felt the need of enlisting even more strength in this campaign so he approached Ferreira to urge him to offer the War Ministry once more to Captain Duarte—as insurance against any possible Radical plots to prevent a smooth transition. Duarte, refreshed from his trip to Europe, allowed himself to be talked into taking the job this time. Once in the cabinet, Duarte found himself inevitably colliding with the ubiquitous Soler. The latter would brook no rival and Duarte was too independent to be overridden.[33] Ugly personal clashes occurred almost daily. Finally Duarte appealed to Taboada, as party leader, to mediate the conflict. Either Ferreira must dismiss Soler, he warned, or he himself would resign. Taboada went to the president, but he found Ferreira unwilling to govern without Soler—although he did not want to lose Duarte either.[34]

In the meantime, a tragedy drove the Cívicos and Radicals further apart. The leader of the Liga de la Juventud Independiente was Carlos García, who also edited *Alón*. His broadsides against President Ferreira were answered with personal attacks on his own character by the young, and equally hotheaded, editor of the progovernment *El Liberal*, Gómez Freire Esteves. Their quarrel escalated until finally, on 12 January 1908, the two fought a duel. When it was over García, who was only twenty, was dead. Freire Esteves, twenty-two, was sent abroad as secretary of the legation in Paris.

García's friends vowed revenge against all the Cívicos. The latter, distracted by their internal quarrels, failed to notice a plot developing. Involved were a group of men connected with *El Diario*: Adolfo Riquelme (also of the Liga), Manuel Franco, Félix Paíva, Gualberto Cardús Huerta, and Eusebio Ayala. Nor were they without military support. Major Albino Jara was always ready to lead a coup. A handsome, dashing officer whose bravery was unquestionable, he was not without his supporters. But it was the willingness of Lieutenant Colonel Patricio Alejandro Escobar to place himself at the head of the revolt that brought over the more moderate officers.

Still, it was Jara's daring that caught the government by surprise and made success possible. Having lined up most of the regimental commanders of the capital's infantry battalion, on the night of 2 July 1908 he sneaked into the artillery barracks with a handful of supporters and took control of it. By the time the government realized what was happening, the rebels were already in strong positions. Ferreira was no quitter, and he still had the cavalry and police. For two days Asunción was rocked by heavy fighting, but on the afternoon of 4 July Ferreira realized that the tide of battle was going against him. He signed his resignation, handing power over to the Radicals, and then went to the port and boarded a ship for exile, never to return to Paraguay.

Ferreira had been a spirited politician with a good grasp of what the nation needed. At sixty-two, he had many more good years ahead and might have provided Paraguay with wise and energetic leadership. But, as Justo Pastor Benítez observes, "in South America politics comes before administration; people are more interested in personal ties and group interests than in the good management of the public interest."[35] With the general's departure a new political generation rose to power and the age of *caudillos* was definitively closed.

six

THE RADICAL LIBERALS IN POWER

The 1908 coup d'état that brought the Radical Liberals to office was more than a mere change of government. It turned over power to a new political generation that was considerably different from all preceding ones because it was the first that had no recollection of the horrible War of the Triple Alliance.

The march of generations can be seen clearly when we compare the birth dates of those who ran the provisional government that took power in July 1908 with those of the dominant figures before then. The cabinet consisted of Albino Jara (War, 1877), Manuel Gondra (Interior, 1871), Eusebio Ayala (Foreign Affairs, 1875), Manuel Franco (Justice and Education, 1871), and Gualberto Cardús Huerta (Finance, 1878). To them we should add two other top Radicals: Adolfo Riquelme (Police, 1876), and Eduardo Schaerer (mayor of Asunción, 1873). These men were, on the average, about thirty years younger than Bernardino Caballero (1839), Patricio Escobar (1843), Benigno Ferreira (1846), José Segundo Decoud (1848), Juan B. Egusquiza (1845), or Antonio Taboada (1848).

In between came those who formed the bulk of the *egusquicista* Colorados and Cívico Liberals: Cecilio Báez (1862), Adolfo Soler (1869), Emilio Aceval (1854), Ignacio Ibarra (1854), Manuel Domínguez (1866), José Tomás Legal (1865). I do not have a precise birth date for Guillermo de los Ríos, but since he founded his Banco de los Ríos in January 1895 we can assume that he was born in the 1850s or early 1860s. These men either were born or lived their early childhood during the war and so were touched by it, but not so thoroughly as their seniors. Most of their youth was spent in the immediate postwar period that was so marked by violence and extreme poverty, which may account for why they placed such a high value on civil order, consensus, and the attraction of foreign capital as the *sine qua non* of economic recovery.[1]

Using the term "generation" in this context assumes that a society like Paraguay's can be divided into age groups whose view of the world is distinctive. Moreover, it assumes that this distinctiveness will persist as the members of those age groups go through the various stages of the life cycle. A generation's outlook is the result of experiences that happen to youths of similar background during their teens and early twenties, their formative years. War, revolution, and economic disaster are the most common examples of such shaping experiences whose effects are enduring and are reflected in a unifying set of tastes, assumptions, attitudes, and behavioral tendencies. Subsequent adult experiences may have a modifying effect on these, and family, career, or class interests may divide a generation's members politically; nevertheless the way they define problems and frame issues will continue to reflect a common Zeitgeist that sets them apart from all other generations.

In the case of the Radical Liberals, not only did they not experience the war, but by the time they reached high school age Paraguay was well along the road to recovery. It was not that these young men were ignorant of or indifferent to that terrible upheaval; indeed, they had grown up hearing about it from their parents and relatives who had been caught up in it. But just as the Russian Revolution means less to young Russians of today than it did to those who fought in it, or the New Deal seems remote to those who were born after the Roosevelt era, so the *Epopeya* (the "Epic") was something that these Paraguayan youths had learned about rather than suffered through. Instead, their generation began unfolding its political consciousness in the era of phony prosperity and the financial scandals of the 1880s. Small wonder, then, that many of these young men would bring a certain puritanical style to politics. Disgusted at the brutal cynicism of the "war generation" (the generation of the 1840s) and impatient with the cautious, pragmatic reformism of the "intermediate generation" (the generation of the late 1850s and early 1860s) that had been shaped by the postwar anarchy, the Radicals tended to be idealistic and intolerant.

Radicalism was personified in its leader, Manuel Gondra. Gómez Freire Esteves, who hated him, called him a "pied piper" (*mago de la juventud*) because he was so popular with the students at the Colegio Nacional and the university, where he taught. After he accepted the party presidency in July 1908, the Liga de la Juventud Independiente dissolved itself and the vast majority became Liberal Party members. There is no doubt that he possessed that rare quality of charisma; yet it was not because he was flamboyant. His appearance was dignified and austere. He always dressed in black and his manners were those of a Spanish *hidalgo*. He was a good speaker, but in the style of a professor explaining with clarity some abstract, theoretical subject, rather than that of an orator. For an intellectual, he wrote little: his best-known works were a short critique of Rubén Dario's poetry and the 1896 Radical Liberal manifesto. He preferred the lecture hall, where he held his young listeners spellbound with his speeches about progress, the equality of men, good government, justice.[2]

The source of his charisma lay, then, in his erudition and sincerity, as well as with the high-mindedness he brought to bear on the discussion of public affairs. For a generation so exposed to governments composed of assassins, thieves, extortionists, double-crossers, and cynics, Gondra immediately claimed great moral authority. He lived simply, even poorly, and no scandal ever attached to his name. Although deeply involved in politics, he displayed a complete indifference to holding public office. Twice he came to the presidency, and twice he resigned soon thereafter, refusing to serve in unacceptable conditions. Some, like Arturo Bray, saw this as evidence of a flaw in Gondra's character. Were his actions really motivated by an idealism that was above politics, or did they reflect a lack of willpower and a desire to avoid responsibilities?

For Bray, Gondra was a man flogged by self-doubt. As an intellectual, he hesitated to commit himself to paper; and in politics he almost never took a firm stand, pretending to be taking the "high road" by giving in to his opponents.[3] More than once his loyal followers would be left exposed by such sudden surrenders.

There were other Radical leaders, of course. The provisional government was headed by Emiliano González Navero, a highly respected former Supreme Court justice. He was known for his ability to work with a wide variety of people, including Cívicos and Colorados. After all, he had served on the Court under Egusquiza and had been Ferreira's vice-president. It was perhaps this very tolerance, together with his age (he was born in 1861, and was therefore about ten years older than the average Radical leader) that disqualified him from the party's topmost position. He was the perfect man to defuse an internal crisis, however, which is why he served twice again as provisional president.

Another influential Radical was Eduardo Schaerer, the well-to-do publisher of *El Diario*. Energetic, tough-minded, and practical, he was just the opposite of Gondra. His excellent connections with Argentine and Paraguayan businessmen were helpful in the 1904 insurrection and the 1908 coup, and would become so again in the future. But although the Radicals admired the free market doctrines of Manchesterian liberalism, they did not like real-life businessmen very much. They found Schaerer just a bit boorish and pushy. What is more, he was tainted by the charges of financial mismanagement that attended his dismissal as director of ports. Although Schaerer claimed he was "framed" by Ferreira, the fact that the investigation was conducted by none other than Emiliano González Navero, then vice-president, lent substance to the accusations.

The man most capable of challenging Gondra for leadership of the Radicals was Colonel Albino Jara, the dashing, mercurial officer most responsible for removing General Ferreira from power. In the flush of triumph, a grateful Gondra had referred to him in a speech as "that most honorable soldier" (*pundonoroso militar*), a phrase he later was to regret. And yet, according to the code of the old *caudillos*, in whose tradition Jara surely followed, he deserved to be called *pundonoroso*. Fearless in a fight, generous to his friends, implacable toward his enemies, quick to take offense at any suspected slight to his honor, a favorite with women, and incorrigibly insubordinate to his superiors, Jara was one of those larger-than-life characters who steal any historical scene. No system could contain him, he would take orders from no one, and he was destined to end both badly and early.

Born on 28 February 1877, he was thirty-one when he toppled Ferreira. The bastard son of Colonel Zacarías Jara, a López soldier who later joined the Paraguayan Legion, he was an unruly child and adolescent. Hoping to discipline his son, Colonel Jara enrolled him in the cavalry at fifteen. The young man took to military life so well that President Egusquiza sent him to Chile for advanced training as one of a select group of junior officers. Although his father was a Colorado, Albino—perhaps because of his rebelliousness—became involved with the Liberals and spent an increasing amount of his time conspiring against the government. That got him cashiered from the army in 1903, and for the next several months he had to make do with a job his father got for him as a librarian at the university (!). During the 1904 rebellion he played a leading part, but was constantly quarreling with his superior officers. He had a particular animus against Ferreira and tried to raise the troops against him both during and after the revolt. Ferreira tolerated him, partly because Jara was so popular with the young Radicals (he was a member of the Liga de la Juventud Independiente) and also because he apparently considered him too unstable to lead a serious revolt. That was a costly mistake, for him as well as for Paraguay.[4]

It was after the July 1908 revolt, when he held Paraguay's political future in his hands, that Jara suddenly discovered his ambition to be president. Viewing himself as the savior of his country, he began in cabinet meetings to make it clear that he considered himself above the other ministers. He drove the finance minister, Gualberto Cardús Huerta, to resign because he refused to recognize any limitations on War Ministry spending. Although some Radicals began to look uneasily at the increasingly megalomaniacal colonel, others surrounded and flattered him.

Although he did not openly challenge Gondra's leadership, Jara acted more and more like a kingmaker, if indeed not a future king. His boisterous behavior on the floor when the Liberal Party opened its nominating convention in August 1910 showed that he was supremely confident, not just of his following in the barracks but among a sizable bloc of the Radical Liberal politicians as well. As usual, Gondra showed little interest in the presidency and even tried to refuse the nomination. As his excuse, he pointed to the fact that he was born in Argentina, of an Argentine father and a Paraguayan mother, whereas the Constitution of 1870 required the president to be native-born. It took much persuasion by his friends to make Gondra change his mind. Warned by Police Chief Adolfo Riquelme that if he did not run the presidency would surely go to Colonel Jara, Gondra bowed to the inevitable. But although he was the party's official choice, there was growing evidence that Jara intended to be the real power behind any future government.

Before elections could be held, however, the provisional government had to crush a revolt of Colorados and Cívicos. The Colorado Party, once stripped of power, had fallen into disarray. General Caballero, now elderly and going blind, was in Buenos Aires and no longer able to lead as he once had done. General Escobar was completely out of politics, now that his son was the ranking military officer on the Liberals' side. Enrique Solano López, the editor of *Patria*, tried to keep an organization intact inside Paraguay and to act as contact man with the exiles, but he lacked the qualities of a strong leader. Consequently, the Colorados welcomed the overtures of the Cívico Liberals, most of whom had been driven into exile by the provisional government. A meeting was held in Buenos Aires at which the two old enemies, Caballero and Ferreira, pledged to join their forces in the face of their common enemy, the Radicals. By February 1909 the Paraguayan Ministry of War was getting reports from its spies that the exiles were preparing an invasion and had already agreed to how the spoils would be divided in their new revolutionary government: Colonel José Gill, the Colorados' field commander, would be war minister; Antolín Irala, foreign minister in the Escurra government, and Antonio Sosa, Escurra's finance minister, would return to those posts; Manuel Benítez would return to the Interior Ministry, where he had served under Ferreira; Adolfo Soler would be justice minister; the infamous Colonel Juan A. Meza would once again be police chief; and Elías García would be Asunción's mayor. General Caballero would preside over the government. There was no provision for vice-president, although presumably it could go to General Ferreira if he wanted it.[5]

The Colorados' new military chief, Colonel José Gill, was the son of assassinated president Juan Bautista Gill, and thus General Caballero's adopted son. He was a true throwback to the age of primitive *caudillos*. Gill and his troops were more like drunken barbaric marauders than soldiers; their atrocities were so notorious that for years the colonel's name was used to frighten disobedient children. Although he fought under the party's red banner, Gill had no political principles. Alfredo Jaeggli describes one of his famous harangues to his troops on the night before battle: "Boys! My children! My only plan for tomorrow's action is this: (a cutting gesture across the throat), (a grasping gesture, of someone robbing), and (an obscene gesture of violation)!"[6]

Near the end of August 1909, armed groups of Colorados began entering the country from the Argentine province of Corrientes, attacking various military outposts in guerrilla fashion. Little by little they consolidated their operations until finally, under Gill's orders, they controlled a wide area in the south, along the Paraná River. Other units, under the command of Eduardo López Moreira and Cayo Romero Pereira, crossed over the Brazilian border and captured some villages in the north. Colonel Jara, perceiving the threat from the south to be greater, marched at the head of the government's forces to meet Gill. On 14 September he dealt the rebels a crushing defeat near the town of Laureles, scattering their forces and executing a number of the rebel prisoners on the spot.[7]

Jara returned from his victory all the more convinced that he was Paraguay's man of destiny and began to show it by presenting to Gondra, as president-elect, a list of demands. To begin with, he wanted assurance that he would remain in the cabinet as war minister. Next, he demanded the appointment of his friends José A. Ortiz and Mario Usher as finance minister and police chief, respectively, in the future cabinet. Deaf to all of Gondra's protestations that he was usurping the president's authority, Jara let it be known that unless these demands were met there might be no inauguration at all.

This piece of blackmail hit the *gondrista* Radicals like a slap in the face. Adolfo Riquelme expected to be Gondra's minister of interior, and he demanded that Jara be removed immediately from the cabinet. Caught between two strong-minded men, Gondra tried to compromise by suggesting that they both resign. Neither would agree to do so. Nor would Jara accept a diplomatic mission to Europe, even when a frustrated Gondra threatened to resign himself unless the colonel accepted. Up to the very night before the inauguration the president-elect tried to cajole the rebellious officer to accept some compromise, but Jara would not bend. On the following day Gondra appointed his cabinet, giving in to all of Jara's demands, but keeping thirty-four-year-old Riquelme as interior minister in an attempt to find a political balance.

A TIME OF TROUBLES

Gondra lasted just two months in office. His relations with Jara deteriorated quickly as it became obvious that the latter was plotting against him. A coalition of maverick Radicals, Cívico Liberals, and Colorados had been meeting with *jarista* army officers, offering to provide civilian support for a new government. Each component of this conspiracy had its own peculiar reasons for joining it: maverick Radicals like Liberato M. Rojas hoped merely to use Jara to replace Gondra in office, the Cívicos aimed to replace the Radicals, and the Colorados intended to return to power by doing away with all Liberal factions. There also was a "silent partner" in the conspiracy: the Paraguayan Central Railway Company.

The Paraguayan Central Railway Company (PCRC) started in 1889 with some state and some private capital, but soon thereafter the burden of keeping it going became too much for local investors and it was sold. Although its headquarters was moved to London, most of its principal shareholders were Argentines. General Ferreira also had acquired a sizable number of shares, which helps account for his favorable attitude toward the company while he was in power. Indeed, this became such a bone of contention between himself and the Radicals that it served to marshal public opinion against his administration, on the grounds that he was betraying the national interest for his own private gain. It was hardly surprising, therefore, that the Radicals' coming to power meant friction between the foreign railway owners and the state.[8]

The PCRC's chief antagonists were Adolfo Riquelme, the interior minister, and Eduardo Schaerer, Asunción's mayor. Together they blocked the company's requests to expand the existing railway system, to install streetcars in the capital, or to build an electric power company. Instead, the Radicals sought to curb its power by fostering competition. They entered into negotiations with Ferrocarril Trans-Paraguayo (FTP), the subsidiary of a Brazilian-based company owned by an American named Percival Farquhar, to build a line from the Brazilian border to Asunción. That would give Paraguay a much-needed alternative to its current dependence on Argentina for access to the outside world. Naturally, both the PCRC and the Argentine government saw this as a threat to their interests, but no amount of pressure could stop Gondra from signing a deal with Farquhar.

Meanwhile, Riquelme was well informed about the goings and comings of the *jarista* conspirators. He decided to strike before they did by arresting Jara. To do so, he needed the police, so he went to Mario Usher. The twenty-six-year-old police chief had been a member of the Liga de la Juventud Independiente, as had Riquelme, and therefore was presumed to be a *gondrista*. The flaw in such logic was that Jara, had been a Liga member too. Besides, Usher was an opportunist who cultivated friends in many different camps. He occasionally wrote articles for the pro-Cívico *El Nacional* and he was on good terms with Jara too. Approached with this plan to seize Jara he carefully weighed the situation and decided that in any showdown the colonel was more likely to win. Thus, he tipped Jara off as to what Gondra and Riquelme intended to do. At dawn on 17 January 1911 the artillery, under Jara's command, declared itself in revolt. Other military units refused Gondra's orders to intervene, and when the police were contacted as a last resort, Usher informed the president that all of the stations throughout the capital had declared for the rebels. With that, Gondra wrote out his resignation and left the country.

Now anarchy began. Jara's government, composed as it was of such contradictory elements, was destined to last fewer than seven months. The Cívicos were represented by Sebastian Ibarra Legal (Interior) and Cecilio Báez (Foreign Affairs); the Colorados had Colonel Carlos Goiburu (War) and former vice-president Manuel Domínguez (Justice and Education); and the maverick Radicals claimed José Ortiz (Finance). The maverick Radicals also controlled the police, through Marcos Caballero Codas, a son of General Caballero's who had deserted the Colorados after the 1908 revolt. Jara appointed him because he didn't trust the much-too-flexible Mario Usher, only to find later that Caballero Codas was equally unreliable. The Supreme Court was composed of two Cívicos (José T. Legal and Pablo Garcete) and a maverick Radical (Francisco Rolón). This unstable mixture was brought together under the banner of a new political party, the Democratic Liberal Party (PLD), which was designed to supplant the traditional Liberals and Colorados. Cecilio Báez, rather unwisely, agreed to serve as the PLD's ostensible head.

Wise, firm leadership might possibly have kept these elements working in tandem, but Jara was a disastrous president. When students from the university and the Colegio Nacional took to the streets to demand Gondra's return, Jara cracked down on them without mercy. Even some of his supporters felt that his toughness went too far. Faced with a hostile Congress, he was equally high-handed. When legislation he wanted was not forthcoming, he simply issued decrees. Jara was thwarted on one symbolic issue, however: he failed to get a promotion to the rank of general. Although the Chamber of Deputies acceded to his demand by one vote—the Chamber's president, Antolín Irala, voting to break a tie—the Senate turned him down flat. Jara even fell out with his financial backers. He discovered that Manuel Rodrígues, a leading shareholder in the PCRC, and Percival Farquhar had made a deal to acquire interest in each other's railroad. With that, Jara canceled all the contracts. Finally, a number of highly placed officers who, like Jara, had been in Chile for advanced training, deserted the government and went over to the Radicals because of personal differences with the temperamental president. Chief among these were lieutenant colonels Adolfo Chirife, Pedro Mendoza, and Manlio Schenoni, all of whom were to play prominent roles on the political scene.

The proximate cause of these desertions, however, was a revolt launched by the Radicals in mid-February 1911. Colonel Goiburu, the war minister, was dispatched to Misiones Territory to suffocate an invasion in the south while Jara himself confronted the main rebel force, which, under Adolfo Riquelme's leadership, had won over the northern garrison of Concepción and was now heading for the capital. This was the sort of action in which Jara excelled. He crushed the revolt in a series of quick but bloody confrontations. In the last battle, fought on 17 March near the small river port of Bonete, Riquelme was captured. Here was the true test of Albino Jara's character: what would he do with his old enemy? After a few hours of thinking it over, he ordered Riquelme to be taken to the riverbank and shot.

It was Jara's worst mistake. With one brutal stroke he destroyed forever the image he had created of the chivalrous young paladin. This was still an age in which the unwritten rules of politics were to permit one's enemies an honorable exile rather than kill them or send them to concentration camps. Riquelme's youth (he was thirty-four), his unquestionable talent, and his family connections all made the murder a shocking affair to everyone. Even Jara's own backers, many of whom were connected by blood, marriage, or acquaintance to the dead man, were disgusted. Young Gómez Freire Esteves, who returned from exile the year before to take over the editorship of the Cívicos' *El Nacional*, protested so vigorously that his paper was closed down and he was expelled from the Democratic Liberal Party. In Congress there was now a sufficient majority against Jara to begin impeachment proceedings against him.

Having gone so far, however, Albino Jara was not going to surrender power peacefully. He nipped the impeachment movement in the bud by arresting its leaders. To secure their release, they had to sign a statement resigning from Congress. One senator, Francisco Campos, a nonagenarian who was the last surviving member of the 1870 Constitutional Convention, was dragged from his home to a nearby barracks and beaten with the flat of a sword until he gave in and signed.[9]

Finding himself increasingly friendless, Jara shuffled his cabinet. Francisco Bareiro, a maverick Radical, became the new finance minister and Cipriano Ibañez, a young Colorado who had been a close companion of Jara's in the Liga de la Juventud Independiente, took over the Interior Ministry. Ibañez quickly became the leading personality in the government because Jara, weary of politics, increasingly entrusted him with the running of affairs. More alert than his master, Ibañez soon uncovered a conspiracy inside the government, led by Police Chief Caballero Codas and War Minister Goiburu, to replace Jara with a more respectable figure. Caballero Codas managed to get to a foreign embassy and claim asylum just ahead of Ibáñez's agents. Colonel Goiburu was not so lucky, but the politic interior minister allowed him to go abroad on a "diplomatic assignment," rather than alienate opinion further by shedding more blood. Meanwhile, he took over the War Ministry himself.

Ibáñez soon realized that his task was hopeless. Jara spent more and more time chasing women and made few appearances at cabinet meetings. The state was adrift. Finally Ibáñez allowed himself to become part of a new plot whose aim was to replace Jara with Liberato Marcial Rojas, leader of the maverick Radicals. The revolt came on 5 July and encountered no resistance. Ibáñez controlled the police and the infantry, while Rojas had the backing of the artillery, where his brother-in-law was in command. Knowing himself to be outgunned, Jara accepted the offer of a "diplomatic mission" and signed his resignation. As he went to board a ship for exile, he was met by "a large, hostile demonstration which suddenly gathered along his path to the docks."[10] The *varón meteórico* was suddenly in eclipse. Even as his ship pulled away from the shore, congressmen were gathering to swear in his successor.

Liberato Marcial Rojas, born in the last year of the war, was raised in extreme poverty. Nevertheless, because he was intelligent and energetic, he obtained degrees from the Colegio Nacional and the university. While still only a teenager, he got into journalism and was one of the founders, along with Blas Garay, Manuel Domínguez, and Fulgencio Moreno, of *El Tiempo*. But Liberalism soon attracted him away from his early friends and he began contributing articles to Liberal journals. In 1887 he participated in the founding of the Centro Democrático and later served on the party directorate. During the 1904 rebellion he commanded one of the small river craft that ferried the rebel soldiers in the movement to encircle Asunción. Afterward he became a deputy and then a senator. Despite all this, Rojas kept up his friendly contacts with Colorados; and it was perhaps because of this that he never was included in Gondra's inner circle.

Although the cabinet personnel was shifted, the new government contained the same mixture of maverick Radicals, Cívicos, and Colorados that Jara's had. To a great extent Freire Esteves is right when he calls it a *jarista* government without Jara. Rojas relied heavily on his brother-in-law, Major Tomás Mendoza, who headed the artillery, and his own brother, Emiliano, who was police chief. Major Mendoza, however, had little faith in the future and soon accepted a lucrative arms-purchasing mission to Europe.

During the eight months Rojas stayed in office, there were many changes in the cabinet as he found himself caught between the Cívicos and the Colorados, each of whom demanded more government posts. Neither a military hero like Jara, who could command support in the barracks, nor the head of a wealthy government able to dispense patronage, Rojas found it impossible to satisfy all the elements of his patchwork coalition. A second invasion by the Radicals, in November 1911, forced him at last to side with the Colorados as the only political organization capable of providing mass support and a corps of trained army officers. On 13 December the Cívicos formally withdrew from the government and were replaced by Colorados. Even the president's brother was forced to give up control of the police to Captain Tomás Romero Pereira, one of the Colorados' toughest militants. From that point on, Rojas was virtually a prisoner, although he managed to get Emiliano out of the country with a hefty portion of the Treasury's funds. The real "brains" behind the scene was Ricardo Brugada, a well-known Colorado politician and writer who had been close to Rojas over the years and now became his trusted advisor.[11]

The second Radical revolt, which caused this government shake-up, was far better organized and financed than the first one. In Buenos Aires a revolutionary junta, formed in September by Manuel Gondra, Eduardo Schaerer, and José P. Montero, had managed to raise a war chest of some 300,000 gold pesos. The money came from a loan provided by Manuel Rodrígues, a Portuguese investor in the Paraguayan Central Railway Company and in the Ferrocarril Trans-Paraguayo. Disillusioned by his flirtation with Jara and distrusting the competence of Jara's successors, Rodrígues—like other foreign capitalists—was anxious to see a stable, business-minded government come to power. Eduardo Schaerer was just the sort of strong, capable businessman to head such a government. Schaerer, chastened by the Radicals' overthrow and needing cash to finance a revolt, was willing to court his former enemies. So a deal was struck by which Rodrígues would supply the money to equip a rebel army in return for the Radicals' promise to install Schaerer as president, renew the contract to build the Brazilian line, and repay the loan as part of Paraguay's foreign debt. After the Radicals' victory, the railway companies did indeed gain lucrative concessions. Although the Brazilian line was never built, they got the streetcar and electric power concessions for Asunción. In addition, they received grants of land in the Chaco and a large bloc of stock on La Industrial Paraguaya, the *yerba mate* company. The government also repaid Rodrígues, at a very high rate of interest. Colorados and Cívicos later pretended to be shocked at the extravagant concessions Schaerer agreed to for getting the so-called Portuguese Loan.[12]

Meanwhile, relations deteriorated between the Argentine and Paraguayan governments. Argentina protested incursions by Paraguayan troops into the Argentine Chaco, and Rojas, after discovering that Argentine ships were transporting rebel units, broke off relations. Brazil, on the other hand, recognized the Rojas government. A Brazilian ship even conveyed Rojas out of danger when, at one point, Asunción fell into rebel hands. Both the Argentine and Brazilian river fleets performed intelligence operations for their respective sides.[13]

As the war began to go against the government, the Colorados decided to sacrifice Rojas as a liability and take over direct control of the government. The coup began with a police roundup of anyone who might resist a Colorado take-over. Even Cívico military officers who so far had fought bravely against the enemy fell into Romero Pereira's net. The last step was Rojas's arrest by his own presidential guard, on 27 February 1912.

This coup paved the way for a twenty-one-day "revival" of the Colorado era. The new president was Pedro Peña (forty-eight), a physician who had spent most of his career at the university, in the diplomatic service, and in politics. His interior minister was Eduardo López Moreira, another physician, who had played an important role in the 1909 Colorado revolt; his war minister was Major Eugenio Garay, the Colorados' most brilliant military tactician and one of that select group of Chilean-trained officers; and his foreign minister was the veteran, Fulgencio Moreno. Two Cívicos also were included in the cabinet, in an effort to broaden the government's base: Rogelio Urizar, at Justice and Education; and Higinio Arbó, at Finance. Tomás Romero Pereira continued to head the police.

This coalition fell apart even before the first cabinet meeting because the more intransigent Colorados opposed it. Colonel Carlos Goiburu, commander of the Colorados' forces in the field, ordered the arrest of Lieutenant Colonel Hipólito Nuñez, the Cívicos' military leader. With that, Urizar resigned from the cabinet and Higinio Arbó, who was still residing in Buenos Aires at the time of his appointment, canceled his plans to return. Although Romero Pereira arrested several of them, many Cívicos managed to flee the capital and take refuge in the south, where their last hope—Colonel Albino Jara—had just reappeared to lead a new revolt.[14]

Meanwhile, the Radicals continued their inexorable march on Asunción, with Colonel Patricio Alejandro Escobar and Adolfo Chirife at the head of their troops. One column drove south from Concepción, the other north from Villa Franca. The rebels also controlled the river with their gunboat, Constitución, which had been impounded from the Paraguayan government by the Argentine authorities at the beginning of the war but then turned over to the Radicals. The Argentine navy also helped transport the rebel troops to Asunción's outskirts and ferried deserters from the government's army to the rebel side. After a bitter, three-day, seesaw battle in the city's suburbs, the Colorado chiefs evacuated Asunción on 22 March by boarding their men on ships and steaming downriver to Argentine territory. The Radicals were once again in control.

The Radicals immediately set up a provisional government under Emiliano González Navero, but they did not take much time to celebrate their victory because Albino Jara was still in the field. At the moment his army was stationed at Humaitá, at the confluence of the Paraguay and Upper Paraná rivers. His strength was growing rapidly, thanks to Cívicos and Colorados who joined his camp for a last challenge to the Radicals. Among those Colorados was the infamous Colonel José Gill, whose passion was war. Feeling confident of victory, Jara began moving his forces northward in April, taking the important town of Villarrica and advancing on the capital by way of the garrison town of Paraguarí. There, on 9 May, he met the Radicals' forces under the command of Colonel Adolfo Chirife. A ferocious two-day battle followed in which the *varón meteórico* finally met his Waterloo. Not only was his army routed but he himself was so badly wounded that he died a few days later, thus putting an end to a particularly dolorous chapter of Paraguay's modern history.

Jara's significance lay in the fact that, like Egusquiza and Ferreira before him, he tried to use his personal prestige to form a third-party movement based on dissidents from the two major parties. In Egusquiza's case, the attempt failed because the 1902 coup upset his fragile coalition of moderates. Ferreira, who took over the remnants of that coalition, was swept aside by the momentum of a revolution he was unable to control. Like them, Jara sought to build a broad coalition based on moderate Colorados and dissident Liberals; and, like them, he was caught between the intransigents of both the traditional parties. His failure was as much due to a lack of political skill as it was to the difficulty of combining so many disparate elements in a single party. It would not be the last time, however, that a charismatic military man attempted to restructure Paraguay's party system.

THE RADICALS DIVIDE AGAIN

Emiliano González Navero, appointed to finish out Gondra's unexpired term, ought to have remained in office until 25 November 1914, but Eduardo Schaerer, who emerged from the revolt as the Radicals' new "strongman," would not wait. At his insistence, the party approved setting the transfer of power for 15 August 1912. From that day forward, all inaugurations took place on Assumption Day instead of 25 November, as had been the practice since 1870.[15]

Schaerer's cabinet drew from the very cream of the Radical faction. His vice-president, Pedro Bobadilla, was the eldest of the top government officials—at the ripe age of forty-seven! Bobadilla, a founding member of the old Centro Democrático, had been minister of justice and education under Emilio Aceval and had served on the Supreme Court during Cecilio Báez's brief presidency. Manuel Gondra returned to the government in the somewhat curious position of minister of war. He moved over to Foreign Affairs the next year, where his talents were more suited, and was replaced by Colonel Patricio Alejandro Escobar. Schaerer's first foreign minister was Eusebio Ayala, who taught philosophy at the Colegio Nacional and law, sociology, and political economy at the university. Ayala came from a wealthy family, had been educated in Europe, and was now vice-president of the Banco Mercantil. José P. Montero, the interior minister, had been a member of the revolutionary junta in the fight against Jara and was a close friend of Schaerer's. Other members of Schaerer's personal entourage were Félix Paíva, the justice minister, and Ernesto Velásquez, the police chief. Paíva, a member of the old *El Diario* group, had been foreign minister in the provisional government. Velásquez also had served in the previous government, as police chief. The top leadership was rounded out by Gerónimo Zubizarreta, the finance minister. Son of the National University's first rector, he had joined the Radical insurrection in 1904 when he was twenty-four and had been an active Gondra supporter ever since.

The average age of these men was thirty-eight, ranging from thirty-two (Zubizarreta) to forty-seven (Bobadilla). Five of the eight had entered politics after 1904. Half had never held a political office before 1912. But despite their youth and inexperience, these men were the undisputed holders of power. Jara was dead, generals Caballero and Escobar had died earlier in the year, and Decoud had taken his own life three years before. Of the Cívicos' great leaders, General Ferreira had died in 1910; Taboada, gravely ill at the time of Schaerer's inauguration, was to die the following May; and Báez had retired to the academy as rector of the National University.

The new administration made rebuilding Paraguay's economy its first priority. Schaerer began by creating a Department of Development (Departamento de Fomento) which launched a great variety of infrastructural projects: new roads; improved port facilities; paved streets, streetcars, and electric lights for the capital; new schools with more teachers; a ferry service linking the Paraguayan and Argentine railways; the reorganization of the Exchange Board to regulate currency transactions; the beautification of parks and plazas; the reform of the Civil Code; the purchase of private radio and telegraph operations. New agricultural colonies were created on estates confiscated from the government's defeated foes, with titles granted to both Paraguayans and immigrants. Congress passed a Homestead Act to protect smallholders.[16]

The money to pay for these improvements was raised, in part, by new taxes on alcohol; but the chief sources of revenue were import and export taxes, whose yield rose greatly because of increased trade with Europe during World War I, thanks to the operations of the new Exchange Board.[17] More meat-packing plants were built and Banco Agrícola was busy loaning money to farmers and ranchers to expand their production. In brief, this was a time of prosperity, and even though the "Portuguese Loan" was scandalously added to the nation's foreign debt, the boom in trade made it easy to finance.

Not all was rosy, however. Cecilio Báez, appointed to the Supreme Court in order to extend an olive branch to the Cívicos, soon resigned, accusing Schaerer of acting high-handedly (a complaint that, in view of events to come, seems plausible). Labor conflicts began to make their appearance, especially on the *yerba mate* plantations, where working conditions were abysmal and the benefits of the new prosperity had yet to trickle down. La Industrial and Barthe & Co. were especially troubled by strikes and violence. The workers' cause was taken up by a young journalist named Leopoldo Ramos Giménez, who was murdered by an unidentified gunman on the night of 5 July 1916.[18] Even more ominous for the future was the chain of forts that Bolivia was building in the Chaco, to back up its claims to that territory.

Since the Chaco issue was to become the cause of the Liberal Party's downfall, it may be useful to review it from the perspective of the time. Bolivia, deprived of its Pacific coastline in 1879 as the result of a war with Chile, had turned eastward to find an alternative outlet to the sea. There were two rivers, lying on opposite edges of the wild Chaco region, which presented possible routes: the Paraguay River to the north and east, and the Pilcomayo River to the south and west. They both flowed into the Paraná, which then ran southward through Argentina to the Atlantic. The Chaco was uninhabited, except by nomadic Indians; the old boundaries between the Spanish colonial provinces of Paraguay and Alto Peru (Bolivia) were poorly described in old documents and were drawn in different places on the old maps. Both countries claimed the region, but neither thought it worthwhile to occupy—until necessity drove Bolivia to take a greater interest.

The first steps to delineate the boundary seemed to start with goodwill on both sides, with the Quijarro-Decoud Treaty of 1879; but when the Bolivians asked for additional concessions, the Paraguayan Congress refused to ratify.[19] Relations between the two states then turned bitter, despite the conclusion of another treaty in 1887 that divided the Chaco in three parts: one for each side and the third to be arbitrated. This never was ratified either, particularly since Paraguay sent a force up the Paraguay River to destroy a Bolivian settlement and replace it with a Paraguayan fort, Bahía Negra. During the next twenty years there was little diplomatic activity concerning the Chaco, but the Bolivians were able to take advantage of Paraguay's unsettled political conditions to build a number of forts in the northwest part of the territory, which became the opening stages of a relentless thrust southward toward the Paraná.

Feeling more confident, Bolivia next sought diplomatic recognition of its fait accompli, whereas Paraguay, feeling itself in a weak military position, was anxious to find a compromise. Through the mediation of Argentina the Pinilla-Soler Protocol was signed in 1907, which ceded about one-fourth of the Chaco to either side and provided for arbitration concerning the remaining half in the middle. Bolivia promised to advance no further and Argentina guaranteed the status quo. This time Paraguay rushed to ratify the pact, but the Bolivian Congress would accept no concessions and refused to go along.

This is where the issue lay in 1913 when Schaerer dispatched Foreign Minister Eusebio Ayala to open negotiations with his opposite, Ricardo Mujía. The result was another protocol calling for arbitration and promising to maintain the status quo referred to in the 1907 accord. Unfortunately for Ayala, he accepted a clause in the new document that asserted that there had been no violations of the status quo established in the Pinilla-Soler Protocol, knowing full well that the Bolivians had since established forts well beyond the old ones. Although he did so in the hope that by being conciliatory he could get a treaty that would guarantee peace, it was a mistake that cost him dearly later on. Even at the time, however, there were concerned citizens in Paraguay who felt that the government was giving away too much to the Bolivians. Former president Emilio Aceval, who was one of these, formed a nonpartisan "Patriotic Union" to bring together people from all parties and factions to study the approaching danger.

War with Bolivia was still remote in 1915, but the potential for internal strife was high. Early on New Year's Day the Cívicos, led by Colonel Manuel J. Duarte and Gómez Freire Esteves, launched another revolt. Schaerer himself was taken prisoner as he hurried to the police barracks to see what was happening, but his wife sped away in their car to give the alarm. Loyal troops, led by Colonel Adolfo Chirife, soon had the rebels surrounded while the gunboat Constitución, captained by Schaerer's brother, began bombarding the rebels' main positions. Although his life was threatened, Schaerer refused to sign any resignation or even concede a place in his cabinet to Colonel Duarte. The most he would offer his captors was an amnesty if they promised to surrender immediately. Perceiving their cause to be hopeless, the Cívicos accepted his terms.[20]

A year after this revolt, a Liberal Party convention nominated Manuel Franco, a close friend of Gondra's, as its presidential candidate. José P. Montero, a friend of Schaerer's, was chosen for vice-president. On 15 August the new government took office in the first peaceful transferal of power between two elected administrations since Egusquiza stood aside for Aceval in 1898; and it was the first such transition between two civilians ever in Paraguay.

Franco was a compromise choice between two wings of the Radical faction that were moving apart. Schaerer had wanted Montero but, even though he was the outgoing president, he was unable to impose his successor. The majority of the Radicals wanted Gondra, but he begged off on the lame excuse that the Constitution required two terms to transpire before a former president was eligible for reelection (as if a president who had been overthrown could be said to have served his term). Thus Franco, who had been director of the Colegio Nacional, rector of the National University, and board member of the Banco Agrícola, and was considered a *gondrista*, became the fallback choice. Even he tried to resist the nomination on the legitimate grounds of poor health (he was to die in office) but was prevailed upon by the *gondristas*, who were determined not to allow the presidency to go to a *schaererista*, although one was permitted to fill the vice-presidency as a sop.

In fact, the government was more of a compromise than the *gondristas* would have liked. Besides Vice-President Montero, there was Ernesto Velásquez at the War Ministry and Félix Paíva at Justice and Education. Nevertheless, the *gondristas* had Gondra at Foreign Affairs, the young and energetic Luís A. Riart at Interior and (*ad interim*) Finance, and the even younger Eliseo da Rosa in charge of the police. The Finance portfolio eventually was taken by Francisco Sosa Gaona, one of the founders of the Liga de la Juventud Independiente and hence supposedly a *gondrista*, although he eventually showed himself to favor neither side.

During Franco's brief administration, which ended with his sudden death from a heart attack on 5 June 1919, there was continual jockeying between the two factions. The *gondristas* seemed to be gaining in January 1918 when Velásquez was replaced at War by Emiliano González Navero, but a year later González Navero turned over the job to Colonel Adolfo Chirife, who was known to be Schaerer's close friend. Shortly before that the police department was placed under Major Francisco Brizuela, another *schaererista* officer. Meanwhile, Manuel Gondra withdrew once again from public office in January 1918, to be succeeded by Eusebio

Ayala. The latter, having served faithfully under both Gondra and Schaerer, was thought to be at least neutral between the factions, if not slightly favorable to Schaerer.

Franco enjoyed great personal popularity as a man of proven honesty and competence, and his administration, like the previous one, basked in the glow of wartime prosperity. Good government and peaceful compromise were his primary goals. His administration was noted for the introduction of the secret ballot, universal suffrage, obligatory voting, and the "incomplete list," which guaranteed minority representation in Congress to the opposition. In May 1917 Congress passed an amnesty law that allowed Colorados, *jaristas,* and Cívicos to return to Paraguay. Naturally, they had to vote, although many preferred to cast blank ballots in protest.

One disturbing incident—a harbinger of trouble to come as well as a factor tilting the balance of power toward Schaerer—was a clash between two army factions that erupted on 19 September 1918. The dispute was between those officers who, like colonels Adolfo Chirife and Manlio Schenoni, had received advanced military training in Chile, and those who had either stayed in Paraguay or had gone to Argentina. The "Chileanists" considered themselves to be more professional because at that time the Chilean armed forces, following their victory over Peru and Bolivia in the War of the Pacific, had the highest reputation in South America. They tended to lord it over their other colleagues who, grouped in a club called the Círculo Militar, looked to General Patricio Alejandro Escobar as their leader.[21]

This rivalry eventually took the form of a personal dispute between Schenoni and Escobar when the general accused his subordinate of being the author of a series of unsigned articles appearing in *El Nacional* that poked fun at the Círculo Militar and himself as being so many incompetent old fogeys. Escobar demanded Schenoni's dismissal from the army. The dispute went to González Navero, the war minister, who was inclined to support his old chum, Escobar; but Schenoni appealed to Franco, providing evidence that that he was innocent of having written the articles. After studying the matter, Franco overruled González Navero, which then touched off a revolt by the Círculo Militar. Loyal troops quickly snuffed it out, and Colonel Chirife took over as war minister the next day.

José P. Montero's succession to the presidency in June 1919 was a setback for the *gondristas,* even though he confirmed all of Franco's cabinet ministers in their posts. There were frequent clashes between the president and his ministers. Riart soon left the cabinet, to be replaced at the key Interior Ministry by Félix Paíva. Sosa Gaona was succeeded by a technocrat, Pastor Ibañez, and Schaerer's brother-in-law, J. Manuel Balteiro, took over the police. Despite these maneuvers, however, in June 1920 the Liberal Party's convention nominated Manuel Gondra as its presidential candidate. It was a stinging defeat for Schaerer, who had been preparing for months. In part, the setback was caused by a postwar economic recession during 1919 that cost President Montero much popular support. In part, too, the *gondrista* victory was due to the efforts of a dynamic young man, José P. Guggiari, who had mobilized the party's youth behind the symbol of Manuel Gondra, the man "above politics." In any case, Schaerer had to content himself with getting Félix Paíva the vice-presidential nomination. Immediately thereafter Paíva had to resign from the cabinet, as the laws commanded, and the *gondristas* got control of both the Interior and Justice ministries.

On 15 August 1920 Manuel Gondra, having campaigned unopposed, began his second term as president. The *gondristas'* elation was to be short-lived, however. Eduardo Schaerer was not giving up his goal of controlling the Liberal Party; the Colorados and dissident Liberals were still unreconciled; and Gondra was to prove once again that he was an unreliable leader. Paraguay was on the edge of another civil war.

seven

THE CLIMAX OF

RADICAL LIBERAL RULE

PARAGUAY ON THE EVE OF CIVIL WAR

Eighteen years of Liberal Party rule had done little to change Paraguay. Asunción, its capital, was still a quaint, somnolent backwater. Only a few buildings—a couple of downtown movie houses and a theater—had electricity or running water, and the appearance of an automobile on one of the shady, unpaved streets was considered quite an event. The one sign of progress was a trolley line that ran from the city's center to the outskirts, its cars clanging at the horses, dogs, and barefoot pedestrians scampering across the tracks.

The pace of life was slow. At midday the tropical heat drove many people indoors for long siestas; others, such as workingmen and street vendors, stretched out on the grass or on benches in the public parks, or found a quiet corner in some arcaded passageway. The gentry lived in tile-roofed, stuccoed houses that presented blank walls and heavily barred windows to the street. This Spanish colonial motif was repeated on a larger scale in the public buildings downtown, many of which dated back to the early nineteenth century, having been expropriated from the López family and converted into ministries, a Congress building, and the presidential palace. There was the National University, with a law school and a medical school, although the latter functioned only feebly and had to be closed from time to time for lack of funds.

City people traveled mostly on foot or horseback along streets picturesquely lined with orange trees. (Those same streets turned into rustbrown rivers of mud after a heavy rain.) Since there were no radios, *asunceños* received their news about national or foreign affairs from one of several partisan newspapers. Most communications within the country were in the form of messages delivered by hand because the post was slow and the telegraph reached only a few places that were considered militarily important. In the absence of plumbing, drinking water was obtained from vendors who sold it from jugs carried from door to door on muleback. Sanitary standards were low, tropical diseases of all kinds were rampant, and the infant mortality rate was very high. There was a Charity Hospital that was serviced by the medical school, but its equipment and services were rudimentary.

Beyond Asunción's city limits life was even more primitive. Travel through the interior was still carried on chiefly by horseback, oxcart, covered wagon, or stagecoach. Many so-called roads were little more than trails consisting of hoofprints or wheelmarks that wound through thick forests and swamps. In the rainy season they were completely impassable. The railway that linked Asunción to the southern port of Encarnación was slow and inefficient: the cars were antiquated and the rails and roadbeds were badly run-down. Outside of a few large ranches and *yerba mate* plantations, run by capitalists for profit, the rural population lived on isolated, subsistence farms. Implements were crude and common agricultural practice was simple in the extreme: you cultivated a small plot of land until the yield declined. Then you either cleared another patch of forest or else moved on, depending on whether you were a smallholder or a squatter. Provincial capitals like Encarnación, Villarrica, Paraguarí, or Concepción were little more than villages where cows grazed on the common green, dogs slept in the road, and chickens scratched in the dirt in front of houses.

Progress was held back by the seemingly endemic political instability, which had worsened under the Liberals. One effect of it was to keep the nation's finances in disarray and lower its foreign credit rating to nil. The reform of the Exchange Board, in 1916, which guaranteed that foreign exchange earnings would go to the state, thus freeing the politicians from their former dependence on the mercantile elites, only meant that those in charge of the state had more patronage to dispense.[1] Top politicians were said to have gained fortunes by manipulating exchange rates, for which reason the best talent was drawn to politics and speculation, rather than to production. Meanwhile, the currency was worthless.

Paraguayan political parties in 1922 were not much different in their organization than they had been in 1887. The system resembled a kind of feudalism in which both Liberals and Colorados were essentially loose alliances of *jefes políticos*. The country was divided into twenty electoral districts, with one deputy elected to Congress from each, and one senator for every two districts. These political representatives were either powerful *jefes políticos* themselves, or else were their delegates. The most powerful of all got cabinet seats. Usually, though not exclusively, the key men came from Asunción or its suburbs and had university degrees in law or medicine. It was considered especially prestigious to combine one's professional and political work with a sideline in journalism or teaching— especially teaching at the Colegio Nacional or the university. Paraguay in

1920 was still a deferential society, where even rough and tumble rural *jefes* paid respect to *universitarios.* Indeed, a university degree was almost essential for admittance to the highest political and social strata.

These trends can be seen most easily by observing the careers of some twenty-one Liberals who served as president, vice-president, or cabinet minister from the end of the civil war in 1912 to the installation of Gondra's government in 1920. Fourteen of them held law degrees and eleven taught law, social science, or philosophy at the National University. Three had served as rectors of the university, one was the private secretary of a rector, one was the dean of the law school, and another was the son of a former rector. Five of the men were also teachers at the Colegio Nacional and one of them had served as the school's director. Almost all wrote for one or more Liberal newspapers, and almost all had served in one or both houses of Congress. Besides the lawyers, there were two physicians and two military officers, one of whom (Colonel Adolfo Chirife) had received advanced military training abroad. Only three of the civilians did not have a university degree, and two of those were graduates of the highly selective Colegio Nacional. It is curious, however, that neither Eduardo Schaerer nor Manuel Gondra, the leaders of the two main factions of Radical Liberalism, had graduated from the university. Approximately half (nine men) of this elite group had been born or raised in Asunción.

Colorado leaders were no different, so far as it is possible to tell from the backgrounds of those who occupied the party's directorate during this same period. There were twenty-two men in this group. Since their party was out of power it was less easy to find out biographical information about them, and for seven of them it was impossible to get any kind of data. Of the other fifteen, however, ten were lawyers, two were physicians, and three were journalists and writers. All but these last three had university degrees, but two of the three were graduates of the Colegio Nacional. The other, Enrique Solano López, son of the fallen tyrant, had gained an education at various schools in Europe and the Middle East while following his mother, Eliza Lynch (his father's former mistress), in her exile. Six of the university graduates also had gone through the Colegio Nacional. Finally, seven of the fifteen Colorados for whom there were adequate data also taught. Two of them were on the faculty of the Colegio Nacional and had served as directors of that institution. Five were university professors, of whom one was medical school dean and the other was rector of the National University.

The Liberal Party's executive committee tended to be composed of cabinet ministers and congressional leaders. They, in turn, bargained among themselves every four years to pick a presidential ticket and parcel out the top government posts. Below these party "princes" were the lesser *jefes políticos*—the baronets, knights, and squires of the system—whose job it was to control the villages, hamlets, and isolated farms of the deep interior. Carrying titles like mayor (*intendente*) or police chief (*comisario*), and nominally under the authority of the Interior Ministry, they collected revenues, kept order, and got out the vote. Until the secret ballot was introduced by President Manuel Franco, voting was done either by writing down one's choice on a piece of paper and handing it to the local *jefe político*, or by declaring it orally. Obviously, this was a system that lent itself easily to fraud and intimidation. Small wonder that the party controlling the government always won and that the opposition usually boycotted elections. In those districts where the opposition was numerous, well organized, and led by its own dynamic *jefe político*, however, the incumbent might face a real local challenge. In that case, violence was the likely result. And when violence threatened to become a general rebellion, which was not infrequently in Paraguay, the *jefes políticos*, like the feudal knights of the Middle Ages, were expected to raise troops among local party or factional members. It would have been bad enough if fighting had been limited to a struggle for power between Liberals and Colorados, but since 1904 the Liberals had been torn apart by bloody factional battles. Their promise of "good government" was rendered inoperative by their apparent inability to govern at all. It was this anarchy that Eduardo Schaerer intended to tame as he took over the presidency of the Liberal Party in 1920—his compensation for having accepted the convention's choice of Manuel Gondra for president of the Republic over Schaerer's man, José P. Montero. And, ironically, it was his attempt to impose order and discipline upon the Liberals that led directly to Paraguay's worst civil war so far.

Schaerer was himself a *jefe político* writ large. A native of Caazapá, the modest capital of an interior province, he had gone to the big city early in life and made good in business. At forty-seven years of age in 1920, he was in the prime of his political career. He was a proven leader, having fought in the 1904 insurrection, administered Asunción as its mayor, headed the Radicals' revolutionary junta that defeated both Jara and the Colorados, and served as president of the Republic from 1912 to 1916. He would have been eligible for reelection in 1920 but hesitated to pit himself against Gondra in a popularity contest. However, he calculated that 1924 was to be his year, and to make sure of that he aimed to use the party presidency to build a disciplined machine that would follow his orders.[2]

As party president, Schaerer was in a position to reward those who supported him; and, knowing Gondra for a weak-willed man, he hoped to run the government from behind the scenes. Among his supporters he counted Enrique Ayala, president of the Chamber of Deputies; Lucio

Mendonça, a *jefe político's* protégé from Concepción who sat in the Chamber; Ernesto Velásquez, Schaerer's former police chief, now a senator; and a number of key army officers who had worked closely with him during the recent civil war: Colonel Adolfo Chirife, the war minister; Colonel Pedro Mendoza, commander of the Encarnación garrison; and Lieutenant Colonel Francisco Brizuela, a former *jarista* who had repented and now, considered a brilliant albeit erratic officer, commanded the Concepción garrison.

Schaerer also enjoyed the support of a "ginger group" of young intellectuals and journalists, most of whom worked for the daily paper, *El Nacional*. The paper's owner, Mario Usher, had a checkered political career. Having served as Gondra's police chief in 1911, he helped Jara overthrow his boss, and then turned against Jara and helped replace him as president with Liberato Rojas.[3] Then, with Marcos Caballero Codas, he staged another coup during the civil war that gave the Radicals temporary control of Asunción, until the Colorado army arrived and drove off them off. This last switch of allegiance, together with his old connections with the Liga de la Juventud Independiente, got him a grudging pardon after the war. He acquired *El Nacional* and hired a brilliant group of young maverick Liberals to work on it: J. Rodolfo Bordón and his younger brother, F. Arturo Bordón, José D. Miranda, and Benjamín Velilla. Some of them would later become involved in the nationalist revolution of 1936 that ended the Liberal Party's rule. Another talented journalist named Policarpo Artaza, who wrote for, and later edited, *El Orden* and *El País*, also became a strong *schaererista*.

On the whole, though, Schaerer tended to stir up resentment among Radical Liberal intellectuals with his thinly disguised contempt for theorizing and his blunt, "self-made man" manner. His somewhat unsavory reputation as a shady financial wheeler-dealer completed the image. Schaerer repaid their contempt by referring to some of the younger, often rich, *gondristas*, many of whom had studied abroad and adopted foreign fashions, as the *saco pucú*—a Guaraní word meaning "long-jackets." Among these were Rodolfo González, a fiery young lawyer and deputy from Luque; Luís and Gerónimo Riart, two brothers bred in the ward politics of Asunción; Modesto Guggiari, a rather larger-than-life *caudillo* from Villarrica, whose extravagant dress, booming oratory, and scandalously advanced ideas attracted a small but devoted following on the party's "left"; Eliseo da Rosa, a suave, cosmopolitan intellectual who had once edited Schaerer's *El Diario* but afterward turned against him; and Belisario Rivarola, a prominent senator, owner of *El Liberal*, *jefe político* of Barrero Grande, and a descendant of ex-president Cirilo A. Rivarola.

Of all Schaerer's opponents, however, two stood out in particular. The first was Lisandro Díaz León, leader of the *gondrista* bloc in the Chamber of Deputies. Extremely tall and powerfully built, with a leonine mane of hair, he was the *jefe político* of Trinidad, a suburban parish of Asunción. Justo Pastor Benítez described him as "a tribune of the people," and Carlos Centurión called him "dantonesque."[4] Díaz León did indeed have the popular touch of a true *caudillo,* having worked as a stevedore in Argentina during a period of exile, before returning to fight against Albino Jara as a common artilleryman. A powerful debater who spoke Spanish and Guaraní with equal fluency, he was classified along with Modesto Guggiari on the left-wing of Radicalism, since he favored more state economic regulation, workers' rights, land reform, and legalized divorce. Díaz León led the fight in Congress against Schaerer's pretensions. Outside of Congress the anti-Schaerer forces were led by the interior minister, José P. Guggiari, Modesto's first-cousin (although the two were frequently at odds). Like many of the younger men around Gondra, he had joined the Liga de la Juventud Independiente, had gotten a law degree, and worked his way up through the party organization. He served as a member of the University Council, criminal prosecutor, attorney general, member of the Liberal Party executive, and finally deputy from Villarrica (his cousin, Modesto, was senator). At the time Gondra chose him to be interior minister, Guggiari was president of the Chamber.[5]

A tireless worker, particularly at organizational tasks, Guggiari had specialized in working with youth clubs during his time on the party executive committee. That had led him to make many trips around the country, during which he came in contact with various local leaders and leaders-to-be. In 1920 he was only thirty-six, yet he had the prestige of having fought in the great revolt of 1904, and he was a gifted speaker and debater besides. His youth, dynamism, and obvious uncompromising commitment to Radical Liberalism appealed to the rising generation of party faithful. But his support did not rest with them alone. Guggiari had the backing of all the older *jefes políticos* who disliked Schaerer, or who admired Gondra. It was this combination that allowed Guggiari, who acted as Gondra's campaign manager, to nail down the nomination at the 1920 convention, even though Schaerer's man was in the presidency.

No sooner was Gondra inaugurated than the long-brewing fight began between Schaerer and Guggiari over who would control the party organization. Guggiari proceeded carefully, lining up his contacts in the party's local committees across the country. Then the *saco pucú* sprung their surprise in September 1921 by mounting a number of challenges during the holding of local assemblies to choose candidates for next March's congressional elections. Schaerer's men, caught by surprise, were ousted as committee chiefs in about half of these confrontations, although in some cases they put up violent resistance. Notable *gondrista* victories were recorded in Villarrica and Encarnación. Seeing the party's organization slipping from his grasp, Schaerer demanded that Gondra dismiss his interior minister. *El Nacional* and *La Tribuna*, a paper recently founded by Schaerer, took up the attack on Guggiari, accusing him of "partisanship" (as if that were something new in Paraguay!) and of sowing discord in the party's ranks.

Gondra appeared to be genuinely distressed by the squabble. He attempted to placate both sides by bringing Guggiari and Schaerer together and urging them to agree on a single list of candidates for the March elections, in which there would be equal representation of *gondristas* and *schaereristas*. After the elections the party would call an extraordinary convention to settle any other differences. Schaerer himself might have been willing to settle for such an arrangement, but he knew that his followers would never go along. Convinced that any delay would lead to further erosion of their position, they were eager to bring the crisis to a head. Already there were rumors that the Concepción garrison was about to revolt.[6]

Unable to back off, Schaerer decided to plunge boldly ahead. On 29 October 1921 he issued an ultimatum demanding that Guggiari be fired. Immediately afterward he and his principal advisor, Ernesto Velásquez, went to the Central Police Headquarters where they would be safe in the event that Gondra issued an arrest order. Velásquez, a former police chief, was popular there and, with the exception of the current chief, Alejandro Arce, all the top officers were *schaereristas*. Faced with this flagrant challenge to his authority, Gondra also took refuge—at the military school, whose commander, Colonel Manlio Schenoni, was the only high-ranking military officer to offer his unqualified support.

The great bulk of the army seemed inert as everyone waited for Colonel Adolfo Chirife to make his position clear. Chirife was cross-pressured. Though much inclined toward Schaerer, he also was a professional. It was he who had suggested that Schaerer go to the police instead of one of the military garrisons, in order not to compromise the army. Now, when Gondra urged him to act, he refused to send his troops to arrest Schaerer. He announced that the armed forces would remain neutral and that the politicians would have to sort out their problems through party channels.[7] On receiving this reply, Gondra resigned.

The president's resignation was entirely unexpected and caught his devoted followers completely unprepared, although it is difficult to understand why. Gondra had resigned the presidency once before and had a long history of ducking out of crises. As Arturo Bray observes, although Gondra was a man of great learning and attractive bearing, in politics he seemed congenitally incapable of taking any firm decision. He preferred lecturing to action and "he always seemed to go about with his resigna- tion in his pocket, just awaiting the right moment to date it."[8] Neverthe- less, everyone was shocked—even Schaerer, who denied any responsi- bility. According to Schaerer's public statement, Gondra had agreed to remove Guggiari from the cabinet, but then had reneged under pressure from his strong-willed interior minister. Thus he, Schaerer, had been forced to act in order to exert counterpressure; but there had been no intention to overthrow the government. Schaerer went on to draw a par- allel with 1911, when Gondra's indecisiveness led to Colonel Jara's coup and all the tragic consequences that followed. Now history was repeating itself with Guggiari playing Jara's role, he claimed. The pushy, power- hungry youngsters who followed Guggiari wanted to use Gondra as a front while they took over the party and the government. Instead of facing down the *saco pucú* and meeting with him to restore sanity to the party, Gondra had abandoned his post.[9]

To be sure, Schaerer's statement was self-serving and designed to cast himself in the best possible light. *La Prensa* of Buenos Aires reported that, in fact, Schaerer had met with Pedro Peña, the Colorados' parliamentary leader, to urge that he not oppose Gondra's resignation.[10] The veracity of this report may be doubted, however, because a resolution calling upon Gondra to reconsider passed both houses of Congress unanimously. It did no good, however. Gondra had made up his mind to step down.

According to the Constitution, it was up to Vice-President Félix Paíva to form a new government that would serve out the remainder of Gon- dra's term. The trouble was that Paíva, like Schaerer, was a native of Caa- zapá and was considered to be the latter's political protégé. Thus, none of the sitting cabinet members would agree to serve under him because they believed that by doing so they would be condoning Schaerer's "coup." Nor would anyone else agree to serve, except for Guillermo Sosa, a *schaererista* deputy, who accepted the post of police chief. After a week of fruitless searching Paíva resigned on 7 November, thereby adding to the confusion.

Colonel Chirife then stepped into the picture. The country was sliding into chaos, he warned, and unless the politicians got together to form a government he would declare martial law. The prospect of military rule was no idle threat. Soldiers already were posted at strategic points throughout the capital and the more nervous *gondristas* were seeking asy- lum at the Argentine and Uruguayan embassies. Once again all parties and factions in Congress called upon Gondra to resume office—and again he refused. With that, the two Liberal factions were forced to agree on a compromise government as the only way to avoid an army coup.

Their stopgap president was to be Eusebio Ayala, Gondra's foreign minister, who seemed to be politically neutral. Although he also had served in 1910 as Gondra's justice minister, he had been in Schaerer's cabinet as well. In between times, he had spent so many years in Europe that he was identified with neither faction. But although Ayala took office with Schaerer's approval he soon raised the latter's suspicions by his cabinet appointments. Two of them had been in Gondra's cabinet: Eligio Ayala (no relation to the president) was retained as finance minister and Rogelio Ibarra Legal moved from Justice to Interior. Alejandro Arce, the new foreign minister, had been Gondra's police chief. Eliseo da Rosa, Ayala's minister of justice, was a prominent *saco pucú*, while the defense minister, Colonel Manuel Rojas, was a compromise between Colonel Manlio Schenoni, the *gondristas'* candidate, and Chirife.

Obviously, the *gondristas* had gotten the best of the bargain, much to the anger and chagrin of the *schaereristas*. Insult was added to injury when the *gondristas* swept the elections for the party directorate in May 1922. It is perhaps revealing, however, that the fifteen men who composed this *gondrista* directorate had an average age of forty-five, which was high when compared with an equal number of leading *schaereristas* drawn from *El Nacional*, Congress, and key military posts.[11] Their average age was thirty-eight. Over half (eight) of the *gondrista* leaders were from the Sixth Promotion—the "Glory Promotion" that triumphed in the 1904 revolution. Four others were recruited before that. One of them, Francisco Campos, was from the Second Promotion. By contrast, seven of the fifteen *schaereristas* were from the Eighth, or most recent, Promotion. That is to say, they had joined after the Radicals' return to power in 1912. Only five were from the Sixth Promotion or earlier, and none had joined before the Fifth Promotion. Therefore, if the *gondristas* can be considered as the Radical Liberal "mainstream," the party was beginning to show signs of aging. It was far from being a gerontocracy, but nevertheless there was a tendency for the men of the "Glory Promotion" to dominate high office in the party and government. It was a tendency that became clearer when it was kept in mind that the leading Liberal military officers and civilians who brought about the 1904 revolution had an average age of only thirty-seven, even including men in their fifties like General Benigno Ferreira and Antonio Taboada.

As the *schaereristas* and *gondristas* resumed their power struggle, the Colorados decided to take advantage. The party was divided between "abstentionists" who opposed any participation in the political process on the ground that it would serve only to legitimate Liberal rule, and the "participationists" (or *infiltristas*) who wanted to take advantage of electoral campaigning and congressional representation to spread the party's message. The abstentionists recently had gained the upper hand but then suddenly had adopted their rivals' platform. Their leader, Pedro Peña, decided that maintaining the party's representatives in Congress would offer a favorable opportunity to drive even deeper the wedge between the two Liberal factions.[12] They found the *schaereristas* willing to join them in demanding the calling of immediate presidential elections, two years before the end of the constitutional term, and in backing the candidacy of the very popular Colonel Adolfo Chirife.

By working together, the Colorados and *schaereristas* were able to steer a bill through both houses of Congress that would require elections to be held on 16 July. The *gondristas* were outraged. Belisario Rivarola, the Liberal Party's president, wrote a series of vituperative editorials against Chirife in *El Libertad*, while Lisandro Díaz León stood up in the Chamber of Deputies to call the colonel "a traitor" and accuse him of having plotted against ex-president Gondra. Although inaccurate for the most part, the charges were not wholly without substance. Although Chirife had neither planned or supported Schaerer's challenge to Gondra, nor had wished for the latter's resignation, neither had he acted decisively to defend the constitutional order. Also, for some months past Manuel Domínguez had acted as the Colorados' emissary in trying to win over Colonel Chirife to the idea of a coup. Although the colonel kept refusing, he did not break off the contacts. In his own mind, however, he was innocent of any wrongdoing. Unaware that he was being used, he had been flattered by the Colorado-*schaererista* presidential nomination. Now the *gondristas'* insults wounded his military honor. And as he grew angrier, he became more dangerous.

Indeed, Chirife's actions were raising deep suspicions in the government. At the beginning of May 1922 he had gone to the Paraguarí garrison and placed himself in command, without permission either from President Ayala or the war minister. When Ayala demanded that Colonel Rojas call him back to Asunción and discipline him, Rojas—knowing that he had no real authority over his nominal subordinate—preferred to resign. Ayala then decided to enlist the help of the *schaereristas* to get Chirife back in line, and so he offered the War Ministry to ex-vice-president Paíva. Although Paíva declined, he offered to act as an intermediary with Eduardo Schaerer, whom he considered the only man in Paraguay with any influence over Chirife. The upshot was that Schaerer let Ayala know, through Paíva, that he opposed any disciplinary action against Chirife. And there the matter lay.

Meanwhile, the *gondristas* demanded that President Ayala veto the election bill. To emphasize the point, Rogelio Ibarra, Eligio Ayala, Alejandro Arce, and Eliseo da Rosa all resigned from the cabinet. The President then sought to replace them with men such as Paíva and Gualberto Cardús Huerta, who were more acceptable to Schaerer, but they also refused to accept office, unless Ayala promised to sign the bill. On 22 May Ayala finally took his stand and vetoed the election bill, arguing that he had a constitutional right to remain in office until the end of Gondra's term. With that, both houses of Congress approved a resolution that called upon the armed forces to intervene in support of the people's elected representatives. That was enough for Chirife, who already was goaded to anger by the *gondristas'* intemperate attacks. After ringing up the Concepción and Encarnación garrisons to assure himself of their support, he raised the troops in Paraguarí, "in defense of the Constitution."

Seeing the nation teetering on the edge of yet another fratricidal war, President Ayala reversed himself on 29 May and withdrew his veto. But it was too late. The opposition was no longer willing to compromise. The issue would be settled by arms.

THE CIVIL WAR OF 1922–1923

Although much of the army went over to the side of Schaerer and Chirife, it was, on the eve of civil war, in deplorable shape. Soldiers received no real training and there was no functioning general staff to coordinate strategy. Although the nation was divided into five military regions, each with its own headquarters, three of those were severely understaffed. Only the main base at Paraguarí and the southern command post at Encarnación had the full complement of troops, consisting of an infantry regiment, a cavalry squadron, and an artillery squadron. Skeleton units were posted to the Concepción and Pilar bases, while the Chaco garrison in Fuerte Olimpo had scarcely a handful of men. In fact, it could almost be said that a truly national army did not exist. Decades of political interference in promotions and assignments had weakened morale and prevented the spread of professionalism. Top officers tended to be partisan, like the *jefes políticos* of the interior, because rewards depended so much on good political contacts. In turn, the men under them followed their leaders largely out of personal loyalty and the expectation of some crumbs of patronage. Thus, the army was much like a loose coalition of semi-autonomous units headed by *caudillos*. When choosing sides in the nation's frequent civil wars, those officers heading key units negotiated with each other and with the politicians for the best terms.[13]

Intelligent, professionally minded officers like Colonel Manlio Schenoni naturally resented this state of affairs. Schenoni, the commander of the loyalist troops in the 1922–23 civil war, had a serious personal clash with José P. Guggiari, then serving as head of the *gondrista* faction of the Liberal Party, about the appointment of officers. Guggiari insisted on having only those who were known as "good party men." Schenoni wrote in his diary of Guggiari that:

His psychology as a politician and *caudillo* makes him think that vulgar *caudillo* leadership has more influence than discipline in promoting the cohesion and military virtues that make armies strong. Dr. Guggiari is a believer in a partisan army, rather than a national army. He thinks that the [party] "colors" strengthen the sense of duty more than the healthy, moral education that forms the basis of true discipline. He is convinced that governments are better sustained by uniformed party men than by army soldiers. He has learned nothing from past experience, which shows that political armies have served only to promote revolts, and that such armies never are motivated by patriotism.[14]

It would take another generation and the experience of war with Bolivia before sentiments like Schenoni's would spread far enough through the officers' corps to impel the army to throw off partisan meddling in its professional concerns. Unhappily, though, the pendulum would then swing to the opposite extreme and lead to government by praetorians. In the meantime, Schenoni had no choice but to buttress his forces, as Chirife was doing, by accepting the irregular militia provided by various local *jefes políticos*. Such units, ranging in size from three to thirty men, could be used to police occupied areas or sabotage the enemy's communications lines. In a pinch, they could fight alongside the regular conscripts—who were not highly trained anyway—to stiffen a defensive position.[15]

It was just that sort of hastily thrown-together defense that saved the government when Colonel Chirife launched the war on 9 June 1922 with an attack on Asunción. The overconfident *schaereristas* were met with a surprisingly ferocious resistance by a combined force of cadets from the military school, navy and police units, a corps of army engineers, and a citizens' militia of *gondrista* Liberals. Schenoni got crucial support from retired general Patricio Alejandro Escobar, who used his influence with the officers of the Círculo Militar to keep them on the government's side. Many of those officers attached themselves to the civilian contingents to advise them in organizing proper defensive works. After several hours of fighting the loyalists were rewarded by seeing Chirife halt the attack and retreat back to Paraguarí.

This defeat seemed to shake the rebels' morale. Several weeks of skirmishing followed, during which Schenoni drilled his forces. Then, at the end of July, he took the offensive. Though inferior in both men and artillery, he dealt the rebels a stinging defeat at Itapé. Another lull followed, but then, on 13 November, he routed Chirife again, at Caí Puente. In both of these battles Schenoni was helped by the brilliant tactical maneuvers of Captain José Félix Estigarribia, who swept around the rebels' flank and caught them from behind. Chirife was forced to retreat to the central mountain range of Caaguazú and dig in.

Had the loyalists pressed their attack, they might have ended the rebellion quickly, but President Eusebio Ayala was a doctrinaire pacifist who refused to allocate enough money for a real military buildup or to prosecute the war with vigor. And, being a true libertarian, he even refused to proclaim a state of siege that would have allowed the police to arrest suspected spies and saboteurs in the capital. Placing his faith in negotiations, now that he had the upper hand, he sent emissaries to Schaerer and Chirife, urging them to spare lives and property by accepting an honorable surrender.[16] Chirife strung Ayala along while he patiently rebuilt his army. Then, in the following March, he showed there still was life in the rebellion by seizing the key provincial town of Villarrica.

Villarrica's fall sent a great shock through the *gondrista* ranks. Both Ayala and Schenoni were criticized for lack of vigor. Nor did the latter's explanation that he was short of men and supplies mollify them; indeed, it smacked to them of disloyalty. Determined to rid the country of its present leadership, but unwilling to act illegally, they hit upon a scheme to induce Ayala to resign. Belisario Rivarola, the Liberal Party's president, let it be known that the party intended to run him as its presidential candidate. However, for appearances' sake it would be better for Ayala to resign so it would not look as if he had used his position to keep himself in power. Ayala, a strict legalist, swallowed the bait. It was not long after his farewell banquet, when he was out of office and serving as a corporation lawyer for one of the big Argentine-owned estates in the Chaco, that he was told that the party leaders had changed their mind. The nomination now would go to the man who replaced him at the presidential palace: Eligio Ayala (no relation). As Rogelio Urizar, a chronicler of the period observed: "After half a century the case of don Cirilo Rivarola had repeated itself."[17]

By this gentle coup the Liberal Party carried on its tradition of chronic fragmentation, for in effect the *gondristas* were now divided. Eligio Ayala had long attracted the loyalties of those *gondristas* who were opposed to José P. Guggiari as Gondra's heir apparent. His interior minister, Modesto Guggiari, was José P's first-cousin, but bitter rival. In his new post he conceived his job to be mainly to loosen his cousin's hold on the party organization by appointing new *jefes políticos* in all the newly "liberated" war zones. In addition, anti-Guggiari men like Raúl Casal Ribeiro and Gerónimo Riart were appointed the Interior Ministry's "roving agents" with the task of connecting the party's base organizations more tightly to the central authorities. Casal Ribeiro, who was a close friend of Eligio Ayala since their days in the Liga de la Juventud Independiente, also served as the president's secretary. Luís Riart, the finance minister (and Gerónimo's elder brother), was another Guggiari opponent. So were foreign minister Rogelio Ibarra Legal and justice minister Lisandro Díaz León. The former was editor of Casal Ribeiro's newspaper, *El Liberal*, and the latter was a close ally of Modesto Guggiari's.

Most galling of all to the pro-"José P" *gondristas* was Eligio Ayala's decision to retain Colonel Manlio Schenoni as army commander, in addition to appointing him war minister. Schenoni had convinced the new president that his removal would set back the loyalist army's morale, especially now that the war was entering its decisive phase. Not only did Ayala retain Schenoni, but he spared no expense in prosecuting the war. Military spending was given top priority.

Schenoni was proved to be right: the rebel cause suffered a terrible setback after its victory at Villarrica when Colonel Chirife came down with pneumonia. Unable to get proper medical treatment on the battlefield, he worsened until finally, on 18 May, he died. With that, the rebels lost their most attractive and capable leader. Chirife's successor, Colonel Pedro Mendoza, was not considered to be a man of great talent. Events were to show that he probably was much underestimated, but up to this point he had spent most of his career tending his political fiefdom as *jefe militar* of the southern region. Perhaps to retain the morale of his troops, Colonel Mendoza quickly went on the offensive. Several minor victories in the interior bolstered their confidence, but it was obvious that they would have to take Asunción to win the war. Accordingly, Mendoza began preparing for the decisive battle.

Between the rebels and the capital lay the government's main forces. The headquarters were at Paraguarí, protecting the southeastern approach, while another strong contingent was stationed at Ypacaraí, to defend against an attack from the northeast. Any attempt to drive through the center would be caught in a crossfire. Despite these strong positions, on 9 July 1923 Colonel Mendoza executed an intricate and brilliant series of feints that completely fooled the Ypacaraí troops under Captain Estigarribia and allowed the rebels to break through and fall upon the capital. For two days fighting raged in the streets as a desperate defense by hastily assembled civilian militiamen was pushed back, block by block, until the rebels had penetrated to the very heart of the city—as far as the Plaza Uruguaya and the Plaza Independencia.

The invaders went no further, however. A withering machine-gun fire from the railroad station and fortresslike government buildings pinned them down while cannon, which the rebels lacked, began blasting them without regard to the surrounding destruction being caused. Meanwhile, the outmaneuvered forces at Ypacaraí and Paraguarí were now closing in from the rear. Caught in between, the rebels panicked and ran. Those who were able crossed the river to Argentina and exile; the others surrendered.

ELIGIO AYALA: A STUDY IN LEADERSHIP

Credited with winning the war by his vigorous leadership and support of the army, Eligio Ayala was the "man of the hour" and the party's logical choice as its candidate in 1924.[18] His career was that of a typical *gondrista* loyalist. Born in 1880 in the village of Mbuyapey, he was educated at the Colegio Nacional before taking a law degree at the National University. Like many young Paraguayan men of the middle class, he had to work at many different jobs after graduation. He was a librarian at the National Archives and also a public attorney for the indigent. After the 1904 revolution, in which he played a minor part, the Liberal government made him a civil court judge. He joined the Liga de la Juventud Independiente and, along with most of its members, supported the 1908 revolt that ousted Ferreira and the Cívicos. For his reward, he was appointed attorney for the city of Asunción. In 1909 he won election to the Chamber of Deputies, but when Albino Jara took over, Ayala went to Europe. There he remained, traveling and studying until Gondra returned to power and offered him the post of finance minister.

On taking up his duties he found Paraguay's finances in a mess. Determined to rectify this, he used his powers as finance minister to impose austerity on all the agencies of the government. His remedy was bitter medicine to many *políticos*: corruption and favoritism would not be countenanced, and all spending requests he considered unessential were refused. His own asceticism and scrupulousness in the handling of the public's money gave him considerable moral authority, so he soon became, along with José P. Guggiari, a dominant figure in the cabinet. Unlike Guggiari, however, he headed no faction. Ayala was a solitary man, mistrustful of everyone, a bit egoistic, and even somewhat misanthropic. But although he had no friends he had a strong sense of purpose and had written a book called *Migraciones* while in Europe, which considered Paraguay's problems and offered sharp analyses. Thus, like Gondra, he was viewed as a man of honor and a thoughtful reformer whose patriotism placed him above politics. But though less agreeable than Gondra, he was more steely. When the former caved in, Eligio Ayala found himself with a body of *gondrista* supporters ready to follow him as the new *conductor.*

He wanted the presidency, but political mores dictated that he would have to resign as provisional president before starting his campaign. In order to prevent what had happened to Eusebio Ayala, he turned the government over to a man he could trust, Luís A. Riart. As finance minister, Riart had worked closely with Eligio Ayala and shared his views. Accordingly, in April 1924 he took over, making a few adjustments in the cabinet. Interestingly, Modesto Guggiari was dropped as interior minister in favor of Belisario Rivarola, president of the Liberal Party; and J. Eliseo da Rosa succeeded Riart as finance minister. Ayala, meanwhile, campaigned without opposition, supported by every Liberal faction—even the old Cívicos. Moreover, in the victorious army Ayala's popularity was unprecedented. Not only were the soldiers grateful for his firm support during the civil war but they also perceived that he alone, among all the top Liberals, was aware of the growing threat of Bolivian encroachment in the Chaco.

Thus, as Eligio Ayala assumed the presidency on 15 August 1924, Paraguay already was heading for another bloodletting. It was largely because of his energy and perspicacity over the next four years that the nation was at all prepared to meet it when it came.

ELIGIO AYALA AND THE RADICAL LIBERAL APOGEE

Ayala's cabinet was staffed with familiar Radical Liberal faces. Vice-President Manuel Burgos had presided over the Supreme Court under both Schaerer and Gondra. Belisario Rivarola, the interior minister, had, like Burgos, been a senator at the time of his appointment and had served as president of the party during the recent civil war. In a move to placate José P. Guggiari's faction, Colonel Manlio Schenoni was not made war minister, although he was surely the logical choice. Instead, Ayala picked his trusted lieutenant, Luís A. Riart. Foreign Affairs was entrusted to Manuel Peña, who had served in that post before, under President Montero. Enrique Bordenave, Eusebio Ayala's half-brother, was elevated from the Chamber of Deputies to the Justice Ministry.[19] The government's finances were placed under the care of Manuel Benítez, an old Cívico, as a reward for that faction's support. Although Benítez was honest and competent, his appointment roused a protest from José P. Guggiari's faction. Ayala, who felt he had compromised enough by not giving Schenoni the War Ministry, refused to budge in this case—at the cost of a permanent political rift.[20]

Although the cabinet was staffed by men of proven worth, it also reflected the *gondrista* tendency toward aging. Of the seven men heading the government, two were from the Fifth Promotion, associated with the Egusquiza era; three were from the Sixth ("Glory") Promotion that carried out the 1904 revolution; and two were from the Eighth Promotion that rose after the 1912 revolution and ended with the 1922–23 civil war. The aging tendency can be seen, also, if we compare the average age of ministers for each elected government following the 1912 revolution: Eduardo Schaerer, 39; Manuel Franco, 41; Manuel Gondra, 41; and Eligio Ayala, 45. Despite this, the Eligio Ayala administration is considered today, among people from all of Paraguay's different parties, to have been the most dynamic and successful of any Liberal Party government.

Ayala himself was a strange man. A solitary, austere bachelor with a bitter, sarcastic humor that stung all those around him—even cabinet ministers and high party officials—he bore a strange resemblance to Paraguay's first great dictator: Doctor José Gaspar Rodríguez de Francia. Like Francia, he had no friends and sought none, but he was absolutely honest and dedicated to public service. Like Francia, too, he saw a foreign threat looming over Paraguay and was determined to meet it by making military preparedness his highest priority. That earned him criticism from most Liberals, who were deeply antimilitary and impatient to return to a peaceful "normalcy" after the recent civil war. Rising early, Ayala liked to spend his mornings alone in his office, writing down his thoughts. Unlike Francia, we have in his case some record of his ideas about what kind of government Paraguay needed.

Ayala's political views were a mixture of laissez-faire liberalism and deep pessimism. In *Migraciones*[21] he identified two principal causes of Paraguay's poverty and backwardness. The first, which is deeply imbedded in the culture, is the Paraguayans' total preoccupation with politics, to which everything else is willingly sacrificed. "Our national religion is the passion for political control," he wrote. "Paraguayans are not concerned about religion, or industry, or farming, or war. In Paraguay, one pursues politics and nothing but politics."

> The merchant who, through a brilliant talent for business and his persevering labor, has made a fortune; the poet who has written inspired verse; the university professor who teaches and writes with penetrating wisdom; the honest and upright judge; the soldier; the

journalist—all live in sad obscurity, ignored and disdained if they fail to get a high political post, such as deputy, senator, or minister.[22]

By contrast, the village idiot, the butt of jokes, will be admitted to "society" if suddenly he is raised to office. Furthermore, in a country with limited economic opportunities, politics is one of the few lucrative professions; and since patronage is concentrated in the presidency, it becomes necessary to control that office. Those who succeed in doing so fight to stay in power and exclude those outside their circle, whereas those who are excluded plot to overthrow the incumbents or at least hinder them in their exercise of power. Parties stand for no principles; they are simply shifting alliances of egoists who quickly betray one another in their scramble for jobs. Consequently, "there is no system, no plan, no method, no economic goals for the government. Every revolution, every new minister, the intrigues of the powerful—all break the continuity, coherence, and ordinary processes of economic policy."[23]

Obviously, a trait so deeply embedded in the political culture admitted of no easy remedy, nor did Ayala suggest one in his *Migraciones*. So far as his actual policies afford a clue to his thinking, it appears that he hoped to make politics less attractive by keeping government lean and by developing alternative opportunities in the private economy. He insisted upon a balanced budget, which he achieved by raising taxes and reducing expenditures. When drawing up his budgets, Ayala always calculated the coming year's revenues on the low side. All payments to the government had to be made in gold, but all government expenditures were made in paper money. The exchange rate was fixed so as to overvalue gold, but the issuance of paper money was strictly controlled.[24] The treasury also was built up by strengthening the Foreign Exchange Office's ability to collect tariffs. The rapid increase in foreign exchange reserves allowed Ayala to pay off Paraguay's most pressing overseas debts, while at the same time stabilizing the currency.

Ayala's tight budget policies did not mean a sacrifice in essential spending, either. The financing of new schools, roads, bridges, and other internal improvments actually rose. Charity Hospital's facilities were expanded and a school of engineering was started at the university. Although the government payroll was trimmed, more talented people were now recruited and—a rare feat in Paraguay up to then—administrative salaries were paid on time.[25]

Still more might have been accomplished had the government financed even more infrastructural changes, but that would have required more taxes and Ayala was afraid that this would discourage investment. Also, as a good laissez-faire Liberal, he believed in strictly limiting the state's power to maintaining order, furnishing a legal structure that would facilitate private economic initiative, and preserving national sovereignty. Beyond those functions, it might act to foster an educational system and carry out physical improvments ("public goods") that were either unattractive to private initiative or beyond the latter's ability to finance—but that was all.[26]

Consequently, neither Ayala nor his successors did much to help the more unfortunate members of society. In a country where about 80 percent of the population lived from agriculture, fewer than 6 percent were landowners. The vast majority of the small farmers whose parcels constituted 99.6 percent of all farms, but only 1.9 percent of all the land, held no title to the earth they tilled—they were, technically, squatters.[27] Under Ayala, Congress passed in 1926 a law requiring the state to foster small holdings of between six and twenty hectares (15 to 120 acres) by either colonizing public lands or by expropriating private holdings.[28] Here again, more could have been done had the state taken a vigorous role in land reform. But although Ayala recognized in *Migraciones* the evils of the unreformed *latifundio* system, he was cautious as to solutions. Breaking up all the big estates to make small farms was not the answer because small farmers lacked the capital and education to exploit the land efficiently. Conversely, collectivized agriculture was utopian. Both reforms would simply carry Paraguay back to a primitive, precapitalist state. The proper solution was to convert the present *latifundia* into efficient, large-scale capitalist farms oriented toward export agriculture, while encouraging the small and medium-sized farms to produce for the domestic market.[29] He had no specific answer, however, as to how this might be accomplished.

As with landless peasants, so with urban labor: the Ayala administration was tolerant and even sympathetic to a certain degree, but unwilling to support real reforms. Unions had begun to appear just before World War I, concentrating on mainly skilled and semiskilled labor: railwaymen, trolley drivers, dockworkers, maritime workers in the river fleets, construction workers, bakers, and printers. Strikes in the 1920s were more frequent, and more violent too—especially when led by the anarcho-syndicalists or communists. In 1927 the moderate and revolutionary wings of the labor movement set aside their differences long enough to form a nationwide confederation called the Unión Obrera Paraguaya (UOP). Compared with other Liberal Party presidents, then or later, Eligio Ayala was benign toward labor. There were no states of siege called, no harsh police crackdowns, no smashing of the proletarian press or closures of union locals. But there was no protective legislation, either. Thus, another opportunity was missed to expand the Liberal Party's social base by incorporating either the urban or the rural working classes. Liberalism remained the ideology of the urban bourgeoisie and its supporters among certain *jefes políticos* and the intelligentsia. As George Pendle observed later, when comparing them with a resurgent Colorado Party:

> The Liberals were Liberal in their ideas, after the nineteenth century fashion; but they made little or no attempt to enter into contact with the less privileged classes of society. Because the leading members of the party had traveled widely and were known to have financial and commercial connections abroad . . . they were accused of serving foreign interests; and because they failed to introduce drastic social and economic reforms, they never won the sympathy of the mass of the population.[30]

In fairness to Eligio Ayala, however, his attention was almost completely absorbed by a terrible new threat that was descending on Paraguay: the relentless approach of a well-trained and well-equipped Bolivian army through the Chaco, patiently spreading and extending its network of forts in the direction of the Paraguay River. Ayala's reputation as the outstanding statesman of the whole Radical Liberal period rests upon his largely successful efforts in preparing Paraguay for this challenge.

The seriousness of the approaching crisis was brought home dramatically in 1927, when a clash between Paraguayan and Bolivian patrols in Chaco resulted in the death of a Paraguayan soldier, Lieutenant Adolfo Rojas Silva, son of ex-president Liberato Rojas. An outburst of nationalist emotion swept through the armed forces and through the elite students of the Colegio Nacional, from which Lieutenant Rojas Silva recently had graduated. Angry demonstrations presaged even worse outbursts in the years to follow, which Liberals would find increasingly difficult to understand or manage. Ayala, however, already was embarked on a program of military spending to put Paraguay on a war footing. His careful husbanding of Paraguay's finances now paid off, for he had money to spend for European arms purchases, building forts in the path of Bolivia's advance, running telegraph lines from Asunción to strategic points in the Chaco, and hiring a French mission to train the army.

Such policies made Ayala so popular among the armed forces that he probably could have stayed in power with their backing if he had chosen to do so. He was wise enough to see, however, that if he did he would split the country. What Paraguay needed above all else was political unity, for it was precisely the many decades of distracting civil strife that had allowed the Bolivian threat to catch it unaware. Accordingly, Ayala sought political peace at home by guaranteeing fair elections and finally coaxing the abstentionist Colorados to participate. After testing the government's goodwill in the 1927 legislative elections, the Colorados were sufficiently satisfied to agree to run again in the 1928 presidential race.

Although it is generally agreed that the 1928 elections were the freest Paraguay had ever known until then—and the first presidential elections in which there was an opposition candidate—they did not break the old unwritten rule that, in Paraguay, the incumbent party always wins. More disturbing still was the Liberal Party's choice of José P. Guggiari as its standard-bearer. A tireless proselytizer who had used his time since leaving the government in 1922 to solidify his hold on the party's local organizations, he now emerged as the new Radical Liberal "strongman." Ayala, a loner who had relied too much on his own personal will and intelligence, found himself outmaneuvered in his attempt to get the nomination for Riart.

In the postconvention negotiations to select a cabinet, Guggiari offered to patch up differences by offering Ayala the Finance Ministry. The latter accepted, hoping thereby to exert a moderating influence on Guggiari's dogmatic, partisan leadership style. It would do no good. Both Ayala and Guggiari would be swallowed up by fate, while Paraguay was swept along in a flood of events that would end the Liberal Era.

eight

THE RISE OF NATIONALISM

Paraguay in 1928 was entering the denouement of its Liberal Era. Despite all the bloodletting and intrigue that characterized its politics since the end of the War of the Triple Alliance, all the factions and parties contending for power had shared a broad liberal consensus: a belief in limited government, free enterprise, free trade, and individualism. Colorados and Liberals might dispute about which of them was more patriotic or competent, and politicians could fight over how generous the government ought to be with respect to land or railway concessions, but none would dispute the absolute sanctity of private property. It was not ideology that made Paraguayan politics so violent, but the desperate need to govern in order to control the few sources of wealth in an otherwise impoverished country—together with the inherited hatreds, passed down through family lines, arising out of that violent struggle to conquer the state. But by 1928 that was already beginning to change.

One source of change was the growing social criticism directed by writers like Rafael Barrett against the *latifundio* system, especially the *yerba mate* plantations, where the laborers (*mensú*) worked for low wages in unspeakable conditions.[1] Similarly, the increase in the size and importance of urban labor made it all the more difficult for Asunción's middle-class intellectuals to ignore "the social question." The Communist Party, founded in February 1928, quickly attracted some of the most prominent and promising young men of the new generation. Oscar Creydt, heir to a large fortune, related on his mother's side to one of Paraguay's oldest and most aristocratic families, educated in Germany, and possessor of a law degree, converted to communism after returning from Europe. Cultured and extremely intelligent, he became the party's chief ideologist and devoted the remainder of his life—as well as his fortune—to spreading its gospel. Another *niño bién* who joined the party was Obdúlio Barthe. His family, one of the richest in the whole La Plata region, owned vast *yerba mate* plantations, cattle ranches, and one of the two principal river fleets. A good speaker and debater, who also possessed organizing skills, he gave the party a dynamic image and helped to extend its influence both to the labor unions and the university intellectuals.[2]

The Liberal Party was not wholly immune to this new concern with questions of social justice. For some time there had been a socially conscious left wing headed by Modesto Guggiari. Some of these *modestistas,* like Policarpo Artaza, J. Rodolfo Bordón, and F. Arturo Bordón, were rehabilitated followers of Eduardo Schaerer. Others, like Roque Gaona, Salvador García Melgarejo, and Anselmo Jover Peralta, represented a new breed of intellectual that reflected the current upsurge of emotional nationalism combined with an insistence that national unity required social and economic reforms. Jover Peralta, in particular, was so eager to move the Liberals leftward that he became a frequent collaborator in Communist Party rallies. A respected Guaraní linguist and literary figure, he represented the *modestistas* in the Chamber of Deputies, which he used as a pulpit to profess his Marxist views.[3] Other "fellow travelers" who hovered somewhere between the Liberal "left" and the Communists were Francisco Sánchez Palacios and Francisco Gaona. The former had succeeded Creydt as president of the University Student Federation and also worked closely with him in organizing the law school students; the latter was a self-taught intellectual, head of the railway workers' union, and an influential figure in the Centro Obrero Regional del Paraguay, a broad federation of maritime workers, stevedores, and skilled construction workers that was gravitating from *modestismo* toward Marxism.

Integral nationalism, provoked by the relentless approach of Bolivian forts in the Chaco, constituted the other volatile factor of change in the late 1920s. Although it spread rapidly throughout the politically active public, its principal voice was a newspaper called *La Nación,* founded in 1925 by two law school professors, Adriano Irala and Juan Stefanich. *La Nación* had become increasingly influential, especially after the March 1927 clash between Paraguayan and Bolivian soldiers at Fortín Sorpresa, in which Lieutenant Adolfo Rojas Silva was killed. That incident had so inflamed Paraguayan public opinion that only Argentina's diplomatic intervention prevented a war. Thereafter, *La Nación's* readership grew rapidly, prompting Irala and Stefanich to start a political movement in 1928 called the Liga Nacional Independiente, whose chief purpose was to alert Paraguayans to the Bolivian threat and pressure the government to do even more to prepare for war.

But the Liga went beyond nationalist claims to the Chaco in its first manifesto, dated 14 May (Independence Day) and called for (1) state intervention to secure and humane working conditions for labor, (2) equal rights for women, (3) the abolition of child labor, (4) protection for Paraguay's Indian tribes, (5) agrarian reform to give titles to those who worked the land, and (6) educational reform, to modernize the curriculum and extend the opportunity for schooling to all. What the Liga wanted, the manifesto said, was a completely united nation, with all classes cooperating to achieve their common independence and well-being. Social reform was necessary in order to give the workers and peasants a stake in society, which in turn would keep communists from pitting class against class.[4]

National solidarity required symbols to rally around, and here Liga intellectuals joined with Colorado writers like Juan O'Leary to promote revisionist history that extolled the figure of Marshal Francisco Solano López as the martyred hero of Paraguay. Rather than the megalomaniacal monster of the Liberal textbooks, then being taught in the schools, López was a brave statesman who had fought to preserve the nation's sovereignty. Those who opposed him—above all, the Legionnaires—were traitors. By now, through the incessant propaganda of Colorado historians, the Legion was identified as the direct precursor of the Liberal Party! So effective was this propaganda that even today no amount of empirical evidence to the contrary seems able to shake it from the popular consciousness.

As with ideas of social reform, nationalism had begun to penetrate the Liberals' ranks. As early as 1926 a sufficient number of Liberals in the Chamber of Deputies was willing to join with the Colorados to pass a resolution canceling the old Triumvirate's 1869 decree declaring López to be an outlaw. It was killed in the Senate, however, where older, more traditional Liberals dominated. The government itself was divided on the matter. President Eligio Ayala favored the resolution as a way of mobilizing more support for his stepped-up defense program. Nevertheless, he failed to support it with his full influence, which allowed his interior minister, Belisario Rivarola, a fervent anti-*lopista*, to quietly marshal the Liberal senators against it.[5]

As for the Colorados, it should not be assumed that they had undergone any profound change of mentality. Intellectuals like O'Leary, Enrique Solano López, or Ignacio Pane, who had contributed so much to Marshal López's rehabilitation, might have a sincere ideological commitment to integral nationalism; but for most Colorado politicians nationalism was simply a weapon to be used to weaken the Liberals' hold on power. The bulk of the party, especially its younger leaders, had accepted Eligio Ayala's offer of participation in 1926 and were committed to playing the parliamentary game by the Liberals' rules. By 1928 the party was following a new charismatic personality, Juan Natalicio González, who headed a group of energetic young men calling themselves the "Club Republicano." Taking advantage of the fact that the old leadership of Pedro Peña, Eduardo López Moreira, and Eduardo Fleitas had been discredited by joining Schaerer on the losing side in the 1922–23 civil war, González had thrust himself to the top. The first Colorado to accept Ayala's offer, he ran in 1926 for the Chamber in an off-year election, and won. By the following February he had convinced the Colorado executive committee that electoral abstentionism was a dead-end street and that only participation opened up the possibility of breaking out of the current stagnation and isolation. Even the old leadership split, with Fleitas and López Moreira composing the party's electoral ticket in 1928, while Peña and his protégé, Juan León Mallorquín, convinced many party members to abstain. As the new government took over, the majority of Colorados were willing to continue experimenting with democracy, on the assumption that Guggiari would play fair, just as Ayala had.

In brief, although new and powerful currents of opinion were gaining ground among the public, Paraguay's two traditional parties were only vaguely aware of them. They still were committed to the liberal rules of the game. Neither was prepared for, or understood, the events that were to marginalize them in the political process.

TOWARD THE 23RD OF OCTOBER

José P. Guggiari had devoted his life to the Liberal Party: that is, to the *gondrista* wing of the Radical faction of the Liberal Party. He was a man of undoubted courage, having fought in the 1904 rebellion, opposed General Ferreira through the founding of the Liga de la Juventud Independiente, participated in the 1911–12 campaign against Colonel Jara, and opposed the pretensions of Schaerer and Chirife. His energy and forceful personality tended to polarize those around him, however, into either dedicated followers or sworn enemies. In comparing him with Eligio Ayala, one can say that he was more of a politician than a statesman. Ayala's colleagues overlooked his bitter disdain for them in their admiration for his Olympian objectivity and his unquestioned devotion to the public good. Guggiari was more partisan, vindictive, and intolerant. One example of this was his treatment of the abstentionist Colorados. Unlike Ayala, who trusted in fair play to bring the *abstencionistas* around eventually, Guggiari had their leaders arrested and exiled.[6]

The new president had not been the Liberals' unanimous choice, either. The party's left wing had opposed him; indeed, Modesto Guggiari, his cousin, regarded him with a visceral hatred. Eligio Ayala and the top military officers doubted his willingness to continue the rearmament program, and with good reason as we shall see. Despite General Manlio Schenoni's desire to keep the army out of politics, the soldiers would have staged a coup to keep Ayala in office, had he shown any inclination to go along.[7] Others in the party regarded Guggiari with unease too: Belisario Rivarola, Ayala's interior minister, and even some of the *saco pucú* like Eliseo da Rosa and Rodolfo González. However much they regarded Guggiari's tirelessly devoted party work, they doubted his breadth of vision and moral sense of balance.

Unfortunately, these different factions were not able to combine effectively to stop Guggiari from using his position as party president to obtain the official nomination. The one man who might have claimed the undisputed leadership, Manuel Gondra, died in 1927, and no one else was available to fill the vacuum. Eligio Ayala was not eligible to run and his handpicked choice, Luís Riart, was considered to be a useful party workhorse rather than an independent leader in his own right. Also, Guggiari was able to obtain the crucial backing of Eusebio Ayala, who had his own following and was still smarting from being shunted out of the presidency in 1923. Unprepared at the moment to make a run for the presidency himself, he evened scores with Eligio Ayala and Luís Riart by throwing his support to Guggiari.[8]

Guggiari was surprisingly astute and conciliatory in composing his first cabinet. Eligio Ayala was offered, and accepted, the Finance Ministry. Rodolfo González, a close friend of Eusebio Ayala's half-brother, Enrique Bordenave, got the Justice portfolio. In appointing them, Guggiari seemed to be gambling that it was better to have his enemies inside the government, where he could watch them. Luís de Gasperi became the new interior minister, and Eliseo da Rosa became war minister. Neither was closely identified with Guggiari. Indeed, in the months to come they would oppose him openly in the cabinet. Gerónimo Zubizarreta rounded out the governing team at Foreign Affairs, where he was expected to follow Guggiari's lead. Vice-President Emiliano González Navero, an old Radical Liberal warhorse, could be counted on for loyalty too. Thus, just about every Radical Liberal faction, except the *modestistas*, was represented in the new government.

The average age of these top government officials was forty-seven, which compared with forty-five in Eligio Ayala's first cabinet, forty-one in Gondra's 1920 cabinet, forty-one in Manuel Franco's, and thirty-nine in Eduardo Schaerer's. Three of the seven men were from the Sixth, or "Glory," Promotion, and one (González Navero) was from the Fourth.

Less than four months after taking office Guggiari was faced with a new crisis in the Chaco that nearly brought on war with Bolivia. Ever since the Fortín Sorpresa incident, the two countries had been meeting in diplomatic negotiations held in Buenos Aires, but without success. Bolivia was determined to get access to the Atlantic by way of the Paraguay River, and both countries were certain that vast reserves of oil lay beneath the Chaco's wasteland. Thus, when the negotiations were broken off in

July 1928 both resumed their military preparations. Tension rose as reports of skirmishes were sent back to Asunción. Finally, on 5 December 1928, Major Rafael Franco, commander of the Bahía Negra garrison on the upper Paraguay River, took matters into his own hands and attacked a recently built Bolivian outpost, Fortín Vanguardia, which lay a short distance to the north. The Bolivian troops were driven off and the fort was burned. In reply, the Bolivians captured two Paraguayan forts, upon which both countries ordered the full mobilization of their armies. Before any actual fighting broke out, however, the International Conference of American States on Conciliation and Arbitration, then meeting in Washington, was able to get the belligerents to the negotiating table again.[9]

Meanwhile, the troop call-up in December proved embarrassing for the government. There was a shortage of everything: weapons, ammunition, uniforms, medical supplies, and food. The Colorados and the Liga Nacional Independiente raised an outcry: here were the results of a quarter century of Liberal Party rule! Guggiari tried to calm the situation by setting up a National Defense Council, with representation for all of the major political groups except the Communists. But the Council was a failure from its very first meeting. Eduardo Schaerer, representing the dissident Liberals, refused to collaborate with his old enemy; the Colorados, as usual, were divided; and the Liga Nacional's representative, Stefanich, presented what the government considered to be a fantastically ambitious plan of military purchases.[10]

Both sides accused the other of bad faith. Stefanich defended his "shopping list" on the grounds that it had been drawn up with the cooperation of Colonel Camilo Recalde, the director of the military school. Guggiari, however, pleaded the government's inability to finance a war and could only offer the suggestion that the arms purchases might be covered by taking up a public subscription. Failing that, he trusted in diplomacy to preserve the nation's interests. The National Defense Council ended its short life soon afterward, when diplomacy failed. On 3 January the International Conference of American States on Conciliation and Arbitration named Paraguay as the aggressor and ordered it to rebuild Fortín Vanguardia for the Bolivians. When it was learned that the Paraguayan government accepted the terms, the Colorado and Liga Nacional Independiente representatives on the Council resigned.[11]

From that point on the Guggiari administration was assailed by charges of appeasement. The military was so disaffected that only the lack of a willing leader kept it from a coup. General Manlio Schenoni, the war minister, might have served the purpose, and so might have Eligio Ayala. Indeed, Ayala apparently approached Schenoni with the suggestion.[12] But Schenoni, ever the professional soldier, refused to go along, even though Guggiari was plotting to undermine him by bringing Colonel Patricio Alejandro Escobar out of retirement and appointing him the army's commander in chief.[13] As for Ayala, whom many considered to be Guggiari's logical replacement, he was eliminated in a sudden and dramatic manner on 24 October 1930 when he was shot to death in a lovers' quarrel.

Plotting now revolved around the tempestuous Major Rafael Franco, who had been relieved of his Chaco command and posted to the strategic Campo Grande base outside the capital. Though officially in disgrace, he was a popular hero and a natural ally for all those in the opposition—*schaereristas, modestistas,* and *abstencionista* Colorados—seeking military support to overthrow the government. Gradually Franco and Major Arturo Bray, a former aide-de-camp to President Eligio Ayala, formulated a plan to seize both Guggiari and Schenoni and take power. The coup was scheduled for the night of 19 March 1930, but at the last minute Bray betrayed the plot to Guggiari. Franco was forced to resign his commission and the interior minister, Luís de Gasperi, was accused of being part of the conspiracy and dismissed.[14]

Another military crisis broke out in April when the soldiers at the Chaco outpost of El Galpón mutinied. Although the mutiny was suppressed three days later, at the cost of three men killed and eight wounded, subsequent investigations revealed that the incident was caused by severe shortages of food and clothing, and the fact that the soldiers had been been forced to remain in the army beyond the proper length of service. War Minister Schenoni admitted all this to the press, but defended the government on the grounds that the army's food and clothing allotments had to be cut in order to save money. As for keeping the draftees in the army, he explained that the system of conscription was deficient and therefore it was difficult to find replacements. That press interview added fuel to the fire of public indignation, forcing Guggiari to ask for Schenoni's resignation. On 14 April he was replaced by Raúl Casal Ribeiro, a civilian.[15]

A much worse blowup came in October, provoked by another Bolivian advance in the Chaco. On 7 September the Bolivians took the Paraguayan fort of Samaklay, but the news was suppressed by government censors. Almost four weeks went by before the news leaked out by way of Bolivian radio broadcasts, rumors coming from field hospitals where the wounded soldiers were brought, and letters smuggled back from officers serving in the Chaco. The government's attempts to deceive the public only made matters worse as the details became more widely known.

The National University and the Colegio Nacional became the centers of protest. Popular teachers like Adriano Irala, Anselmo Jover Peralta, Juan O'Leary, and Juan Stefanich already had created considerable intellectual ferment there. Depending on the individual professor, the glories of Russian communism, Italian fascism, Peruvian *aprismo,* or the Mexican Revolution were held up as superior in dynamism and idealism to the shoddy deceptions of traditional liberalism. And the students responded by forming a variety of nationalist and/or social revolutionary clubs.[16]

Following the Fortín Sorpresa incident, President Eligio Ayala had instituted a Reserve Officers' Training Program, headed by Colonel Camilo Recalde, which all male university and high school students were required to join. Colonel Recalde, who had started the Paraguayan Boy Scouts back in 1920, was popular and the program was successful in instilling patriotism into Paraguay's youth. Besides weekly drills, the young men were taken to the Chaco during school vacations to get firsthand experience of military life. All of this forged a strong bond among them that was to set them apart from their elders. That bond would be strengthened even more after war broke out in 1932 and they were sent off to fight. Many of them came back from the front determined to have nothing more to do with Liberalism, and they helped to start new political groupings such as the socialistic Febrerista Party or the Christian Democratic Movement. Even those who stayed with the Liberals and Colorados would challenge the old leaders and try to inject more nationalistic and socially minded ideas into the party program.

On the night of 22 October 1931 these students took to the streets to demonstrate against the government. Having been refused an audience with the president earlier in the day, they were in an ugly mood, which Stefanich and Jover Peralta whipped into a fury with their impassioned speeches. From the Plaza Uruguaya and the Plaza Independencia the crowd marched to Guggiari's home where they were dispersed by bayonet-wielding troops, after pitching a barrage of stones at the building. The mob then vented its anger by attacking and burning the pro-government newspaper, *El Liberal.*[17]

The next day Asunción's center was filled with students listening to harangues by Stefanich and Jover Peralta, and also by Juan Natalicio González, who by now had abandoned "participationism" for nationalism. Their passions stirred, they marched to Major Franco's home, where he spoke to them about the grave situation in the Chaco. Afterward, Franco advised them to return to their homes peacefully; but about 450 of the demonstrators decided to march on the presidential palace. Met by a cordon of soldiers guarding the entry, the angry demonstrators tried to break through. As the mob surged forward, one of the nervous soldiers opened fire. The others, thinking that the demonstrators were shooting at them, raked the crowd with rifles and machine guns. The protesters fled, leaving eleven people dead. Another twenty-nine were later reported as wounded. The city was placed under martial law. Major Arturo Bray, whom Guggiari placed in charge of the police, quickly rounded up and deported major opposition figures like Stefanich, Natalicio González, Jover Peralta, and Major Franco. Modesto Guggiari, who was identified as one of those who urged the students to action, also was arrested. After being summoned before the Liberal Party's executive committee to explain his part in the events, he was expelled.

President Guggiari did not escape criticism, however, even from those in his own government. Justo Prieto, the minister of justice and education, resigned. In a pamphlet explaining his action, he admitted that the students had been influenced by agitators, but held Guggiari responsible for contributing to the confrontation by refusing to meet with the student leaders. In doing so, Guggiari, at the urging of his secretary, Efraím Cardoso, had overruled Prieto's suggestion that such a meeting would help to defuse the tension.[18] Prieto was not alone in his criticism of Guggiari. Shock and indignation were so widespread that, on 25 October, the president agreed to step down temporarily and face a congressional investigation. Vice-President Emiliano González Navero took over and tried to restore public confidence in the regime by changing the cabinet.

The new ministerial team was a coalition of Liberal Party factions in which Guggiari's influence was much reduced. Gerónimo Zubizarreta, at Foreign Affairs, was the only survivor from the previous cabinet. Even he was not clearly identified as a Guggiari man. Below the cabinet level, Major Arturo Bray was retained as police chief of Asunción, from which post he became one of the "strongmen" behind the government. Though efficient in suppressing Guggiari's opposition after the "23rd of October," he also had served as Eligio Ayala's aide-de-camp and therefore had other factional ties. The man Bray replaced, Luís Escobar, was now interior minister, but his relationship to Guggiari was doubtful too. On the other hand, Luís Riart, the war minister, was clearly anti-Guggiari. Rodolfo González, the finance minister, and Victor Rojas, the justice minister, were followers of Eusebio Ayala and therefore tepid, at best, toward Guggiari.

Meanwhile, the events of 23 October were investigated by a special committee of the Chamber of Deputies, composed entirely of Liberals, since the Colorados had withdrawn all their representatives from Congress. The committee's hearings began on 16 December and ended on 23 January. The testimony was one-sidedly favorable to Guggiari, who was exonerated as expected. He resumed his duties as president on 28 January 1932, but there was little left for him to do. The party's convention already had been held the week before, while Guggiari's grip was still weakened by his being out of power. Unable to impose a successor from his own faction, he had to content himself with preventing the old Eligio Ayala faction from taking over.[19]

The *eligistas'* candidate, Luís Riart, combined the powerful posts of war minister and party president, and enjoyed the backing of such *jefes políticos* as Zubizarreta, Rodolfo González, Eliseo da Rosa, and Belisario Rivarola. Yet, even from the sidelines Guggiari retained enough of his old influence to throw the nomination to Eusebio Ayala, who, like him, had no love for the *eligistas*. Had the Eligio Ayala faction been able to join forces with the *modestistas* the outcome might have been different, but Bray's efficient persecution of the latter had destroyed their influence.[20]

On 15 August 1932 Eusebio Ayala, having run unopposed, was inaugurated as president of the Republic. The Liberals began their last real term in power.

THE QUINTESSENTIAL LIBERAL

Eusebio Ayala was, in many respects, the perfect embodiment of civilized, cosmopolitan liberalism. Born in 1874 in Barrero Grande, a small town near Asunción that today bears his name, he was educated at the Colegio Nacional and received his law degree from the National University at the age of twenty-five.[21] After graduating he dabbled in politics as part of the Liberal Party's Radical wing but then married a Frenchwoman and moved to Europe. There he expanded his education. According to George Pendle, "He was acquainted with the German universities, attended lectures by Bergson, and subsequently specialized in political economy and international law." He was especially well read in the works of Charles Darwin and Herbert Spencer.[22]

After the Liberals came to power he returned to Paraguay and accepted a chair in philosophy at the Colegio Nacional. Later, he taught law, sociology, and political economy at the university as well. As a Radical, he participated, in a minor way, in the 1908 revolt that toppled President Ferreira. His reward was to be appointed minister of foreign affairs in González Navero's provisional government and minister of justice and education under Gondra. When Jara overthrew Gondra the following year, Ayala returned to Europe and stayed there until the Radicals came back to power. From 1912 to 1923 he served in every Radical Liberal government: as minister of justice and education under Schaerer; as minister of foreign affairs under Schaerer, Franco, Montero, and Gondra; and finally as head of the provisional government in the 1922–23 civil war.

At home equally in Europe or South America, the master of several languages, and a man of considerable culture and education, Eusebio

Ayala was the perfect choice to represent Paraguay at international conferences. And with his knowledge of international law and economics,
together with his political influence, he was the bankers' and foreign
investors' obvious pick as a lawyer to represent them. He became the vice-
president of the Banco Mercantil and the legal representative of the Puerto
Pinasco cattle and quebracho company. As a good liberal, Ayala believed
in free trade, free enterprise, the sanctity of contracts, and very, very limited government.

Best of all, Ayala was so well-to-do that he literally was "above politics." So, when he was maneuvered out of the provisional presidency in
1923, he simply retired to Europe to resume the life of an intellectual of
independent means. He might have remained there, but the approach of
war made it imperative to find someone with good international connections to head the government, and so he got the party's nomination. He
did not even have to campaign for it.

Unfortunately for him, Ayala's obvious virtues were counterbalanced
by other qualities that, under the changing circumstances of the 1930s,
would be held against him. His enemies turned his cosmopolitanism
against him by spreading around the rumor that he had Jewish ancestry.
That created suspicion in the minds of many Paraguayans that he was
unwilling to fight for the nation's interests. If it is true, as alleged, that
Ayala once said "I don't believe in patriotism, I believe in conveniences,"
then he clearly was out of touch with his times. Even if he never said it,
it was widely believed anyway. The Colorados' revisionist historian, Juan
O'Leary, though he treated Ayala cordially in public, is quoted as saying
in private: "This Jew is going to sell out all of our Chaco." And Arturo
Bray quotes Benjamín Banks, Ayala's future finance minister, as saying
after the nominating convention: "Not even with the help of German
schnapps can I swallow that Jew!" (Nevertheless, he accepted the cabinet
appointment when Ayala offered it to him.) Bray himself displays no little
anti-Semitism when summarizing Ayala's political character: "His [or-
dinarily] clear intelligence was clouded at times as the result of seeing
problems from an angle that accentuated characteristics of semitic idio-
syncracy. He thought he could govern Paraguayans with the style of a
bank manager, or the director of an industrial or commercial enterprise."
And Bray adds, further, that "his personality lacked popular fervor and
was resisted by the army. On the other hand, he was supported by the
so-called *fuerzas vivas*: that is to say, banking, large-scale commerce, and
the big companies."[23]

If we leave aside the anti-Semitism, there is some truth in this assess-
ment. Eusebio Ayala was a true child of the Enlightenment, who believed
that the world's problems could be solved by reason and logical consis-

tency. He had no understanding of, or sympathy with, the kinds of passions that gave nationalism its force. Bray is correct in saying that Ayala was never a popular president. Although he conducted his presidency with dignity and skill, he was also hardheaded and impatient with people who held different views. He expected his cabinet ministers to carry out his orders without discussion; they worked *for* him, not *with* him. And, like other members of the Liberal Party elite, he was viewed in the popular mind as a spokesman for rich foreign interests. Above all, he leaned strongly toward pacifism, believing that reasonable parties could resolve their disputes through negotiation rather than by fighting. That had been the reason for his weak leadership in the 1922–23 civil war, for which he was removed from the presidency. Now again, even though fighting broke out in the Chaco on 15 June 1932, Eusebio Ayala as president-elect called on Congress to vote down war credits. He was convinced that, since the Inter-American Conference in Washington had just branded Bolivia as an aggressor, Argentina and Brazil would force Bolivia to stop shooting and pull back.[24]

After the inauguration, on 15 August, Ayala proposed a suspension of hostilities and the creation of a demilitarized zone. Although Bolivia rejected this, he repeated the offer time and again. Only on 1 May 1933, nine months after taking office, did he recognize the futility of his efforts and declare war. As might be expected, Ayala's pacifism was especially unpopular in the armed forces. Many officers were visceral anti-Liberals, holding that party responsible for Paraguay's lack of preparedness. For them, Ayala was the *reductio ad absurdum* of Liberalism's unrealistic faith in reasonableness.

Much ink has been expended in the debate over whether the Liberals really did fail to prepare Paraguay for war. David Zook follows Policarpo Artaza in arguing that the Guggiari government had a secret plan for building up the army and that almost 60 percent of its budget was spent on it.[25] On the other hand, Waltrud Morales dismisses claims of secret purchases as "unconvincing" and calls the Liberals' defense efforts "timid and inadequate."[26] Even Liberal army officers cast doubt in their memoirs about the Liberals' commitment to defense. Colonel Carlos Fernández, in his lengthy study of the Chaco War, noted that the army lacked telephones, vehicles, medical supplies—indeed, just about everything. The little equipment it did have was old and in poor condition.[27] General José Félix Estigarribia, the Paraguayan commander in chief, recalled later that "Everything was lacking: men, units, arms, munitions, equipment, money. . . . My men often fought on empty stomachs; we didn't have trucks, only oxen, and rains held up our convoys. There was no medicine to fight epidemics and our ambulances were miserably equipped. We operated on the wounded without anesthesia. . . . Yet, not once did my men fail me. Fortín Toledo was retaken by men decimated by dysentery and fever."[28]

CONDUCT OF THE WAR, CONDUCT OF THE PEACE

Paraguay's army was badly equipped but it had the advantage of shorter supply lines. Topography neutralized Bolivia's military advantage by making it necessary to move troops and equipment over difficult mountainous terrain. Also, the Paraguayan troops enjoyed higher morale. The average Bolivian soldier was a bewildered Indian, pulled out of his traditional community and forced to fight for his *criollo* masters in a cause he could not understand. Accustomed to the cold *altiplano*, he quickly deteriorated in the Chaco's steamy swamps. In Paraguay, by contrast, ties of marriage and godfathership (*compadrazgo*) knitted social classes together. At the start of the war all parties and factions set aside their quarrels and pledged themselves to back the cause. Accustomed to the tropical climate, Paraguayan soldiers outperformed their enemies so markedly that by December 1933 the Bolivian army was pushed back to the margins of the Chaco. This surprising string of victories was capped by a spectacular triumph at Campo Vía, in the northwest corner of the disputed territory, on 11 December.

The demoralized Bolivian army seemed on the verge of surrender. Indeed, many Paraguayan officers were certain that a hotter pursuit of the retreating foe and another sharp rout would bring the war to a close. Instead, President Ayala, with General Estigarribia's approval, offered the Bolivians a ten-day truce, which then was extended for another five days. During that time Ayala appealed to the League of Nations to help negotiate a peace treaty. But instead of asking for peace, the Bolivians used the breathing space to regroup their forces and change their commanders. Unwilling to negotiate from such a disadvantageous position, the Bolivian government renewed hostilities on 6 January 1934. Fighting continued for another year and a half, with many more casualties on both sides. Although Ayala and Estigarribia justified the Truce of Campo Vía on the grounds that the Paraguayan lines were overextended, many other officers and politicians interpreted it as another example of diplomatic bungling by the Liberal oligarchy. Some went so far as to mutter about pacifist "treason."[29]

The war finally ended with the signing of an armistice on 14 June 1935. Both sides were exhausted. Bolivia had been pushed out of almost all of the Chaco, but Paraguay's advance stalled in the foothills of the Andes.

No sooner had the armistice been signed, however, than political intrigues began.

THE COUP OF 17 FEBRUARY 1936

The end of the war coincided with the approach of elections, which in Paraguay always give a boost to political passions. The Liberal Party was deeply divided as it prepared to hold its nominating convention. With the war ended, the *schaereristas* and *modestistas* were free to attack the incumbents once more. The *gondristas* were split between those who belonged to the Ayala-Guggiari axis and the former backers of Eligio Ayala, who continued to support Luís A. Riart as his successor. In brief, it promised to be a replay of the 1932 convention, except that Eusebio Ayala was ineligible to run. Logically, he could have repaid Guggiari by securing him the nomination, but Guggiari was too controversial. How, then, to stop Riart? Increasingly it looked as though there was only one way: amend the Constitution to allow President Ayala to stay in office. As rumors spread that such a scheme was afoot, reporters asked the president what he knew about it and received an ambiguous reply. He had no wish to serve another term, Ayala assured them. But if his country needed him, and if public opinion demanded such a change in the Constitution, he would not stand in the way.[30]

Meanwhile, Ayala had decreed a rapid demobilization of Paraguay's armed forces, even though opponents pointed out that no peace treaty had been signed yet. The government replied that the treasury was empty and therefore it was necessary to cut expenses. For the same reason, Congress voted down a bill to provide pensions for disabled war veterans, although it saw fit to vote a life pension to General Estigarribia of 1,500 gold pesos annually—more than any Paraguayan ambassador got to operate an embassy! Estigarribia himself was widely unpopular with many army officers. During the war, personal dislike or anger over the failure of a mission had caused him to punish highly regarded colonels like Luís Irrazábal, Arturo Bray, and Carlos Fernández by stripping them of their commands, and in the case of the first two, ordering them courtmartialed. The commander in chief was also notoriously stingy with promotions and saw to it that he was the only general in the army. Colonel Federico W. Smith, who was to lead the coup that overthrew the government, opined later that this was one of the principal reasons why so many officers supported his action.[31]

All of these incidents raised suspicions that Ayala was planning to keep himself in office with Estigarribia's backing. The units being demobilized, it was said, were those whose loyalty was suspect. The main source of such criticism was Colonel Rafael Franco, who had been brought back from exile at the start of the war and given command of the Second Army. He was one of those who was quickly demobilized; but, being an extremely popular officer, he was elected president of the Chaco War Veterans' Association (Asociación Nacional de Ex-Combatientes, or ANEC), from which post he continued to be a thorn in the government's side.

Ayala, meanwhile, inflamed nationalist opinion by agreeing, in the peace talks then being held in Buenos Aires, to the repatriation of all war prisoners. Since there were some 17,000 captured Bolivians to only 2,500 Paraguayans, hard-line army officers had urged a man-for-man exchange, which would have left thousands of Bolivians to be used as hostages in future negotiations. By ignoring them, Ayala only confirmed their suspicions about his lack of patriotism.

Discontent with the government found its most vocal outlet in Colonel Franco, around whom there now gathered a circle of conspirators. Instead of being squelched, however, Franco was appointed as director of the military school, largely on Estigarribia's urging. The latter admired Franco as a good soldier who had served him loyally and brilliantly during the war; but if he imagined that Franco would be appeased by this appointment he soon realized his mistake, for Franco quickly used the job as a pulpit. At the beginning of February 1936, Estigarribia told Franco that President Ayala wanted him removed and suggested a long trip abroad at the government's expense. Franco indignantly refused and a few nights later made a violent speech attacking the government. The next day he was arrested and deported to Argentina.

Franco's fate spurred his friends into action. Their connections included the naval base at the edge of the capital, the nearby army air base, the arsenal, and an artillery regiment across the river. None of them commanded large enough units to carry off the coup, however, so it was necessary to bring in a senior officer. Colonel Camilo Recalde, Franco's close friend, would have been the logical choice but the authorities were now keeping him incommunicado at the military hospital, under the pretext of "holding him for treatment." Colonel Recalde's younger brother, Facundo, who edited the *Revista Militar*, then contacted Colonel Federico W. Smith, the commander of the Campo Grande base. To the surprise of all, the taciturn and seemingly unpolitical colonel agreed to lead the coup.[32]

At half past ten in the evening of 16 February Smith and his aides went to Campo Grande to begin the revolt. Troops were roused from the barracks and put aboard trains bound for the capital. By three o'clock in the morning they were in control of downtown Asunción. Ayala, awakened with the news that a revolt was in progress, hurriedly dressed and fled in a car toward the police barracks, just ahead of the soldiers sent to arrest him. After a brief but bitter battle, the police surrendered and Ayala was forced to take refuge, first in the post office and then in the naval ministry. Finally he was taken aboard a gunboat, which held the rebels off for a few hours while telegrams were sent to the Chaco urging General Estigarribia to hurry back with reinforcements. But the request was vain because there was no time to move troops from their forward positions in the Chaco to relieve the capital. Instead, Estigarribia gambled on his personal authority to restore order and flew back to Asunción. Upon landing, he was placed under arrest, along with other high government and military figures. Ayala, seeing the situation to be hopeless, surrendered and resigned the presidency.

In less than a day, more than three decades of Liberal Party rule were brought to a close. But the February Revolution was more than just a change of officeholders. It was the triumph of nationalism, a rejection of the whole body of political ideas and institutions that characterized the period between the War of the Triple Alliance and the Chaco War. The change received symbolic emphasis when, in August 1936, the president of the revolutionary government, Colonel Rafael Franco, sent a party to Cerro Corá to locate the forgotten grave of Marshal Francisco Solano López, exhume his body, and carry the remains back to Asunción. There, after a lavish parade and many speeches by leading revolutionary figures, they were deposited in a small chapel once built by Carlos Antonio López in the main plaza. Renamed the "Pantheon of Heroes," the little chapel became the shrine of a renascent Paraguayan nationalism, with the marshal as its principal saint. It was the end of one era and the start of another.[33]

nine

REVOLUTIONARY PARAGUAY

THE FEBRUARY REVOLUTION: A FAILED EXPERIMENT

Immediately following the February 17 coup the military leaders sent an airplane to Buenos Aires to bring Colonel Franco back from exile to head the new government, although the somewhat naive Colonel Smith had expected to name his friend, Gómez Freire Esteves, the Cívico leader, as the new president. Freire Esteves was wise enough not to challenge Franco, however, and contented himself with writing up a revolutionary proclamation justifying the coup.[1] The "Proclamation of the Liberating Army" is a document worth studying for what it reveals of the nationalist military viewpoint in 1936.[2]

Although the proclamation was addressed to "the Nation," it quickly becomes apparent that the armed forces alone had the right (and capability) to interpret accurately the sovereign national will. This was justified by a thumbnail sketch of Paraguay's history, which emphasized that in every crucial event it was the army that played the central role. Next, the proclamation indicted the Liberal Party's three decades of rule, focusing especially on Eusebio Ayala's career, which was taken to be typical of "that group of declassed politicians' long hegemony, which has brought this country to the brink of disaster." Finally, the proclamation contained clues as to the new revolutionary government's orientation. There would be no more concessions made at the Chaco Peace Conference. Steps would be taken to reduce the power of foreign economic interests in Paraguay and to raise the living standards of workers and peasants. Strong, active government would replace laissez-faire liberalism.

After Franco was offered the presidency, on 19 February, he had to pledge himself to honor the sentiments of this proclamation in a so-called "Plebiscitary Decree." The "plebiscite" referred to was a kind of "sense of the will of the armed forces," as expressed through "We, the Chiefs and Officers of the Army and Navy of the Republic, meeting together in a General Junta to deliberate on those emergency measures required to meet the urgent needs of our national reorganization, and interpreting the aspirations of the Liberating Army as expressed in its plebescitary proclamation."[3] The Plebiscitary Decree then authorized Franco to form a provisional government and to call a national constitutional convention to establish a "definitive modern organization" of the Republic. In brief, Franco derived his authority, not directly from the nation, but from the armed forces chiefs who spoke for the nation—a crucial point, as we shall see.

The first revolutionary government was as follows: Colonel Rafael Franco (president), Gómez Freire Esteves (Interior), Luís Freire Esteves (Finance), Juan Stefanich (Foreign Affairs and, *ad interim*, War), Anselmo Jover Peralta (Justice and Education), Bernardino Caballero (Agriculture), and Colonel Pedro Duarte Ortellado (Public Health). This cabinet was surprising, not the least because of those who were left out of it. Colonel Smith refused any government or military appointment and requested retirement from active service. Colonel Camilo Recalde, who had been a key plotter, accepted an ambassadorship to Chile and never returned to Paraguay.

Two other features stood out about this cabinet: the men were young and few of them had any experience in government. Gómez Freire Esteves's forty-nine years made him the oldest. He was also the only one with any previous governmental experience. Stefanich was the next oldest, at forty-eight. Since his colleague, Adriano Irala, had died in the Chaco War, he was now the undisputed chief of the Liga Nacional Independiente. I do not have birth dates for Luís Freire Esteves or for Bernardino Caballero, the grandson of the Colorados' great figure; however, the former was slightly younger than his brother, which would place him in his forties. As for Caballero, if we use twenty years as being about the average span of a generation, we can assume he was in his forties too. All the other cabinet ministers were in their thirties. Jover Peralta was thirty-nine, Franco thirty-eight, and Duarte Ortellado thirty-five. The last-named had distinguished himself as an army doctor during the Chaco War and was an officer in ANEC, the Veterans' Association. All these ministers, except for the Freire Esteves brothers, were from the Ninth and Tenth Promotions (the latter having begun with the 17 February coup), and only Gómez Freire Esteves, Juan Stefanich, and of course Franco, could be said to have achieved any political prominence before coming to office.

Contrast these features with those of the government that was overthrown. President Ayala was sixty in early 1936 and Belisario Rivarola, who moved from the Justice Ministry to Interior just before the coup, was about to turn sixty. Luís Riart (foreign affairs) was fifty-five. Those in their forties were Vice-President Raúl Casal Ribeiro (forty-eight), War Minister Victor Rojas (forty-seven), and Finance Minister Benjamín Banks (forty-six). Justo Prieto (thirty-eight), the new minister of justice, was the youngster of the cabinet. All these men were seasoned veterans of politics and government service. Ayala, Rivarola, and Riart were from the Sixth Promotion, while Casal Ribeiro, Banks, and Rojas were from the Eighth. Only Prieto came from a recent promotion: the Ninth.

Franco's first cabinet was largely a product of his personal whims. The Freire Esteves brothers were taken on to satisfy Colonel Smith, while Caballero's appointment was intended to enlist the Colorados' support. Caballero himself was a peculiar sort of nationalist radical whose many years spent in Germany had bred in him an admiration for national socialism. Stefanich was an old acquaintance from prewar days. He was to exercise an immense influence over Franco in the months to come, especially with the help of Elpidio Yegros, who was Franco's second-in-command at the ANEC. Yegros had been a student of Stefanich's at the Colegio Nacional, was a reserve officer before the war, and served as Franco's aide-de-camp in the Chaco. When Franco took over the government, Yegros became de facto head of the ANEC and was useful in mobilizing the war veterans to support Stefanich's position during cabinet crises. Finally, Jover Peralta had been included, despite his pacifism during the war, because he had spent time in exile with Franco after the infamous "23rd of October" and had succeeded in opening that simple army officer's mind to the "social issue." Unfortunately, the only thing these men had in common was their hatred for the Radical Liberals. Apart from that, they were ideologically and personally antagonistic.

During the revolutionary government's first month in power Gómez Freire Esteves played the role of "strongman" in the cabinet, backed as he was by the military's most nationalistic wing. Freire Esteves had lived for a time in Mussolini's Italy, which he considered to be a model for Paraguay to imitate. As a result of his influence, phrases like "organic democracy" began appearing in Franco's speeches. But on 10 March he overplayed his hand by issuing Decree Law 152, which abolished all political organizations—parties, movements, clubs, or interest groups—for one year, if they did not emanate directly from the government. All questions concerning the relations of labor to capital were placed under the control of the Interior Ministry, which would handle them through a newly created Department of Labor. The Ministry also would create a Committee of Civil Mobilization, whose duties were left vague. Gómez Freire Esteves's intentions can be gleaned, however, by reading the decree's preamble, which declared that the revolution was of "the same type as the totalitarian social transformations of contemporary Europe."[4]

It may be wondered how the rest of the cabinet approved this decree. To begin with, none of the ministers believed in a pluralistic liberal democracy—although Stefanich later claimed that he did. Caballero was sympathetic to the creation of a fascist state, and both Stefanich and Jover Peralta wanted to abolish the traditional parties to make way for a new one-party regime. Thus, they agreed with Freire Esteves on the need for a revolutionary sweep of the political board, although they disagreed on the nature of the future official party. Caballero naturally expected that a purged and disciplined Colorado Party would rule alone, as the "natural" representative of Paraguayan nationalism: the offspring of the *lopista* tradition. Stefanich wanted to ground the revolution on an entirely new organization formed out of the Liga Nacional Independiente and the ANEC, with no ties to the traditional party system. Jover Peralta also wanted to break with the past, but his vision was Marxist. Second, the decree was issued as a response to a rapidly deteriorating political situation, punctuated by strikes and street violence. As Stefanich recalled later:

> Those were the first days of the February government and one lived in times of anxiety and agitation. It was extremely difficult to get coordinated action or to channel the popular and individual activities that had been unleashed on all sides. Meetings, assemblies, and improvised debates heated the atmosphere; the most divergent opinions were expounded in the streets; labor unions acted tumultuously at the service of their own ends; the ranks of the army were incited by these trends, while the students found themselves laboring for the most disparate and antagonistic doctrines.
>
> This anarchy sapped our strength and it became necessary to give direction, definition, and organization to the popular forces of the revolution. Delegations of unknown origin were appearing in the towns and cities of the interior, sowing discord with their exalted discourse. Orators with suspicious affiliations became self-appointed tribunes and announced drastic revolutionary measures: the division of land, the confiscation of property, factories, and industries; and announced extremist programs behind the backs of the authorities.[5]

Obviously, the revolutionary government was not as revolutionary as it pretended to be. In any case, as soon as the decree was published each of the ministers came under pressure from his constituency to repeal it. The Colorados told Caballero they would resist any attempt to abolish them. The Federation of University Students protested to Jover Peralta. And the 106,000-member ANEC, whose branch organizations spreading throughout the country made it the true basis of popular support for the revolution, made it clear that Freire Esteves had to go.

Franco tried to hold the line in a speech on 14 March (Independence

Day), promising that Paraguay would not become fascist, racist, or communist. Its government would not be a copy of any other, but rather a faithful expression of the natural democratic culture of its people. Decree Law 152 was but a "political truce," he explained. It was needed to help stabilize the revolution. He went on to say that he believed that the traditional parties had completed their historical mission and should now make way for new organizations, but he would not use force to abolish them.

Even Franco could not stem the tide of protest, however. That night all the cabinet ministers handed in their resignations. On the following morning Franco dismissed the Freire Esteves brothers and replaced them with Germán Soler at Interior and Emilio Gardel at Finance. Those were significant appointments because both men were members of the Liga Nacional Independiente. Though small in membership, the Liga now controlled three of the seven cabinet posts and Stefanich became the new "strongman."

Even before Decree Law 152 was issued, there had been a move by Stefanich and Jover Peralta to form an official party of the revolution. Early in March the Liga, the ANEC, the National Confederation of Workers (CNT), and the Paraguayan Students' Federation (FEP) had joined in launching the National Revolutionary Party (PNR). Francisco Gaona, the CNT's general secretary, was elected chairman of the new party's Provisional Executive Committee. He and Jover Peralta, the hero of the Student Federation, quickly steered the PNR leftward. Its "Declaration of Principles" called for the socialization of "certain" goods, industries, and services that might be designated as "indispensable" or of "supreme necessity" for the economy and the people's welfare. The protection of the rights of workers and peasants was declared to be the revolution's basic goal, which would be achieved by the "scientific planning of production."[6]

The PNR was jubilant over the Freire Esteves brothers' fall from power, but it soon learned that their replacements were no more favorable toward radical social reform. Germán Soler, the new interior minister, set up a Department of Labor and issued a labor code that seemed to encourage the unions, but in reality his intentions were to exert a firm control over the workers. The Paraguayan labor code actually used the Italian Fascist labor code as its model. Like that model, it required unions to get government recognition in order to function as legal entities. Without such "juridical personality" a union could not sign a binding labor contract, represent its members in court, own property, or have a bank account. Strikes were forbidden unless previously approved by the Interior Ministry. Instead of allowing collective bargaining, the Department of Labor would set the terms of all labor agreements.

Soler also moved quickly to suppress all "radical agitation" in the countryside by turning the ANEC's branch organizations into a kind of rural militia. The Republic was divided into ten police districts, each with an ANEC officer appointed to insure order.

Finally, Soler moved against the PNR itself. Using the new labor code, he undermined Gaona by setting up an officially recognized labor federation, the Paraguayan Confederation of Workers (CPT), in opposition to the old CNT, and gave it the exclusive right to speak for the workers.[7] On 12 May the CNT called a protest strike, but informers already had prepared the government for such a confrontation. Gaona was arrested the night before, and on the following day the police rounded up the other strike leaders. Also arrested were a couple of prominent journalists, J. Rodolfo Bordón and Arnaldo Valdovinos, who had been severely critical of the government for its unrevolutionary attitude. All of those arrested were exiled. Jover Peralta followed them abroad a few weeks later when Franco, under pressure from the ANEC and the military, dropped him from the cabinet. In his case, however, exile was softened by an ambassadorial appointment to Mexico.[8] His place in the cabinet was taken over by Crescencio Lezcano, a founding member of the Liga Nacional Independiente.

By the end of June 1936 all of Franco's cabinet ministers, except for Bernardino Caballero, were Liga men. Caballero was able to resist Stefanich's machinations because he had a strong, independent power base in the Colorado Party, and also because he was the popular author of the Agrarian Reform Law of 5 May 1936. The most ambitious attempt so far to encourage a class of small farmers, it provided for the expropriation of about 5 million acres of land, to be redistributed as family farms. Over the next few months some half a million acres were actually distributed to around 10,000 smallholders.[9]

But even Caballero was to fall victim eventually to Stefanich's determination to rule the cabinet without opposition. At the Ministry of Interior Germán Soler was using Decree Law 152, which never had been repealed, to close down all independent newspapers. Soler's police stormed the offices of El Liberal, edited by Modesto Guggiari's son, who committed suicide afterward. They also closed down the Paraguayan Student Federation's El Estudiante and Facundo Recalde's Verde Olivo, which reflected the views of the ANEC's left wing. More important, the Colorado Party's Patria, edited by Juan Natalicio González, was proscribed. That signaled the beginning of the Liga's attempt to eliminate the Colorados from the revolutionary coalition.

On 25 August 1936 La Nación, the Liga's newspaper, announced a "new stage" in the revolution: the founding of the National Revolutionary

Union (UNR). Although this organization was not to be formally brought into being until November, *La Nación's* readers were assured that the first steps were already being taken. Indeed, five days later this still-to-be-established party issued (somehow) its Declaration of Principles, many of which were lifted straight from its predecessor, the PNR.[10] Following this proclamation, the Colorados withdrew their support from the government. Caballero resigned as minister of agriculture, to be replaced by a Liga man, Guillermo Tell Bertoni. Another highly placed Colorado, Felipe Molas López, resigned as intendant of Asunción. He was replaced by Elpidio Yegros, the head of the ANEC and Stefanich's close ally. Both Caballero and Molas López were arrested and charged with plotting against the state.[11]

The Liga Nacional Independiente was now fully in control of the revolutionary government. But, being essentially a club of intellectuals, it provided no popular base for the regime. Only the ANEC could do that, which meant that it had to be coopted into the UNR. But would its membership go along? At the UNR's founding convention, held on 15 November at the National Theater, spokesmen for the ANEC declared their organization's willingness to support the new official party of the revolution. Out of the seventeen men forming the ANEC's executive committee, nine were incorporated into the UNR's thirty-man directorate. As for the ANEC's mass membership, it seems that only about a third ever joined the UNR. The ANEC claimed 106,000 members, while Stefanich's highest estimate of the UNR's membership was 38,000—and of the latter, many were from groups other than the ANEC. Furthermore, it may be supposed that a large number of the UNR's membership joined mainly out of personal sympathy with Colonel Franco and had little loyalty toward the organization.[12]

Despite its flawed beginnings, however, the UNR was led by a group whose youth and energy contrasted sharply with the contemporary leadership of the Liberal Party. Of the twenty-three men on the UNR directorate for whom birth dates could be found, the average age was slightly less than thirty-three. By contrast, for the fourteen Liberals out of fifteen on the party's executive committee for whom birth dates could be located, the average was just over fifty-one. It is also worth noting that sixteen of the UNR directors had been students at the Colegio Nacional in the "23rd of October" period, served in the reserve officers training program, and fought in the Chaco. Eight of them also were on the ANEC executive committee. The president of the UNR, Stefanich, had been their professor at the Colegio and, of course, a prominent participant in the "23rd of October." Thus do events like the one in 1931 often have long fuses. Whatever else the February 1936 revolution may have been, it clearly represented the rise to power of a new reformist generation, much as the Liberal Party had been a couple of generations before.[13]

THE COUNTERREVOLUTION

By the beginning of 1937 it was becoming clear that Franco's government had lost its way and that Franco himself, though a fine soldier and an honest man, was no political leader. As the revolution narrowed its base, its former friends began to mutter that Franco had fallen into the hands of bad advisors. The Liberals were quick to seize on this thesis, for Stefanich, with his air of superiority and his didactic manner toward those around him, was widely unpopular. It was with considerable glee that his enemies learned, in January 1937, that he had granted concessions at the Chaco Peace Conference, after having excoriated the Ayala government for doing so. Specifically, he agreed to pull back Paraguayan troops from their forward positions controlling a strategic road between two towns in the Chaco in order to allow the passage of Bolivian supply trucks. Although the agreement was supposed to be secret, rumors leaked out and eventually Stefanich was forced to defend himself in a three-hour public address at the National Theater. But although he explained that a neutral peacekeeping mission would supervise all transit along the road, public opinion was not appeased. Inevitable comparisons were drawn with the Truce of Campo Vía.[14] Military nationalists were alarmed enough to speculate whether it might be necessary to move forcefully to free Franco from the ministers surrounding him.

Stefanich, in his memoirs of the revolution, claims that the January agreement was previously approved by Colonel Ramón Paredes, the commander of Paraguay's Chaco forces, and that the latter held back what he knew because he secretly was conspiring to put the Liberals back in power. It seems that Paredes was disaffected from the revolution after his wife wrote him from Asunción to inform him that Franco had taken away an official car she was using. (Actually, the order came from Colonel Aristides Rivas Ortellado, the newly appointed war minister, who issued it as an austerity measure.) Although he was a personal friend of Colonel Franco and linked to him through *compadrazgo* (godparentage), both Paredes's father and brother were Liberal activists and were in touch with many Liberals in exile, such as Eduardo Schaerer. According to one version, the Argentine government, then led by the conservative General Agustín P. Justo, was so concerned about the possibility of Franco's nationalizing Argentine landholdings in Paraguay that it was supplying

Schaerer with funds to pass along to Paredes. Other versions leave out Justo but confirm the connection between Schaerer and Paredes.[15]

There already was much grumbling among the soldiers in the Chaco about the shortage of food and clothing. Friends of the February Revolution, who later called themselves Febreristas, have accused Paredes and another army conspirator, Colonel Damaso Sosa Valdéz, the commander of the Puerto Pinasco garrison, of deliberately holding up supplies in order to sow discontent. It is likely, however, that the shortages were real and that the Franco government was simply too short of money to supply adequately its troops in the field. Sosa Valdéz later insisted that he was never an original part of the plot, but was simply leading the Chaco troops in their protests. According to him, Paredes fooled him into marching on Asunción to "save" Franco from the clique surrounding him. This version is the one generally accepted at present.[16]

There were other aspects of the countercoup of 13 August 1937 that suggest more direct reasons for the military's disenchantment with Franco's cabinet. Years later General Amáncio Pampliega, a prominent nationalist officer in 1937, suggested that the Colorados' defection from the government was a turning point. In his view, the attempt to create a third political party only spread confusion. Had Franco made the Colorados his official party, he would have captured for the revolution a mass-based party with esprit de corps and a cadre of administrators who would at least have possessed the virtue of a common party loyalty. What Pampliega did not address, however, was whether such a move might not have entailed sacrificing much of the government's reform program and, more important, whether the bulk of the military would have supported putting the government back into the Colorados' hands.[17]

Clearly, there were Colorado officers willing to oust Franco after their party was suppressed by the government. Colonel Emilio Díaz de Vivar, the head of Colonel Paredes's staff, and Captain Ramón Martino, the head of the navy, were both central to the coup of 13 August 1937. But they could not have carried out their plans without the support, or at least the acquiescence, of the great bulk of the military officers, who identified themselves more as nationalist patriots than as members of any party. By August these men had also turned against the government and accepted the proposition that Franco had to be rescued from bad advisors. What had happened?

In addition to giving ground at the peace conference and failing to provide adequately for the Chaco troops, the Liga-dominated cabinet had angered nationalist military officers by opposing a generous offer of economic and technical aid from Nazi Germany.[18] The offer was made in May. Franco himself welcomed the aid, but Stefanich, who was pro–United

States, argued against it. When the top military chiefs learned of that, they demanded Stefanich's removal from the government. Colonel Aristides Rivas Ortellado, the war minister, sided with them.

Caught between his reliance on Stefanich as a political advisor and his wish to satisfy the military, Franco shuttled back and forth throughout June, trying unsuccessfully to find a compromise. Finally forced to choose, he decided to jettison his foreign minister. But when he called the fateful cabinet meeting on 5 July, Stefanich outwitted him by announcing suddenly that he had information that Bolivia was about to renew the war and that it was necessary to send all available troops to the Chaco for a show of strength. Astounded by this news, Franco and Rivas Ortellado ordered two infantry regiments and one cavalry regiment, then stationed near Asunción, to the front. On reaching Puerto Casado, the troops were to be dispersed to different parts of the Chaco. But the orders were drafted so vaguely that it was clear a civilian had written them. With that, the officers held a council to decide their next move. It was at this point that Colonel Sosa Valdéz entered the picture. As the ranking officer on the scene, he took it upon himself to phone Paredes, the supreme commander of the Chaco forces. Upon being informed that troops were being sent to the Chaco to stop an expected Bolivian attack, Paredes answered that such a thing was absurd: he had spoken only a few days before with Paraguay's chief negotiator in Buenos Aires, who told him that the talks were proceeding constructively. "That," Sosa Valdéz recalled, years later, "let the entire army know that we had been fooled, that nothing serious was going to happen in the Chaco that would justify so many pains to send us there—and that was the fundamental cause of the revolt."[19]

After that, events moved quickly. Paredes hurried to Concepción, where he found Sosa Valdéz ready to lead a march on Asunción. The various unit commanders had met, on 2 August, to sign an agreement that they would force Franco to dismiss his current cabinet and replace it with one composed exclusively of military officers. If Franco agreed, he could stay on as president; otherwise, the armed forces would annul his mandate under the Plebiscitary Decree.[20] Paredes then flew to Asunción to inform Franco of what was about to happen and urge him to dismiss Stefanich and the other ministers before the troops arrived. But Franco refused to meet him. Instead, Colonel Rivas Ortellado ordered Paredes to prepare the city's defenses!

Gathering the officers and units still left in the capital, Paredes told them that they would have to act to save the revolution by removing Franco's cabinet before Sosa Valdéz did. Not until 12 August were all the *trabajos* for a coup completed; however, by that time the Chaco units were at the outskirts of the city. Paredes's revolt began in the early morning hours of 13 August with a warning salvo from the gunboat Humaitá. Franco and Elpidio Yegros hurried out to Campo Grande to rally support, only to learn that its troops were part of the revolt. Franco then returned to the presidential palace to meet with his cabinet. All the ministers turned in their resignations, so as to give him a free hand. But when Paredes arrived to propose that Franco stay on at the head of a new government, the latter called him a traitor and flatly refused the offer. With that he was arrested, along with his ministers.[21] The February Revolution was over.

With the fall of Franco, Stefanich's attempt to supplant the traditional political parties with the UNR came to an end as well. Although Stefanich tried to revive the organization in exile, he had no success. A similar attempt by Jover Peralta to revive the PNR failed as well. Both proved to be ephemeral experiments. Nevertheless, the revolutionary fervor remained. It had penetrated deeply into the labor movement and student revolutionary clubs. Many of those activists went underground after the 13 August 1937 coup, and in October 1945 they joined with the exiles to set up a confederation of revolutionary organizations called the Concentración Revolucionaria Febrerista, with Franco and Stefanich as copresidents. Finally, in December 1951 the Concentración converted itself into a true party: the Partido Revolucionario Febrerista.[22] Under this name it is still active in Paraguay as a party of the democratic socialist left. But thirty years of almost constant exile, from 1937 to 1964, stunted Febrerismo's growth. It became the banner of a particular revolutionary generation, which was unable to replenish its ranks.

But politics would never be the same after the February Revolution. The Liberals would briefly regain power, and eventually the Colorados would take their turn. But the old system dominated by traditional party politicians was dead. Nationalism had unleashed the military on civil society like a genie let out of the bottle, and there would never again be a retreat back to the barracks.

THE PAÍVA INTERLUDE

A few hours after Franco's arrest, Paredes and Sosa Valdéz were at the home of Félix Paíva, dean of the law school, asking him to form a provisional government. In choosing Paíva, they bowed to the influence of Eduardo Schaerer, Paíva's old friend, whose money had helped make the counterrevolution possible. The cabinet Paíva formed was intended to be nonpartisan. Paredes assumed the crucial post of interior minister. Two other professional soldiers, Colonel Juan B. Ayala and Lieutenant Colonel Alfredo Ramos, became war minister and police chief, respectively. Foreign Affairs was turned over to Cecilio Báez, the Liberal Party's "grand old man," while Finance and Economy went to two law school colleagues of Paíva's, Luís P. Frescura and Francisco Rolón, both of whom were academicians rather than politicians. The Justice and Education portfolio was given to Luís Argaña, another law school professor, but one identified with the Catholic nationalist right.

Although the new government aspired to be "above politics," this quickly proved to be impossible. The Liberal Party, considering itself to have been unjustly deprived of power the year before, was determined to get the government back. Nationalists were equally determined to prevent them. Meanwhile, the ousted Febreristas turned to violence, which they exercised through sympathizers among the army officer corps and through underground student clubs. One of their attempted coups, led by Major Juan Martincich, actually captured the central police station on 7 September 1937 and was crushed only by the intervention of the Campo Grande cavalry under Colonel Sosa Valdéz. This close call led to the resignation of War Minister Ayala and his replacement by a more committed Liberal, Navy Captain José Bozzano. A couple of weeks later Colonel Ramos resigned as police chief after a Febrerista student died during an interrogation. He was replaced by Colonel Arturo Bray, another militant Liberal.

Bray immediately resorted to the tactics he had used before as police chief during the "23rd of October": imposing censorship and a curfew, forbidding public meetings without permission from the police, and mass arrests of political suspects. He also presented Paíva with a long list of judges and civil servants whom he wanted dismissed. His highhandedness soon generated numerous enemies. The Colorados, many of whom were jailed, objected to being treated as subversives. Cecilio Báez, who had protested Bray's appointment in the first place, on the grounds that it "signified the return of the Liberal Party to power," was joined in his suspicions by Luís Argaña when he protested to Paíva that Bray was forming a special squad of police, loyal to him personally, without the cabinet's approval. The nationalist military officers, led by men like colonels Sosa Valdéz and Higinio Morínigo, also viewed Bray's acts as part of a strategy to give the Liberals control. Even Paredes began to perceive that Bray, his nominal subordinate, refused to obey him.

Finally, Bray was opposed by a group of young Liberals who were hoping to steer their party away from its traditional laissez-faire and toward the sort of reformism that the February Revolution had begun. Rather than allow the Febreristas to monopolize the progressive position, they argued, Liberals ought to take the lead in making overdue changes in labor and welfare legislation, land tenure, and the writing of a more socially enlightened, government-interventionist constitution. Prominent among these New Liberals were men like Efraím Cardoso, who once had been Manuel Gondra's presidential secretary; Alejandro Marín Iglesias, Artemio Merles, Carlos Centurión, Julio César Cháves, Rogelio Pavón, and Luís Chase Sosa. Born between 1900 and 1912, they were of the same generation as the Febreristas, and like them had—in most cases—passed through the Colegio Nacional, the reserve officers' training course, and the Chaco War. Hence, there was a close similarity of outlook, but unlike the Febreristas they had remained in the Liberal Party, intending to reform it from within. Some of them were destined to become cabinet ministers; others would be famous literary figures. The New Liberals also included a few slightly older figures like Justo Pastor Benítez, Justo Prieto, and Lucio Mendonça, all of them born between 1895 and 1900.

The New Liberals considered it essential to have a prestigious figure, unconnected with the party's past, at the head of the ticket when the next elections were held. At the moment, the choice seemed to lie between two veterans: Luís A. Riart and Gerónimo Zubizarreta. For the New Liberals, however, only one man could capture the public's imagination while also defying the party regulars, and that was General José Félix Estigarribia. But the party's Old Guard, aware of their plans, was determined to thwart them. Estigarribia had been kept in Argentina by the Paíva government on the grounds that political conditions in Paraguay made it too risky for him to return. Every time the subject was raised, Colonel Bray told Estigarribia that he could not guarantee his security. Estigarribia took the hint, knowing full well that after arresting and court-martialing Bray during the war his own life might now be at risk if he went back—not from the Febreristas, but from Bray's special police.

Not until 9 February 1938 did Estigarribia finally take the risk. On his arrival he was met by large, enthusiastic crowds, despite Bray's ban on public demonstrations. But he did not stay long in Paraguay for Paíva quickly appointed him as minister plenipotentiary to the United States, on the grounds that his personal prestige might influence the Americans to take a more favorable stance at the Chaco Peace Conference.

Estigarribia did not return to South America until early July. En route to Paraguay he stopped in Buenos Aires to observe the peace conference proceedings. He found the negotiations deadlocked, chiefly because of Paraguay's refusal to countenance any further concessions. The neutral participants—Argentina, Brazil, Chile, Peru, and the United States— were increasingly frustrated with the Paraguayan diplomatic team, headed by Gerónimo Zubizarreta, and Bolivia was even threatening to renew the war. Whether the threat was serious or not, it had a depressing effect on the Paraguayan government. Its military was fragmented, its treasury was empty, its foreign debts were enormous, and there was little prospect of foreign aid in the event of more fighting. The public mood, war-weary and exhausted from two years of political turmoil, was unlikely to support the return of conscription either.[23]

Even the Paraguayan negotiating team had begun to splinter. Zubizarreta discovered that Efraím Cardoso was working behind his back on a compromise plan. The confrontation that followed became so serious that Cecilio Báez had to fly in to patch things up. While in Buenos Aires he asked Estigarribia to read Cardoso's proposal and give his opinion. The next day he received Estigarribia's favorable report, which he then forwarded to war minister Bozzano (who was also Cardoso's brother-in-law). When Bozzano let it be known that the armed forces would accept the compromise, Zubizarreta resigned as both head of the delegation and as president of the Liberal Party. Báez then appointed Estigarribia as chief Paraguayan negotiator. By 21 July a final draft of Cardoso's peace plan had been signed by all the parties to the conference, whereupon Paíva scheduled a plebiscite on whether to ratify it. Although Zubizarreta and other old *gondristas* opposed it, it had Estigarribia's imprimatur and, equally important, it accorded with a strong desire in the public for peace. It passed, on 10 August, by 135,385 votes to 13,204.[24]

Their victory in the plebiscite convinced the New Liberals that Estigarribia could win the next presidential election. The Liberal Party "old guard" favored Zubizarreta, however, and opposed Estigarribia on the grounds that he was not officially a party member and that his candidacy would violate the party's *civilista* tradition. As convention-time approached the party was split along generational lines: New Liberals versus Old Liberals.

The Old Liberals were indeed old, by the standards of Paraguayan politics and in comparison with the Franco government, or even Eusebio Ayala's, as the data in Table 2, on all the ministers that served under Ayala, Franco, and Paíva, illustrate. Determined to retain control of their party, the Old Liberals began a campaign to depict their young challengers as "ambitious, irreverent, pushy vulgarians."[25] At first they had the support of Colonel Paredes, who used all his influence as interior minister to discourage the New Liberals' plans to nominate Estigarribia; but as a military officer he quickly became aware that out at Campo Grande, in the navy yards, and throughout the regional army bases the prevailing sentiment was running strongly against the traditional Liberal Party. Most officers still embraced the nationalistic and reformist ideas of the February Revolution. Although they might hold Colonel Franco to be in-

TABLE 2. AGE AT TIME OF APPOINTMENT (PRESIDENTS, VICE-PRESIDENTS, AND CABINET MINISTERS)

	Paíva		Franco		Ayala	
	average	(n)	average	(n)	average	(n)
All officials	50	(14)	42	(8)	46	(8)
Civilians only	56	(8)	42	(7)	46	(8)
No data	—	—	—	(4)	—	(1)
		(22)		(19)		(17)
			Range			
All officials	35–75		34–50		36–57	
Civilians only	39–75		34–50		36–57	

competent and harbor doubts as to whether Estigarribia was really the man to set things right, one thing was certain: no other candidate the Liberal Party might nominate, other than Estigarribia, would be allowed to take office.

The Old Liberals pushed ahead anyway. Gerónimo Riart, the party's new president, talked President Paíva into a major cabinet change on 1 November that replaced Colonel Paredes at Interior with the more politically reliable Colonel Bray. The Old Liberals also gained ground elsewhere, as Juan Francisco Recalde replaced the *tiempista* Luís Argaña at Justice and Enrique Bordenave, Eusebio Ayala's half-brother, replaced Luís P. Frescura, a technocrat, at Finance. At Foreign Affairs one old Cívico replaced another when Elías Ayala took over from the aged Cecilio Báez, who was seen as too pro-Estigarribia. The nationalists were not completely shut out, however. No one but a nationalist would have been acceptable to the officers as head of the War Ministry, so Colonel Nicolás Delgado, an Estigarribia supporter, was appointed. Nor was Colonel Bray able to pick his successor as police chief. The job went to Major Mushuito Villasboa, a strident nationalist.

Bray's strategy was to postpone the Liberal Party's convention and keep Paíva in power for another year in the hope that by that time the enthusiasm for Estigarribia would die down. But who then would be the Liberals' choice? Not Zubizarreta, whose ill-tempered resignation as leader of the Chaco peace delegation and party president had hurt his reputation. As for Luís Riart, his main rival, it was unlikely that the military would accept him. Although too modest to admit it in his memoirs, Bray seems to have fancied the nomination for himself as a compromise acceptable to both the Old Liberals and the army. His frequent trips around the country as interior minister awakened suspicions among some party leaders that he indeed harbored presidential ambitions.[26]

But, for all his scheming, Bray could not get around the war minister, Colonel Delgado, who was determined to have Estigarribia. Delgado was backed in the cabinet by a navy captain, José Bozzano, who had moved from the War Ministry to the Economics Ministry and was, in addition, married to Efraím Cardoso's sister. Thus, there was no way to stop the Estigarribia bandwagon which, by mid-January 1939, clearly would have a majority of the convention delegates, as well as the backing of the top military leaders. Indeed, the latter, to avoid any factionalism that might divide their ranks, decided to endorse Estigarribia unanimously. Since Bray was a high-ranking officer too, he received a visit from Colonel Sosa Valdéz and the new army commander in chief, Colonel Paulino Antola, to get his declaration of support as well. When he refused to give it, they went, together with Colonel Paredes, to President Paíva and asked for his dismissal as interior minister. The very next day Bray was replaced by Colonel Higinio Morínigo, a staunch nationalist.[27]

Estigarribia, meanwhile, had been in the United States. On his return journey, in late February, he was met by a delegation of nationalist officers, led by Sosa Valdéz, who urged him to run as an independent rather than as a Liberal. Estigarribia promised to consider it, but a few days later in Asunción he met again with that group and informed them that he would accept the Liberals' nomination because they were "the only organized party" in the country. On 19 March the Liberals did indeed make him their presidential candidate; on 30 April he was elected unopposed—the Colorados having returned to their policy of abstentionism. With the inauguration, on 15 August, the Young Liberals began to their attempt to rescue the Liberal Era.

ESTIGARRIBIA: FROM PRESIDENT TO DICTATOR

Estigarribia's administration began inauspiciously. Although the Young Liberals were jubilant, the very fact that he had run on the Liberal ticket had pleased almost no one else. The Old Liberals had gone along only grudgingly, the army had viewed his decision with misgivings, and the Colorados, observing that Luís Riart was his running mate, accused him of partisanship. The formation of Estigarribia's first cabinet only deepened the sense of letdown. Five of the seven cabinet posts went to Liberals, of whom three were in the Young Liberal camp: Efraím Cardoso (Justice and Education), Justo Prieto (Foreign Affairs), and Pablo Max

Ynsfrán (Economy). The other two, Cipriano Codas (Finance) and Alejandro Dávalos (Public Health), were men of little political experience but with many personal friendships among the Old Liberals.[28] Besides the Liberals there were two military officers. Delgado was moved to Interior and promoted to general. His replacement at the War Ministry was Colonel Eduardo Torreani Vera. Their appointments also caused some controversy. The Liberals complained that Delgado's appointment to such a sensitive post violated the party's *civilista* tradition. They were upset, too, because the colonel recently had published a book in which he accused the Liberals of failing to prepare Paraguay for the Chaco War.[29] On the other hand, Colonel Torreani Vera was known to be sympathetic toward the Liberal Party and so excited suspicion among the nationalists.

In terms of generations, the average age was forty-six, the same as in Eusebio Ayala's administration, though older than Franco's. The range extended from Cardoso's thirty-three to Riart's fifty-nine. Of the civilians, the three Young Liberals were conceded to be the ministers closest to Estigarribia. Justo Prieto, the oldest of them, was a forty-two-year-old lawyer from Pilar who had been a professor of political economy and sociology at the military school and the superior war school. From there he had gone on to be dean of the law school and then rector of the university. In 1929 Guggiari had appointed him minister of justice and education, but he resigned in 1931 after the "23rd of October." Reappointed to head Justice and Education by Eusebio Ayala, he was arrested and exiled by the Franco government. He was a senator at the time that Estigarribia offered him the Foreign Affairs portfolio. Pablo Max Ynsfrán was the son of Facundo Ynsfrán, who was killed on the floor of Congress in 1902. Like many Colorado children of his generation, the young man had switched to the Liberal Party, although he maintained many friendships with Colorados—among them one with the fiery Juan Natalicio González, with whom he coauthored a book, *El Paraguay Contemporáneo*, in 1929. After serving as a Liberal deputy from 1924 to 1928 he was appointed to the Paraguayan embassy in Washington, where he took classes at Georgetown University's School of Foreign Affairs. When Estigarribia was sent by Paíva to the United States, he took Ynsfrán with him as an advisor. The two were very close friends thereafter and it was conceded that Ynsfrán had an important influence in the new government's deliberations. Efraím Cardoso, former student body president at the Colegio Nacional, son of the former director of public schools, secretary to President Guggiari, and editor of *El Liberal*, owed his influence to the fact that he had been a loyal member of Estigarribia's general staff during the war.

Sensitive to criticism that his government was partisan, Estigarribia ordered Colonel Delgado to sound out the Colorados about their terms for participating in the system. Delgado met with Federico Cháves, leader of the faction most willing to consider collaboration with the government. Cháves's demands included a lifting of the state of siege, freedom of the press, an updating of the voter registration lists, and new elections with full guarantees of fair procedures. Estigarribia was willing to accept all these conditions, as was the Liberal Party directorate.

Just when it seemed that the government and its opponents were about to reach an agreement, however, protest demonstrations led by Febrerista students broke out at the National University over the appointment of Félix Paíva as the rector. The government responded clumsily by sending troops into the university, arresting the demonstrators, and installing an intervenor. Since many of the arrested students were Colorados, Delgado followed up his actions by closing down the party's newspaper, *Patria*. With that, the Colorados broke off the negotiations.

Now the military began to stir. On 13 February Estigarribia received a memorandum signed by a large number of officers demanding that he reorganize his cabinet to represent a broader slice of political opinion. The memo ended by reaffirming the officers' loyalty to the president (although not to his government), but also hinted strongly that it was time for a change. Meanwhile, the officers warned the police not to deport any of the opposition. Two days later Estigarribia informed Gerónimo Riart, the Liberal Party's president, that the worsening political situation made it impossible to continue within the existing constitutional framework. The Liberals would have to agree to accord him dictatorial powers until a new constitution was in place.

No amount of argument from Riart could shake Estigarribia from the course he had outlined. Deeply depressed by what he clearly perceived to be the end of the Liberal Era in Paraguay, Riart left the presidential palace to call a session of the party directorate. On the following morning Estigarribia held a cabinet meeting to receive his ministers' resignation. The time had come, he informed them, for fundamental constitutional changes, for which he would need a completely free hand; otherwise he could not guarantee the continuation of civilian rule. That afternoon the Liberal Party's directorate met at Riart's home to consider its response. Of the sixteen (out of twenty-six) members present, thirteen voted to go along with Estigarribia's plan to reform his cabinet. Riart and two others were left in the minority, whereupon they resigned their seats in protest. On 17 February 1940—four years to the day after the fall of Eusebio Ayala—the Senate and Chamber of Deputies met in a joint session to pass a resolution calling for the "integral reform" of the 1870 Constitution, after which they dissolved themselves.

The next day Estigarribia issued his famous decree establishing a dictatorship "to save Paraguay from anarchy." Hatred had so divided the nation, he said, that radical solutions were needed to hold it together. A simple change of men at the top would not suffice because there no longer was respect for the existing rules. The individualistic democracy established in 1870 had run its course. Political democracy was not enough: there had to be economic and social democracy as well. It was time to write a new constitution that would establish a wholly different kind of state. As a first step, he would call together the nation's best legal minds to prepare a draft, and in the meantime he would assume plenary powers so as to insure peace and stability. The Constitution was suspended and political parties and clubs were outlawed.

On 19 February a new cabinet was announced. Generals Delgado and Torreani Vera were retained at Interior and War, respectively, but the only civilian to survive the shake-up was Pablo Max Ynsfrán, who moved from the Economics Ministry to the newly created Ministry of Public Works. The Young Liberals were still a force in the government, however: Salvador Villagra Maffiodo was at Justice and Education, Justo Pastor Benítez headed Finance, and Alejandro Marín Iglesias took over the new Government and Labor portfolio. The Colorados were to be appeased by the appointment of Tomás A. Salomoni as foreign affairs minister and Ricardo Odriozola as public health minister. The Economics Ministry, renamed Ministry of Agriculture, Industry, and Commerce went to Francisco Esculies of the Catholic nationalist Tiempista group (after their newspaper, *El Tiempo*). The average age was forty-three, with Odriozola (sixty-two) and Salomoni (twenty-nine) representing the range. With the exception of Odriozola, who had served in Pedro Peña's brief administration in 1912, Benítez, and Ynsfrán, all were from the Tenth Promotion.

But Estigarribia's efforts still did not stop the grumbling against his government. The Old Liberals were unreconciled with the promulgation of a military dictatorship and were further alarmed by a decree issued in mid-March that imposed censorship on all publications and speeches, besides banning political meetings. On the other hand, the army's nationalists resented the Young Liberals' continued influence, for they considered them as simply old wine in new bottles. The most politically active among them—Morínigo, Sosa Valdéz, and Paredes—now seemed to prefer the Tiempistas, whose most articulate spokesman, Luís Argaña, was an admirer of the corporatist experiments in Mussolini's Italy and Salazar's Portugal. In May they pressured Estigarribia into dropping Delgado, his trusted comrade, from the cabinet and moving over Torreani Vera to replace him. General Morínigo then took over the War Ministry.

Meanwhile, Estigarribia plowed ahead with his project to give Paraguay a new constitution. Although a commission was appointed to write a draft, the real writing was done by Pablo Max Ynsfrán and Justo Pastor Benítez. The finished document, presented to Estigarribia at the end of July, rejected the old classical liberal philosophy that had dominated in Paraguay since 1870, substituting for it a powerful regulatory state. Although it provided for an elected unicameral Chamber of Representatives, it gave the president so many powers, including the power to dissolve the legislature and rule by decree, that the new system would be little more than a thinly disguised dictatorship. No longer were the rights of property or contract, or the freedom of speech and press, inviolable. The state could regulate the conditions of labor, the maximum amount of land an individual could own, the publication and circulation of ideas, the use of private property, the content of education, the organization and functioning of "groups of a public character"—whether political, economic, or cultural. Indeed, the state could regulate practically anything, since "all citizens [were] obliged to collaborate for the good of the state and nation." For the same reason, the state could suspend liberties whenever it considered it necessary by decreeing a state of siege. During such periods—and they were frequent in the years to come—the state could claim unbounded emergency powers. Finally, the influence of corporatist ideas was evident in the creation of an appointive Council of State composed of representatives of the military branches, agricultural and commercial entrepreneurs, the Catholic church, and the National University. This consultative chamber was intended to review all legislation from the viewpoint of the leading societal interests.[30]

On 4 August Estigarribia submitted the new constitution to a plebiscite. It was ratified by a large majority, although the electoral turnout was light. On 15 August Estigarribia and his cabinet swore their allegiance to it.

The Constitution of 1940, like the one of 1870, was symbolic of the passing of a political era. In this case it announced the triumph of nationalism over liberalism. It remained in effect until 1967, well into the Alfredo Stroessner regime, when it was replaced by a mere variant of itself in order to allow Stroessner to circumvent the two-term limitation on succession.

Would Estigarribia have used the powers of the Constitution of 1940 to their fullest extent to bring about the reforms that the February Revolution had failed to realize? Would he have ruled as dictatorially as Stroessner? There is no way of knowing because on 7 September, only three weeks after the 1940 Constitution was promulgated, he was killed in an airplane accident.

THE FINAL DEFEAT OF THE LIBERAL PARTY

Upon the news of Estigarribia's death, the chiefs of Paraguay's key military units met to choose a new president. While this may seem an extraordinary procedure, it should be remembered that the 1940 Constitution did not provide for a vice-president, and elections had not yet been held for the Chamber of Representatives. The logical choice to succeed Estigarribia, if rank and seniority were to be respected, was General Torreani Vera, the interior minister, but there was much resistance to him by Colonels Paredes and Sosa Valdéz. Their candidate was the war minister, General Higinio Morínigo, a genial, well-liked figure of the nationalist faction, whom they thought would be easy for them to control. Given the general belief among the officers that Torreani Vera was pro-Liberal, Morínigo got the majority's support and became the new president of Paraguay.[31]

Upon taking over, Morínigo confirmed all of Estigarribia's cabinet ministers in their posts. General Paulino Antola replaced Morínigo as war minister. Another of his first acts was to decree the posthumous promotion of Estigarribia to the rank of field marshal—a rank previously held in Paraguay only by Francisco Solano López.

Despite these conciliatory gestures, Morínigo soon discovered that Paraguayan politics was a nest of vipers. No one took him seriously as anything but a stopgap president. All the factions—Old Liberals, New Liberals, and military nationalists—assumed that he would be removed just as soon as one of them was able to dominate the others. In an autobiographical interview many years later, Morínigo claimed that on the same night that he assumed the presidency he accidentally came across the New Liberal ministers plotting together in one of the rooms of the palace. Moreover, according to him, General Antola informed him a few days later that those same men had approached him about leading a coup.[32] Whatever the truth of those charges, Morínigo prepared for a showdown by checking his support in the barracks and among the Tiempista civilian intellectuals. Then, on 30 September, he suddenly dissolved the cabinet and appointed a new one. All of the New Liberals were purged, arrested, and deported.

The new cabinet, appointed on 1 October 1940, represented the apogee of right-wing Catholic nationalism. Argaña, the Tiempista leader, replaced Salomoni at Foreign Affairs. Aníbal Delmás, another Tiempista, took over Justice and Education from Villagra Maffiodo; and Francisco Esculies, who had been heading Agriculture, Industry, and Commerce, held on to that portfolio while also taking over Finance from Justo Pastor Benítez. The military were well-represented too. Generals Torreani Vera and Antola were retained as ministers of interior and war, respectively. Colonel Ramón Paredes replaced Marín Iglesias at Government and Labor; Captain Ramón Martino of the navy, an extreme nationalist who had helped overthrow the Franco government, took over Public Works from Ynsfrán; and Colonel Gerardo Buongermini, a much-respected army physician, became minister of public health.

Over the next few months Morínigo, who proved to be a much better politician than anyone had suspected, further consolidated his power.[33] On 25 November the Liberal-leaning officers—Torreani Vera, Antola, and Paredes—were dropped from the cabinet. Paredes's political ally, Sosa Valdéz, was removed as commander of Campo Grande in January after a mutiny (encouraged by Morínigo) of his regimental commanders. Morínigo gave him an honorable way out by appointing him minister of interior; but a month later, as soon as the new Campo Grande chief, Major Victoriano Benítez Vera, was firmly in control, Sosa Valdéz was sent to a disguised form of exile—as a military attaché in Buenos Aires. In the meantime, Morínigo suppressed a revolt by two Liberal officers, Colonels Abdón Palacios and Alfredo Ramos, in Concepción. Another revolt, backed by the Colorados and led by Colonel Federico Smith and Gómez Freire Esteves, was snuffed out before it ever got to the action stage.

Many military officers were concerned about the regime's lack of a broad civilian base, for the Tiempistas were no more than a small circle of elitist intellectuals. Their leading spokesman was the chief of the general staff, Colonel Isias Báez Allende, who urged the opening of negotiations with the Febreristas. Morínigo agreed to send Luís Argaña to Montevideo to discuss with Colonel Rafael Franco the possibility of an alliance, but when the foreign affairs minister got there Franco refused to see him. Instead, he made it clear that he would accept nothing less than his complete restoration to the presidency. Such conditions obviously could not please Morínigo or the Tiempistas, but at a 17 April meeting of the top sixteen unit commanders Colonel Báez Allende's proposal that Morínigo hand over power to Franco received thirteen votes! Morínigo, who was present, disclaimed any political ambitions of his own and declared himself ready to do as his colleagues wished. He only asked for a little time to make the necessary arrangements for the transition. That night, however, Colonel Benítez Vera's Campo Grande troops, supported by well-armed police units, rounded up the pro-Febrerista commanders and their chief subordinates. Later in the month a Febrerista-inspired revolt broke out at the southern garrison of Pilar and was supported by labor and student strikes in Asunción. All were put down ruthlessly by Morínigo's new commanders.[34]

By the end of April 1941, therefore, Morínigo had succeeded in marginalizing both of the traditional political parties as well as the upstart Febreristas. Exactly a year later he put the last symbolic touch to the end of the Liberal Era. Toward the end of 1940 the Argentine government had published the documents of the Chaco Peace Conference, which included a statement by the U.S. ambassador to the effect that a group of Paraguayan exiles had approached the Bolivian representative in 1936 with a proposal to join forces in overthrowing the Franco government. Although the Bolivian minister, Enrique Finot, subsequently published a letter identifying those Paraguayans as "extremist elements" completely unrepresentative of the Paraguayan Liberal Party, the Liberals could not escape having their mythical "Legionnaire" origins flung once again in their face. At the time, Morínigo was too preoccupied in shoring up his own position to take action; but by the beginning of 1942 his hands were free, and now he struck. Using the Argentine publication as his evidence, on 25 April he decreed the Liberal Party to be an enemy of the Republic and proscribed it. All prominent Liberals still in Paraguay were arrested and exiled.[35]

This was not really the end of the Liberal Party, of course. It, together with the Colorado and Febrerista parties, continued to live in a legal twilight until near the end of the Morínigo period. A brief revival of party activity, under an amnesty by Morínigo in 1946—more or less forced upon him by the United States—permitted old hatreds to reemerge, and led very soon to a civil war in 1947. Although Morínigo survived the conflict, he was forced to rely on the Colorados for the necessary mass support. Once they had defeated the Liberals and Febreristas and driven them back into exile, the Colorados got rid of Morínigo too and set up a one-party state. Their return to power proved to be a disaster, for they quickly divided into factions whose power struggles resulted in a series of unstable dictatorships between 1948 and 1954. Eventually the military, led by General Alfredo Stroessner, took power again. Although the Colorados were permitted to continue holding most of the important public positions as the regime's official party, Stroessner purged all of their independently minded figures and converted their organization into an obedient machine for distributing patronage and mobilizing activities in support of his personal rule. Eventually, the Liberals and Febreristas were allowed to come back to Paraguay, much weakened by years of exile, to act as a docile opposition in Congress. Stroessner's own fall from power in 1989 has so far brought no fundamental change in the military-dominated system he erected.

The period from 1936 to 1940, or from the overthrow of Eusebio Ayala to the promulgation of Estigarribia's new constitution, represents a real watershed in the history of Paraguay's political parties. With the coup of

17 February 1936 the principle of civilian supremacy came to an end. The military entered the scene as the ultimate arbiter of who shall rule, and it has not relinquished that role since. Indeed, the military has ruled the nation directly for the last three decades. As a consequence of their marginalization from the political process, the parties' organizational development stalled out.

The importance of this can hardly be understated, especially today, as Paraguay moves slowly toward democracy. Political parties, if properly organized, may perform functions that facilitate the institutionalization of democracy in developing nations. They provide a continuity of personnel and policies that cannot be obtained in a system where only personalities count. Their symbols and propaganda, especially in nations where many people are poorly educated and have little time to inform themselves, may help voters to make choices—if on no other basis than that of group interest. And finally, to the extent that they are cohesive, parties are crucial in forming governments and coordinating the actions of the executive and legislative branches.

For all these reasons, the final collapse of the Liberal Era in 1940, for all of its many defects, was a tragedy for Paraguay. Two—almost three—subsequent generations of citizens have lived under a system that denies them the opportunity to acquire the political skills necessary for democracy, skills that could best be learned through political parties. If Paraguay is lucky, the next generation may have its chance.

SUMMARY AND CONCLUSION

The Liberal Era in Paraguay, viewed from the perspective of its political parties, was characterized by a process of institutional development, the impact of generational conflict, and changing political agendas in response to new ideas. The early chapters of this study showed the emergence of political clubs, before, during, and after the War of the Triple Alliance. In the beginning they were organized primarily around clusters of families: Decouds, Machaíns, Iturburus, Recaldes, and the like. This phase lasted approximately through the Constitutional Convention of 1870, to be replaced by clubs headed by *caudillos*: powerful individuals commanding a personal following. Old family names still figured in the executive committees of these clubs, but real leadership rested with men like Cándido Bareiro, Bernardino Caballero, Juan Bautista Gill, and Benigno Ferreira, whose authority was personal, not familial.

By 1880 all of the leading *caudillos* had been eliminated, save for General Caballero, who was unchallenged as head of the state, head of the army, and head of the dominant political coalition. Under him, politics changed from a battle of personalities to the distribution of patronage through a political machine. This proved to be a transitional phase, however, because by the mid-1880s a new opposition began to take shape. When in July 1887 the regime's opponents coalesced to form the Centro Democrático, forerunner of the Liberal Party, Caballero and his supporters responded the following month by inaugurating the Colorado Party. Thus, true political parties now took the place of ephemeral clubs and have continued to shape the political process ever since.

Paraguay's two-party system has not always gone unchallenged. Both the Colorados and the Liberals splintered in the 1890s into moderate and extreme factions. Among the Colorados, those who remained loyal to General Caballero stood at the conservative extreme of the political system, resisting all change. Opposing them were the followers of General Egusquiza, who wanted to replace the high-handed rule of *lopista* army officers with civilian rule. Among the Liberals the split was between the Cívicos, led by General Ferreira, who were willing to collaborate with Egusquiza, and the intransigent Radicals, for whom nothing would do short of a clean sweep of the Colorados from power. For a time it seemed that the *egusquicistas* and Cívicos might compose a "third force" between the two original parties, but the *caballerista* coup of 1902, Egusquiza's death that same year, and the overthrow of Ferreira in 1908 prevented that. Another attempt by Albino Jara to patch together a coalition of Cívicos, moderate Colorados, and maverick Radicals, from 1910 to 1912, failed through his own personal ineptitude.

The power struggle that split the dominant Radical Liberals in the early 1920s, between the *schaereristas* and the *gondristas*, was not an attempt to form a third party. Rather, it was about which leader, Eduardo Schaerer or José P. Guggiari, Manuel Gondra's "grand vizier," would lead the process of gathering the loosely structured Liberal Party into a more cohesive, centralized, and disciplined organization. It was not until the February Revolution and the rise of a new nationalist-socialist movement, subsequently known as Febrerismo, that another serious attempt was made to start a third party. The Febreristas' first party, the Unión Nacional Revolucionaria, failed to survive the fall of the revolutionary government. Febrerismo continued as a vital third force well into the 1940s, but eventually its many years in exile cut it off from the sources of renewal. The Partido Revolucionario Febrerista remains today a stunted minor party.

The Liberal Era was not characterized by deep ideological divisions. Paraguay's defeat in war and occupation by the Allied armies so discredited the old autocratic and statist regime of Francisco Solano López that even those who fought for it repudiated it afterward. The liberal principles embodied in the Constitution of 1870 enjoyed almost universal support, at least among the political class. Nor, despite the conventional wisdom in today's Paraguay, did the political divisions that gave rise to the Colorado and Liberal parties run along the lines of "patriots" versus Legionnaires. What really led to the original Liberal-Colorado split, besides personal conflicts, was a challenge to General Caballero's political machine by a rising generation disgusted at the regime's blatant corruption and easy recourse to fraud and violence.

Generational differences provided the motive for much of the partisan conflict of the Liberal Era. What is surprising about this period is how young its politicians were. Men in their fifties were normally considered old, past their prime. Politicians who stayed in the forefront until their sixties were relatively rare. By the same token, many men became prominent in their twenties, and a few even began to attract notice in their teens. As a rule, the peak years of a political career tended to occur in the late thirties to late forties—rather sooner than generational theorists like Ortega y Gasset would predict.

The men who came to prominence directly after the War of the Triple Alliance were a remarkably young generation. At the time of the Constitutional Convention, in 1870, Benigno Ferreira was twenty-four; Facundo Machaín, twenty-three; José Segundo Decoud, twenty-two; Cayo Miltos, twenty-seven; Juansilvano Godoi, twenty; Rufino Taboada, twenty-six; Cirilo Rivarola, twenty-nine; Juan Bautista Gill, thirty; Bernardino Caballero, thirty-one; and Cándido Bareiro, a venerable oldster of thirty-six! These were the men who dominated the period up to 1880, as opposed to the elderly figures from the Sociedad Libertadora, Asociación Paraguaya, or Paraguayan Legion. Lieutenant Colonel Juan Francisco Decoud, at fifty-nine, as well as Colonel Fernando Iturburu, his senior, were typical of a generation destined to be marginalized by the outburst of youth *enragés* unleashed by Paraguay's defeat.

The dominant coalition that controlled the state, first through General Caballero's political machine and later through the Colorado Party, from 1880 to 1890 was mainly composed of the middle-aged survivors of the immediate postwar struggles. Caballero and his military cronies made their peace with ex-Legionnaires like José Segundo Decoud and Higinio Uriarte. At the time the Colorado Party was founded, Caballero was forty-eight; General Patricio Escobar was forty-four, Colonel Juan Crisóstomo Centurión was forty-five, and Decoud was thirty-nine. These men were at the zenith of their power and were not to be challenged in any effective way for another seven years.

By contrast, the Centro Democrático was primarily an organization of men in their twenties and thirties. Though it contained a few old soldiers like Pedro V. Gill, Ignacio Ibarra, Cirilo Solalinde, and José Mateo Collar, its dynamism came from the young men who quickly became the most prominent opposition figures: Cecilio Báez, who was twenty-five in 1887; José de la Cruz Ayala, twenty-three; Fabio Queirolo, twenty-five; and Adolfo Soler, eighteen. The Centro's president, Antonio Taboada, was a mature thirty-nine.

The beginnings of political realignment, during the 1890s, reflected generational change. General Caballero's faction of the Colorado Party was clearly showing signs of aging. The general himself was sixty-one in 1900, an advanced age in Paraguayan politics. His closest political friend, General Escobar, was fifty-seven; and another political ally of many, many years, Agustín Cañete, was in his seventies. There were some attempts to attract youth: Fulgencio R. Moreno was only twenty-eight as the decade opened. But two promising young *caballeristas* had their careers cut tragically short. Blas Garay was killed in a duel in 1899, at the age of twenty-six; and Facundo Ynsfrán died in a shoot-out on the floor of Congress in 1902. Egusquiza's following was more youthful, on the whole. Although he was fifty-five in 1900, his followers in the Club Popular Egusquicista were almost all in their twenties and thirties. Emilio Aceval, who also represented the rising mercantile interests, was the oldest among those whose birth dates could be found, at forty-six years of age in 1900. Rufino Mazó, the Club's president, was in his early forties, as was Guillermo de los Ríos, another figure from the business and banking world; and Benigno Riveros, the Club's secretary, was twenty-nine. Other prominent *egusquicistas* in 1894 were Héctor Velásquez, thirty-seven; Arsenio López Decoud, thirty-two; Manuel Amarilla, thirty-six; and Manuel Domínguez, thirty-one.

Over in the Liberal Party, the leader of the Cívico wing, General Ferreira, was fifty-four in 1900, but his following was somewhat younger. In 1900 Adolfo Soler was thirty-one; José T. Legal, thirty-five; and Manuel Benítez, thirty. Besides these, he had the support of Antonio Taboada, who by this time was fifty-two, and he had won over Cecilio Báez, now thirty-eight. Báez's desertion to the Cívicos meant that the leadership of the Radicals gravitated into even younger hands. The man who was to replace him as the Radical's grand chieftain, Manuel Gondra, was only twenty-nine in 1900, but already was a charismatic figure. The man who would be Gondra's greatest rival for the leadership of the Radicals, Eduardo Schaerer, was twenty-seven. Other activists who became prominent Radicals were Manuel Franco, twenty-seven; Albino Jara, twenty-three; Gualberto Cardús Huerta, twenty-two; Eusebio Ayala, twenty-five; and Adolfo Riquelme, twenty-four.

In the opinion of the present writer, it is 1908, even more than 1904, that marks a watershed in Paraguayan politics. Although the 1904 revolution ousted the Colorados from power, the governments of Gaona, Báez, and Ferreira that followed did not pose a sharp break with the past. Essentially, they were coalition governments composed of former Egusquiza followers and Cívicos. In 1908, however, the Radicals swept clean the political board and established a hegemony that lasted over a quarter of a century. It is true that Albino Jara's defection got this period off to a shaky start, but it quickly became clear that no other political force beside the mainstream Radicals could govern the country.

The period of Radical hegemony saw a gradual but distinct aging tendency in the country's political leadership. The average age of each administration, from Schaerer's to Eusebio Ayala's, rose steadily, even though it is possible to speak of a new generation of Radicals succeeding to power after 1923. By the time the generation of the 1880s (Eligio Ayala, Luís A. Riart, José P. Guggiari, Modesto Guggiari, Gerónimo Zubizarreta) took over from that of the 1870s (Gondra, Schaerer, Paíva, Eusebio Ayala), it was already well into its forties. Stable government promotes gerontocracy, it seems.

Leaving aside the Paíva interregnum, the events touched off by the February Revolution brought about a rejuvenation of the political system. The men around Colonel Franco were, for the most part, young and uncompromised by previous experience in power—both a virtue and a shortcoming. With the exception of Gómez Freire Esteves (1886) and Juan Stefanich (1889), they had been born in the 1890s or in the first decade of the twentieth century. Nor did the fall of the revolutionary government permit the Old Liberals to turn back the clock. The New Liberals who steered General Estigarribia into the presidency were of the same generation as the revolutionaries of 1936. Indeed, in many cases they had been classmates at the Colegio Nacional. To a great extent the shift away from the classical liberalism that had been dominant since 1869 toward the new social-reformist nationalism that penetrated even the Liberal Party was as much a generational struggle as it was an ideological one.

The march of generations affected, and was affected by, changing political agendas. Dominant coalitions formed to pursue compatible goals among their component elements only to lose power when a new conjunction of interests, with different perspectives and a different political agenda, pushed them aside. A summary of those changes is contained in Table 3.

In every instance a change in the dominant coalition and the political agenda required an act of violence to become definitive. Sometimes there were other symbolic acts of violence that punctuated the fact that the old coalition had lost its hold. Thus, the first period may be said to have ended with Benigno Ferreira's defeat and exile in 1874; but some elements of the original dominant coalition failed to perceive that their power was broken until Facundo Machaín's tragic death in prison in 1877. By the same token, General Caballero's coup of 1880, by arresting Vice-President Adolfo Saguier, the constitutionally designated successor to Bareiro, put a definitive end to factional politics and made it clear that a single machine now controlled the state.

The fourth political period, beginning in 1894, had its origins in José Segundo Decoud's creation of the Colorado Party in 1887, which paved the way for the first *civilista* president, Juan G. González, to be elected in 1890. But the power of the *lopista* army officers was not broken until the failed Liberal coup of 1891 gave General Juan B. Egusquiza the opportunity to establish himself as the new "strongman" of the political system. The new dominant coalition he constructed was fatally crippled, however, by the *caballeristas'* "last hurrah" in 1902, which drove the Cívicos and Radicals back into each other's arms. The 1904 revolution brought the Cívicos, the other political component of the coalition, to power; however, by that time the *egusquicista* Colorados were but a small piece of a badly shattered party and could bring little strength to the government.

TABLE 3. DOMINANT COALITIONS AND POLITICAL AGENDAS

Period (Promotion)	Dominant Coalition	Political Agenda
1869–74 (1, 2)	Legionnaire families of Gran Club del Pueblo	Establish a new constitutional order
1874–80 (2)	So-called National Party of Gill, Bareiro, and Caballero	Departure of allied forces, recovery of sovereignty, political pacification
1880–94 (3, 4)	*Caballerista* Colorados, composed of *lopista* army officers and most Legionnaires	Financial recovery through land sales; orderly distribution of patronage to maintain political stability
1894–1908 (5, 6)	*Egusquicista* Colorados, Cívico Liberals, and new business class	Promote trade and economic growth; political peace through incorporating Liberals into the government (or Colorados, after 1904)
1908–32 (7, 8, 9)	Radical Liberals, especially the *gondrista* wing	Political democracy based on limited government; a more unified and disciplined Liberal Party to insure Radical hegemony
1932–40 (9, 10)	Nationalist elements of the military, with support of dissident Liberals, Colorados, and Liga Nacional Independiente	Defend national claims to the Chaco; agrarian reform; labor reform

Despite the support of the rising business class, this progressive elite coalition was overturned by the much more popular Radicals.

It took another bloody civil war, from 1911 to 1912, to establish the definitive end of the Cívico-*egusquicista* coalition; and it may well be that it was Eduardo Schaerer's business contacts that really made the difference. Clearly, more research is required on this period of Radical hegemony, especially about the relationship of the dominant party faction to the business interests. A more focused investigation may turn up evidence that would cast the Schaerer-Gondra struggle in a new light. In the absence of hard data, however, the awful civil war of 1922–23 must be viewed as a power struggle in the Radicals' ranks rather than an attempt to bring a new dominant coalition into being.

By dating the last period of the Liberal Era from 1932 I am accepting the "23rd of October" incident as a symbolic watershed. It was the climax of a buildup of nationalistic frenzy in the prewar period, and its effects—on student reserve officers, intellectuals, and young regular military officers—can be traced directly to the February Revolution of 1936. It was the turning point for the old dominant coalition: never again would it enjoy majority backing from Paraguay's political class. If the Chaco War acted as a catalyst for the February Revolution, it also constituted a reprieve for the Liberals. The failure to revive Liberal rule, from 1937 to 1940, revealed the unpopularity of the old order. Nationalism had supplanted liberalism as the prevailing ideology.

Generation succeeded generation more rapidly, in many cases, than the fifteen-year rule of thumb suggested by Ortega y Gasset. Eight to ten years was more often the spread between one political generation and the next. In the case of the Bareiro-Gill-Caballero "National Party"—the core of the group I have labeled as Second Promotion—these men were, on the average, about seven years older than the Decoud-Ferreira-Machaín group of the First Promotion that formed the nucleus of the Gran Club del Pueblo. This difference in their ages may help to explain, in addition to other important variables, their political allegiance. The young men of the First Promotion reached their adolescence in the early 1860s. José Segundo Decoud became fifteen in 1863, Benigno Ferreira and Jaime Sosa Escalada in 1861, Facundo Machaín in 1860. Their early youth coincided with the first years of the Solano López tyranny, and it was spent in exile. Their hatred for the regime is hardly surprising. By contrast, Bareiro was fifteen in 1848 (the same year Decoud was born), Caballero in 1854, Gill in 1855, and Escobar in 1858: all within the heyday of Carlos Antonio López's peaceful and prosperous rule. Except for Bareiro, they seldom left Paraguay. Cirilo A. Rivarola, who reached fifteen in 1856, shared the same background. But his father had been persecuted by Carlos Antonio and he himself had been tortured by Francisco Solano. Consequently, he fit into neither of the postwar political camps.

If the generation of the fifties pushed aside that of the sixties as Caballero established his control, it soon found itself under attack from the generation of the seventies. Cecilio Báez (fifteen years old in 1877), Fabio Queirolo (1877), and José de la Cruz Ayala (1879) were the driving force behind the Centro Democrático. But it took the leadership of two men from the sixties generation, Benigno Ferreira (1861) and Antonio Taboada (1863), plus the crucial participation of many from the eighties generation such as Manuel Duarte (1888), Patricio Alejandro Escobar (1889), Elías Ayala (1885), and Adolfo Soler (1884) to bring off the 1904 revolution. There were even two prominent revolutionaries from the nineties generation: Albino Jara (1892) and Adolfo Riquelme (1891). What they shared was the disgust and humiliation at the *caballerista* governments' rampant corruption, cynicism, and alienation of the public lands.

Theorists like Karl Mannheim hold that the experiences of early youth stamp a "generational unit" with its particular outlook. If that is true, then the period from the first law for the sale of public lands, in 1883, to the beginning of the Egusquiza administration in 1894 should have provided the pool of teenagers from which future Radical Liberal reformism would find its leadership. And that was indeed the case: Manuel Gondra and Manuel Franco were fifteen in 1886, Eduardo Schaerer in 1888, José P. Montero in 1888, Liberato Rojas in 1885, Ramón Lara Castro in 1888, Eusebio Ayala in 1890, Adolfo Riquelme in 1891, Albino Jara in 1892. Self-righteous and intransigent, that generation finally won power in 1908 and swept away all opposition to the margins of the political system. Then, ironically, its unity dissolved in two vicious civil wars that put the Liberal Party's capacity to rule in grave doubt.

Before it came to power, however, the Radical faction had to battle the Cívicos for supremacy within the Liberal Party. Ever since the 1890 election, the Liberals had been divided over whether to cooperate with moderate, *civilista* Colorados to get Caballero and his cronies out of power. But it was in 1894—when the incumbent Liberal directorate, desperate to find a military leader capable of replacing the fallen Major Eduardo Vera, picked General Ferreira as the new party president—that the split turned into a schism. Though forced to accept Ferreira's leadership in the 1904 revolution, the Radicals would not tolerate him, either as party president or as president of the Republic. Thus, another generation of Radicals emerged having been exposed to the party struggles of 1894 to 1908. Many of them were so opposed to General Ferreira because of his allegedly shady past that, rather than affiliate with the Liberal Party, they belonged to the Liga de la Juventud Independiente. Among the future presidents and cabinet ministers from this generation were: Eligio Ayala, who was fifteen in 1895; José P. Guggiari, in 1899; Modesto Guggiari, in 1900; Luís A. Riart, in 1895; J. Eliseo da Rosa, in 1898; Belisario Rivarola, in 1901; Raúl Casal Ribeiro, in 1902; and Lisandro Díaz León, in 1904. All but Riart and Rivarola were Liga members. This was the generation that took over in 1923.

The new forces that challenged liberalism in the 1930s—communists, socialists, nationalists—were led by the generational elites of the following decade: those whose early youth was marked either by the civil war of 1911–12 or by that of 1922–23. The first group, coming to early youth between 1908 and 1916, includes such Febreristas as Anselmo Jover Peralta, Colonel Rafael Franco, Crescencio Lezcano, Emilio Gardel, and

Pedro Duarte Ortellado; "New Liberals" like Pablo Max Ynsfrán, Justo Prieto, and Justo Pastor Benítez; and nationalists like Colonel Higinio Morínigo and Luís Argaña, the Tiempista chief. The second group, which reached the age of fifteen between 1919 and 1927 includes second-line Febreristas like Elpidio Yegros, Arnaldo Valdovinos, Francisco Sánchez Palacios, Ruperto Resquín, and Francisco Gaona. Many of these younger Febreristas were critical of the Franco government and were exiled by it. The 1919–1927 generation also includes New Liberals like Efraím Cardoso and Alejandro Marín Iglesias; and both of the top Communist Party leaders, Oscar Creydt and Obdúlio Barthe. On the whole, this latter generation was more radical in outlook, but both generations shared the conviction that traditional Liberal Party rule was bankrupt.

Is there any pattern to this all? Curiously, Paraguayan politics seems to go through major transitions about every thirty years. If we take 1870 as a pivotal date—the death of Solano López and the promulgation of a new constitution—then thirty-four years elapse until the 1904 revolution. And if we date the Colorado period from 1874, we have a span of exactly thirty years. After that the Liberal Party rules for thirty-two years and then comes the February Revolution. Working back from 1870, it is thirty years to the death of Doctor Francia, and fifty-nine to the Independence revolt. All of that is most likely coincidental, however. After all, nothing much happened in 1966, as might be expected if we were dealing with a scientific theory. It is true that President Alfredo Stroessner had the constitution changed in 1967, but that was hardly a watershed event. But for those who believe in portents, there should be a major regime change toward the end of the 1990s.

In the meantime, within those grand cycles covering the Liberal Era generations followed each other, if not with clocklike regularity, at least with enough regularity to suggest a pattern. A simple example can be had by taking the outstanding figure from each generation and checking the difference in ages. Between Caballero and Decoud the spread is nine years; between Decoud and Báez it is fourteen; between Báez and Gondra it is eleven; between Gondra and Guggiari it is thirteen, and it is the same between Guggiari and Rafael Franco; from Franco to Efraím Cardoso, the most famous of the New Liberals, it is nine. In other words, the spread between one generation in politics and the next is about ten or eleven years. Each generation modifies the agenda of the previous one, and about every three generations one may expect (though not with certainty) a really major change of regime.

Such are the tentative conclusions about Paraguayan politics that one might offer from this examination of a particularly significant and complex period of its history. Much more work needs to be done on the Liberal

Era in order to fully understand this fertile seedtime of modern Paraguay, but the effort is certain to be rewarding. Paraguayan politics is not a random affair; it is not mere anarchy. There are "rules of the game" that govern interparty as well as intraparty politics that are as familiar to practicing politicians today as they were to Bernardino Caballero, Benigno Ferreira, or Eduardo Schaerer. They are the "constants" in an interminable game whose ongoing interest derives from the steady replacement of generational teams on the field of play.

INTRODUCTION

1. Diego Abente, "Foreign Capital, Economic Elites and the State in Paraguay during the Liberal Republic (1870–1936)," *Journal of Latin American Studies* 21, no. 1 (February 1989): 61.

2. Samuel Huntington, *Political Order in Changing Societies* (New Haven: Yale University Press, 1968), 412–20.

3. Maurice Duverger, *Political Parties* (New York: John Wiley & Sons, 1963), xxiii, notes that the term "party" is often applied erroneously to personalistic factions in the ancient Greek and Roman republics, to the followers of the various *condottiere* of Renaissance Italy, the clandestine clubs of revolutionary France, and the local electoral committees, or caucuses, that formed in the late eighteenth and early nineteenth century in the United States and England. But true parties, as we now know them, came into existence only with the extension of the suffrage, around 1830 in the United States and about three decades later in England.

4. Huntington, *Political Order*, 414–15. Huntington's discussion of the origins of factions follows closely that of Duverger, *Political Parties*, xxiv. For a different theory of factional and party origins, see Angelo Panebianco, *Political Parties: Organization and Power* (Cambridge: Cambridge University Press, 1988), 50. Panebianco prefers to divide parties as to whether they emerge from factions based on "territorial diffusion" or "territorial penetration." In the former case, many locally based factions fuse to form a party, usually retaining a federal structure. In the latter case, national political elites form an organization that then extends itself to the local communities.

5. William Nesbit Chambers, *Political Parties in a New Nation* (New York: Oxford University Press, 1963), 45–48.

6. Eric Wolf and Edward C. Hansen, "*Caudillo* Politics: A Structural Analysis," *Comparative Studies in Society and History* 9 (1967): 168–79.

7. Huntington, *Political Order*, 419.

8. Panebianco, *Political Parties*, 53.

9. Ibid., 60–62; Duverger, *Political Parties*, 64.

10. Duverger, *Political Parties*, book II, chap. 1.

11. Ibid., 215.

12. Byron Nichols, "Las espectativas de los partidos políticos en el Paraguay," *Revista Paraguaya de Sociología* 5 (December 1968): 22–61; Frederick Hicks, "Interpersonal Relationships and Caudillismo in Paraguay," *Journal of Inter-American Studies and World Affairs* 13 (January 1971): 89–111.

13. V. O. Key, *Politics, Parties, and Pressure Groups* (New York: Thomas Y. Crowell, 1962), 227–28.

14. Ibid., 229–30.

15. Duverger, *Political Parties*, 300–301.

16. For an extreme example of the disintegrating effects of political persecution in Paraguay, see Paul H. Lewis, *The Politics of Exile: Paraguay's Febrerista Party* (Chapel Hill: University of North Carolina Press, 1968).

17. Everett C. Ladd, Jr., *American Political Parties: Social Change and Political Response* (New York: W. W. Norton, 1970), 2–7.

18. The classic statement on this is, of course, Roberto Michels's *Political Parties* (New York: Dover Publications, 1959).

19. Panebianco, *Political Parties*, 62.

20. Ibid., 243, 246.

21. José Ortega y Gasset, "El tema de nuestro tiempo," in *Obras completas* (Madrid: Revista de Occidente, 1955), 3:145–49.

22. Karl Mannheim, "The Problem of Generations," in *Essays on the Sociology of Knowledge* (London: Routledge & Kegan Paul, 1952), 276–322.

23. José Ortega y Gasset, *Man and Crisis* (London: Allen & Unwin, 1959), 56–59.

24. Ibid., 55–56.

25. See Anthony Esler, *The Generation Gap in Society and History: A Select Bibliography*, vols. 1 and 2 (Monticello, Ill.: Vance Bibliographies, 1984), for an excellent survey and summary of the entire literature on social generations.

CHAPTER I

1. Controversy exists about how many Paraguayans died during the war. Vera Blinn Reber revises sharply downward earlier estimates that about half the population was wiped out, in "The Demographics of Paraguay: A Reinterpretation of the Great War, 1864–1870," *Hispanic American Historical Review* 68, no. 2 (May 1988): 289–319. But see also Thomas L. Whigman and Barbara Potthast, "Some Strong Reservations: A Critique of Vera Blinn Reber's 'The Demographics of Paraguay . . . ,'" *Hispanic American Historical Review* 70, no. 4 (November 1990): 667–75.

2. Justo Prieto, *Manual del ciudadano liberal paraguayo* (Buenos Aires: Editorial Asunción, 1953), 12–13; Epifanio Méndez, *Lo histórico y lo antihistorico en el Paraguay* (Buenos Aires: Artes Gráficos Negri, 1976), 23–70.

3. Juan B. Gill Aguinagua, *La Asociación Paraguaya en la Guerra de la Triple Alianza* (Buenos Aires: n.p., 1959), 24.

4. Ibid., 33–36, 39; Harris Gaylord Warren, *Paraguay and the Triple Alliance: The Postwar Decade, 1869–1878* (Austin: University of Texas Press, 1978), 49–50.

5. Héctor Francisco Decoud, *Sobre los escombros de la guerra: una década de la vida nacional, 1869–1880* (Asunción: n.p., 1925), 68. See also his *Los emigrados paraguayos en la Guerra de la Triple Alianza* (Buenos Aires: L. J. Rosso, 1930). As a very young man, Decoud was a participant in the events he described.

6. This figure is from Decoud, *Sobre los escombros*, 58. Carlos R. Centurión,

Historia de la cultura paraguaya (Asunción: Biblioteca "Ortiz Guerrero," 1961), 1:283–85, and Gill Aguinagua, *La Asociación Paraguaya, 59*, put the Legion's strength at no more than 225. I accept Decoud's figure as being from a primary source.

7. Centurión, *Historia de la cultura*, 1:283–85; Arturo Bray, *Hombres y épocas del Paraguay* (Asunción: El Lector, 1986), 2:129.

8. Decoud, *Sobre los escombros*, 103–5; F. Arturo Bordón, *Historia política del Paraguay* (Asunción: Orbis, 1976), 43; Warren, *Triple Alliance*, 50, 179; Centurión, *Historia de la cultura*, 1:283–85; Bray, *Hombres y épocas*, 2:129.

9. Decoud, *Sobre los escombros*, 57. Among the Liberals who deny any claim between their party and the Legion, see Manuel Pesoa, *Origenes del Partido Liberal Paraguayo, 1870–1887* (Asunción: Criterio Ediciones, 1987), 13; Justo Pastor Benítez, "Progenie de los Liberales," in *Ensayos sobre el liberalismo paraguayo* (Asunción: n.p., 1932), 203; and F. Arturo Bordón, *La verdad en su lugar* (Asunción: Libro del Oro de Liberalismo Paraguayo, 1971), 24.

10. For the politics involved in forming the first postwar provisional government, see Decoud, *Sobre los escombros*, 84–95, 121–44; Gómez Freire Esteves, *Historia contemporánea del Paraguay: lucha de cancillerías en El Plata* (Buenos Aires: n.p., 1921), 2–7; Warren, *Triple Alliance*, 53–56.

11. Freire Esteves, *Historia contemporánea*, 13, records these changes, but the details of the split remain obscure. However, there seems to have been great resentment aroused, for during the elections of 3 July 1870 Rufino Taboada was jailed after physically attacking Facundo Machaín.

12. Rogelio Urizar, *Los dramas de nuestra anarquía* (Asunción: Editorial Fundación Ross, 1989), 1:14; Decoud, *Sobre los escombros*, 145–47.

13. Decoud, *Sobre los escombros*, 121–44.

14. Bordón, *Historia política*, 49–52; John Hoyt Williams, *The Rise and Fall of the Paraguayan Republic, 1800–1870* (Austin: University of Texas Press, 1979), 225.

15. Bordón, *Historia política*, 56–57.

16. Warren, *Triple Alliance*, 161–62.

17. On election violence, see ibid., 78–79; and Bordón, *Historia política*, 59. For the electoral results, see Centurión, *Historia de la cultura*, 1:318–19; and Freire Esteves, *Historia contemporánea*, 13.

18. The events of the session of 31 August, and its immediate consequences, are covered in Freire Esteves, *Historia contemporánea*, 14–18; Warren, *Triple Alliance*, 81–88; and *Revista del Paraguay* 1, no. 7 (July 1892): 313.

19. Pesoa, *Origenes*, 22–23. On the other hand, Juansilvano Godoi, Machaín's right-hand man, was said to be a devotee of French liberal thought. See Centurión, *Historia de la cultura*, 1:328.

CHAPTER 2

1. Diego Abente, "The Liberal Republic and the Failure of Democracy in Paraguay," *The Americas* 45, no. 4 (April 1989): 533.

2. Harris Gaylord Warren, *Paraguay and the Triple Alliance: The Postwar Decade, 1869–1878* (Austin: University of Texas Press, 1978), 56, 64, 100.

3. Manuel Pesoa, *Orígenes del Partido Liberal Paraguayo, 1870–1887* (Asunción: Criterio Ediciones, 1987), 25.

4. Pesoa, *Orígenes,* 25; F. Arturo Bordón, *Historia política del Paraguay* (Asunción: Orbis, 1976), 67. Recalde had been a Legionnaire of the Iturburu faction and had come to know Bareiro through the Club Unión Republicana. He also was elected to the Constitutional Convention on the Club del Pueblo ticket. According to Warren, he was a troublemaker who did his best to disrupt the sessions. See Warren, *Triple Alliance,* 80.

5. Pesoa, *Orígenes,* 27; Warren, *Triple Alliance,* 103.

6. On Ferreira's career, see Carlos R. Centurión, *Historia de la cultura paraguaya* (Asunción: Biblioteca "Ortiz Guerrero," 1961), 2:276–77; Warren, *Triple Alliance,* 179–80; and William Belmont Parker, *Paraguayans of Today* (Buenos Aires: Hispanic Society of America, 1920), 215–18. A very laudatory biography is by Jaime Sosa Escalada, *El General Ferreira* (Asunción: Jordán y Villaamil, 1906); and a highly unfavorable one is Ricardo Brugada's *Benigno Ferreira* (Asunción: El Diario, 1906).

7. Warren, *Triple Alliance,* 139; Teodosio González, *Infortunios del Paraguay* (Buenos Aires: L. J. Rosso, 1931), 103–23.

8. Warren, *Triple Alliance,* 177.

9. Gómez Freire Esteves, *Historia contemporánea del Paraguay: luchas de cancillerías en El Plata* (Buenos Aires: n.p., 1921), 27; Warren, *Triple Alliance,* 121–23.

10. Arturo Bray, *Hombres y épocas del Paraguay* (Asunción: El Lector, 1986), 2:141; Warren, *Triple Alliance,* 201–2.

11. Bordón, *Historia política,* 119–28. See also Rogelio Urizar, *Los dramas de nuestra anarquía* (Asunción: Editorial Fundación Ross, 1989), 1:39.

12. This description of the 1873 revolts is from Freire Esteves, *Historia contemporánea,* 29–30; Bordón, *Historia política,* 81–100; and Warren, *Triple Alliance,* 196–202.

13. The 1874 revolt and its aftermath are recounted in Freire Esteves, *Historia contemporánea,* 30–31; Bordón, *Historia política,* 100–111; Pesoa, *Orígenes,* 37.

14. For the executive committee of Ferreira's Partido Liberal, see Pesoa, *Orígenes,* 31; for Gill's electoral committee, see ibid., 54.

15. Urizar, *Los dramas,* 1:41–42; Freire Esteves, *Historia contemporánea,* 31–33.

16. The revolts of March and April 1874 are covered in greater detail in Bordón, *Historia política,* 111–13, 133–42; Freire Esteves, *Historia contemporánea,* 31–32; Urizar, *Los dramas,* 1:41–42; and Warren, *Triple Alliance,* 213–14.

17. For the best coverage of these diplomatic moves, see Warren, *Triple Alliance,* 241–61. See also Antonio Salúm-Flecha, *Historia diplomática del Paraguay, de 1869 a 1938* (Asunción: Emasa, 1972), 47–66.

18. Juan Carlos Herken Krauer, *El Paraguay rural entre 1869 y 1913* (Asunción: Centro Paraguayo de Estudios Sociológicos, 1984), 108–9, 123–38.

19. Gill's economic policies are discussed in Warren, *Triple Alliance,* 221–27, 264–67, 271; Salúm Flecha, *Historia diplomática,* 61; and Ricardo Caballero Aquino,

La Segunda República Paraguaya, 1869–1906 (Asunción: Arte Nuevo Editores, 1985), 85, 101, 107–8.

20. As the assassins ran from the scene of the crime they encountered, by accident, the president's brother, General Emilio Gill, whom they also killed. Juansilvano Godoi was out of the country when the assassination took place. His brother, Nicanor, who did the actual shooting, managed to escape to exile.

21. On Sociabilidad Paraguaya, see Freire Esteves, *Historia contemporánea,* 45–46.

22. According to Héctor Francisco Decoud, the charges against Machaín were brought by a young man named Ildefonso Benegas, who later helped to found the Liberal Party and to launch the 1904 revolution that brought it to power. See his *Tragedia de la cárcel pública: 29 de octubre 1877* (Asunción: Archivo del Liberalismo, 1988), 21.

23. Freire Esteves, *Historia contemporánea,* 47.

24. See Decoud, *Tragedia de la cárcel pública,* for a thorough description of these events. Also, Freire Esteves, *Historia contemporánea,* 45–49; and Pesoa, *Origenes,* 61.

25. Harris Gaylord Warren, *The Rebirth of the Paraguayan Republic* (Pittsburgh: University of Pittsburgh Press, 1985), 43.

26. Warren, *Rebirth,* 46, does not believe that Bareiro ordered Rivarola's murder. Rather, he puts the blame chiefly on Caballero and Colonel Juan A. Meza. Colonel Meza and General Ignacio Genes are credited with the actual killing. Both were jailed as part of a phony investigation to make it appear that the government was trying to solve the crime. Genes, who apparently was considered unreliable, was murdered in prison, but Meza later became minister of interior (!) when General Caballero became president. See also, Warren, *Triple Alliance,* 279.

27. Freire Esteves, *Historia contemporánea,* 55.

CHAPTER 3

1. The list of Club Libertad executive committee members is from Manuel Pesoa, *Origenes del Partido Liberal Paraguayo, 1870–1887* (Asunción: Criterio Ediciones, 1987), 61–62. The Gran Club men were Agusto Calcena, the Club Libertad's vice-president, and Agustín Cañete, who had served in the Constitutional Convention of 1870. The ex-Gill supporters were José González Granados and Genaro Jovellanos. Those from Bareiro's Club del Pueblo were Cirilo Solalinde, Miguel Haedo (the president of that organization), and Juan G. González, who also had been a Legionnaire.

2. The four novices who later became founders of the Centro Democrático were Antonio Zayas, José Z. Caminos, José M. Meza, and Felipe Torrents. The first two were secretaries of the Club Libertad. The fifth man who became a Centro Democrático founder was Cirilo Solalinde, who had been elected to the 1870 Constitutional Convention on Bareiro's Club del Pueblo ticket.

3. Gómez Freire Esteves, *Historia contemporánea del Paraguay: luchas de cancillerías en El Plata* (Buenos Aires: n.p., 1921), 53. The finance minister at the time was José A. Bazaras, José Segundo Decoud having moved to the Foreign Ministry in July 1879 to replace Benjamín Aceval.

4. F. Arturo Bordón, *Historia política del Paraguay* (Asunción: Orbis, 1976), 191–93.

5. Pesoa, *Origenes*, 71–72.

6. Harris Gaylord Warren, *Paraguay and the Triple Alliance: The Postwar Decade* (Austin: University of Texas Press, 1978), 178–79, 278; and Warren, *The Rebirth of the Paraguayan Republic* (Pittsburgh: University of Pittsburgh Press, 1985), 51–57.

7. Warren, *Triple Alliance*, 279. Bareiro apparently was upset when he heard of Rivarola's murder and denied any complicity in it to the Brazilian ambassador. See Warren, *Rebirth*, 46.

8. Juan Carlos Herken Krauer, *El Paraguay rural entre 1869 y 1913* (Asunción: Centro Paraguayo de Estudios Sociológicos, 1984), 169. See also Diego Abente, "The Liberal Republic and the Failure of Democracy in Paraguay," *The Americas* 45, no. 4 (April 1989): 525–45. Abente (p. 537) specifically locates the *jefes políticos'* influence with the peasants in their control of credit necessary to finance harvests.

9. Abente, "The Liberal Republic and the Failure of Democracy," 536, ascribes the predominance of clientelistic politics over class politics to the power and influence of the *jefes políticos* and to the enfranchisement of the peasants under the 1870 Constitution. The latter provided a mass electorate, which the *jefes políticos* were able to organize to suit their own ends. Although Abente does not make a point of it, the linkage between a *jefe político* and his followers was cemented as much by paternalism, marriage, and god-parentage as it was by economic considerations.

10. Pesoa, *Origenes*, 74.

11. For a roster of the Club Libertad's executive committee, as well as its ordinary members, see Freire Esteves, *Historia contemporánea*, 55; and Bordón, *Historia política*, 195–96.

12. Warren, *Rebirth*, 43–44; Ricardo Caballero Aquino, *La Segunda República Paraguaya, 1869–1906* (Asunción: Arte Nuevo Editores, 1985), 123.

13. On rural conditions in the 1880s, see Herken Krauer, *El Paraguay rural*, 91–92, 94, 115–18, 123–41.

14. Carlos Pastore, *La lucha por la tierra en el Paraguay* (Montevideo: Editorial Antequera, 1972), 251.

15. Decoud's program for Paraguay had been published already in his *Cuestiones políticas y económicas* (Asunción: n.p., 1877).

16. Decoud, *Cuestiones*, 8, 11–13.

17. Pastore, *La lucha por la tierra*, 213–22, 253–56; Efraím Cardoso, *Breve historia del Paraguay* (Buenos Aires: Editorial Universitaria de Buenos Aires, 1965), 112–13.

18. Warren, *Rebirth*, 57, 60–61; Caballero Aquino, *La Segunda República*, 142–44.

19. Freire Esteves, *Historia contemporánea,* 57.

20. Pastore, *La Lucha por la tierra,* 223–32, 234, 245–46.

21. Caballero Aquino, *La Segunda República,* 142–43; Freire Esteves, *Historia contemporánea,* 61.

22. For the Club del Pueblo's membership, see Freire Esteves, *Historia contemporánea,* 60; Pesoa, *Origenes,* 89; Bordón, *Historia política,* 200; and Carlos R. Centurión, *Historia de la cultura paraguaya* (Asunción: Biblioteca "Ortiz Guerrero," 1961), 1:336.

23. Pesoa, *Origenes,* 88–89.

24. In 1887 Decoud was replaced at Foreign Affairs by another military hero, Colonel Juan Crisóstomo Centurión, who was instrumental that year in organizing the Colorado Party. Also in 1887, Cañete was replaced at Finance by former president Higinio Uriarte, who had been in office when the massacre at the Public Prison took place. He had been Gill's cousin, and was now related to Caballero by marriage, since Caballero had married Gill's widow.

25. Pesoa, *Origenes,* 87–92.

26. Ibid., 119–25; Warren, *Rebirth,* 72.

27. Warren, *Rebirth,* 73, puts the number of founding members at 134, but does not give their names. On the other hand, Centurión, *Historia de la cultura,* 1:409–10, lists all 128 of the names on the manifesto announcing the founding of the Centro Democrático. Pesoa, *Origenes,* 165, follows him in this, and I accept their account as being better substantiated.

28. Warren, *Rebirth,* 238.

29. Freire Esteves, *Historia contemporánea,* 64. Colonel Juan Crisóstomo Centurión had been López's "hanging judge" at the trumped-up treason trials held near the end of the war, which sent many an innocent person to his death. An educated man who had studied abroad as a scholarship student under López, he practiced law after the war and served as attorney general under Caballero. He had a leading role in revising the postwar criminal code.

30. Leandro Prieto Yegros, ed., *Enciclopedia Republicana: itinerario colorado de la causa nacional, 1880–1904* (Asunción: Editorial Universo, 1983), 210.

CHAPTER 4

1. Harris Gaylord Warren, *The Rebirth of the Paraguayan Republic* (Pittsburgh: University of Pittsburgh Press, 1985), 74–75; Arturo Bray, *Hombres y épocas del Paraguay* (Asunción: El Lector, 1986), 1:111.

2. Warren, *Rebirth,* 75.

3. Saturnino Ferreira Pérez, *Antecedentes del Centro Democrático: El golpe de 18 de octubre de 1891, su fusión con el Partido Liberal Histórico* (Asunción: Ediciones Comuneros, 1988), 83–96; Warren, *Rebirth,* 77; Rogelio Urizar, *Los dramas de nuestra anarquía* (Asunción: Editorial Fundación Ross, 1989), 1:80.

4. Warren, *Rebirth,* 76.

5. Although a member of the Asociación Paraguaya and the Legion, Egus-

quiza's family was related to the Lópezes, and his brother, Félix, had been Francisco Solano López's diplomatic representative. After the war he settled on an *estancia* near Encarnación and became the region's *jefe político*. During the fighting of 1873–74 he joined in at first on Benigno Ferreira's side and contributed to the victory at Paraguarí; but in the following year he switched over to Caballero. Afterward he returned to his ranch and mixed no more in politics until 1881, when he lent his support to the Club Libertad that was backing Caballero's campaign for the presidency. He also joined the Club del Pueblo that supported Escobar for president. See Héctor Francisco Decoud, *Sobre los escombros de la guerra: une década de la vida nacional, 1869–1880* (Asunción: n.p., 1925), 48; and Pastor Fretes y Britos, "Un hombre de estado," *Revista del Paraguay* 2, no. 8 (1892): part 1, 337–52, and no. 9 (1892): part 2, 385–98.

6. With respect to a more liberal emphasis, it is well to note, however, that Caballero's influence was still strong. As we have seen, President González was his brother-in-law and Vice-President Morínigo was his son-in-law. Moreover, his nephew, Facundo Ynsfrán, would replace Benjamín Aceval at the Justice and Education Ministry the following year. Finally, Venancio López, the foreign affairs minister, was the grandson of Carlos Antonio López and nephew of Francisco Solano López.

7. Ricardo Caballero Aquino, *La Segunda República Paraguaya, 1869–1906* (Asunción: Arte Nuevo Editores, 1985), 161–64.

8. *Revista del Paraguay* 2, no. 3 (March 1892): 83–131, for details of the October 1891 revolt.

9. Besides Facundo Machaín, whose assassination was described in Chapter 2, there was Juan José Machaín, who died in prison under the dictatorship of Dr. Francia.

10. Gómez Freire Esteves, *Historia contemporánea del Paraguay: luchas de cancillerías en El Plata* (Buenos Aires: n.p., 1921), 69–70.

11. Warren, *Rebirth*, 85.

12. Ibid., 37.

13. For the Colorado Party's official history of this campaign, see Leandro Prieto Yegros, ed., *Enciclopedia Republicana: itinerario colorado de la causa nacional, 1880–1904* (Asunción: Editorial Universo, 1983), 330–32.

14. Maciel had served as minister of interior and also as minister of justice under President Escobar.

15. Diego Abente, "Foreign Capital, Economic Elites and the State in Paraguay during the Liberal Republic (1870–1936)," *Journal of Latin American Studies* 21, no. 1 (February 1989): 78–79.

16. Ferreira Pérez, *Antecedentes del Centro Democrático*, 231–36.

17. Warren, *Rebirth*, 90–91; Freire Esteves, *Historia contemporánea*, 75. Ynsfrán had replaced Benjamín Aceval as minister of justice and education and had served for a year in that post. Gondra, wounded by what he considered Eguisquiza's betrayal, later moved permanently to Argentina and became very successful in business.

18. Warren, *Rebirth*, 98–100; Ferreira Pérez, *Antecedentes del Centro Democrático*, 236–37.

19. Caballero Aquino, *La Segunda República*, 183–84, 188.

20. Juan Carlos Herken Krauer, *El Paraguay rural entre 1869 y 1913* (Asunción: Centro Paraguayo de Estudios Sociológicos, 1984), 91, 116; Freire Esteves, *Historia contemporánea*, 77, 79; Warren, *Rebirth*, 189–90.

21. Caballero Aquino, *La Segunda República*, 227.

22. Ibid., 221–22, 231.

23. Freire Esteves, *Historia contemporánea*, 78–80; Caballero Aquino, *La Segunda República*, 239.

24. Paraguay, Ministerio de Relaciones Exteriores, *Datos estadísticos* (1882–1907); Warren, *Rebirth*, 15, 17.

CHAPTER 5

1. Carlos R. Centurión, *Historia de la cultura paraguaya* (Asunción: Biblioteca "Ortiz Guerrero," 1961), 1:433.

2. Efraím Cardoso, *Breve historia del Paraguay* (Buenos Aires: Editorial Universitaria de Buenos Aires, 1965), 127.

3. Leandro Prieto Yegros, ed., *Enciclopedia Republicana: itinerario colorado de la causa nacional, 1880–1904* (Asunción: Editorial Universo, 1983), 361–62; Harris Gaylord Warren, *The Rebirth of the Paraguayan Republic* (Pittsburgh: University of Pittsburgh Press, 1985), 103.

4. Gómez Freire Esteves, *Historia contemporánea del Paraguay: luchas de cancillerías en El Plata* (Buenos Aires: n.p., 1921), 77, 79.

5. Ibid., 77, 79; Centurión, *Historia de la cultura*, 1:528.

6. Centurión, *Historia de la cultura*, 1:427; Warren, *Rebirth*, 100.

7. Ricardo Caballero Aquino, *La Segunda República Paraguaya, 1869–1906* (Asunción: Arte Nuevo Editores, 1985), 190.

8. Ibid., 194; Freire Esteves, *Historia contemporánea*, 82–85; Warren, *Rebirth*, 108; Cardoso, *Breve historia*, 117–18.

9. Freire Esteves, *Historia contemporánea*, 82–85. Warren argues that the reputation Aceval got for indecisiveness was undeserved and that his many achievements in the areas of education, health, agricultural and industrial promotion, and finance "mark him as a very good administrator and the only president since 1869 who approached greatness" (*Rebirth*, 108).

10. Ibid., 109–10.

11. Ibid., 110.

12. V. O. Key, "A Theory of Critical Elections," *Journal of Politics* 17 (February 1955): 4.

13. Angus Campbell, Philip Converse, Warren Miller, and Donald Stokes, *The American Voter* (New York: John Wiley & Sons, 1960), 531–34.

14. Gerald Pomper, "Classification of Presidential Elections," *Journal of Politics* 29 (August 1967): 535–66.

15. Walter Dean Burnham, *Critical Elections and the Mainsprings of American Politics* (New York: W. W. Norton, 1970), 2, 6–8, 10, 26.

16. Mark N. Hagopian, *The Phenomenon of Revolution* (New York: Dodd, Mead, 1974), 6–9, for a classification of coups.

17. On the technique of coups, see Curzio Malaparte, *Coup d'Etat: The Technique of Revolution* (New York: E. P. Dutton, 1932); D. J. Goodspeed, *The Conspirators: A Study of the Coup d'Etat* (Toronto: Macmillan, 1967); Edward Luttwak, *Coup d'Etat: A Practical Handbook* (Cambridge: Harvard University Press, 1979); Samuel E. Finer, *The Man On Horseback* (New York: Frederick A. Praeger, 1962); and Gregor Ferguson, *Coup d'Etat: A Practical Manual* (Dorset, Great Britain: Arms and Armour Press, 1987). But on the particular type of unit needed for rapid success, see especially Eric A. Nordlinger, *Soldiers in Politics: Military Coups and Governments* (Englewood Cliffs, N.J.: Prentice-Hall, 1977), 102–3, 105–6.

18. Freire Esteves, *Historia contemporánea*, 85–86; Warren, *Rebirth*, 116–17.

19. Warren, *Rebirth*, 118.

20. Ibid., 111–14.

21. Diego Abente, "Foreign Capital, Economic Elites and the State in Paraguay during the Liberal Republic (1870–1936)," *Journal of Latin American Studies* 21, no. 1 (February 1989): 81–82, observes that "The defection of the mercantile class was triggered by the July and October 1903 economic policy package." It subsequently lent its support to the revolutionary movement that overthrew the government the following year. One of the new regime's first acts was to repeal those economic measures.

22. Caballero Aquino, *La Segunda República*, 204–7; Juan Carlos Herken Krauer, *La política económica durante la era liberal* (Asunción: Archivo del Liberalismo, 1989), 59.

23. Susana Rodrígues Viana de Quintana, wife of the Argentine president, personally contributed 5,000 gold pesos to the rebels. The Argentine navy opened its arsenal to them too. Argentine volunteers, including some naval officers, accompanied the rebel forces. Caballero Aquino, *La Segunda República*, 208.

24. Freire Esteves, *Historia contemporánea*, 90–98.

25. Caballero Aquino, *La Segunda República*, 215; Freire Esteves, *Historia contemporánea*, 97.

26. For a thorough treatment of the Liberals' debates about the peace treaty (known as the Pact of Pilcomayo), see Rogelio Urizar, *Los dramas de nuestra anarquía* (Asunción: Editorial Fundación Ross, 1989), 1:162–80.

27. Freire Esteves, *Historia contemporánea*, 102; Caballero Aquino, *La Segunda República*, 215.

28. Cardoso, *Breve*, 126.

29. Centurión, *Historia de la cultura*, 1:568–70.

30. Caballero Aquino, *La Segunda República*, 214–15.

31. For a description of Ferreira's policies and the politics inside his government, see Arturo Bray, *Hombres y épocas del Paraguay* (Asunción: El Lector, 1986), 2:145–48; Alfredo L. Jaeggli, *Albino Jara: un varón meteórico* (Buenos Aires: Editorial Lumén, 1963), 89–90, 94–95.

32. Centurión, *Historia de la cultura*, 1:529.

33. Duarte was also a personal enemy of Elías García, the police chief. They had been on opposite sides in the 1905 coup that overthrew President Gaona. García had revolted against Gaona while Duarte had supported him.

34. Freire Esteves, *Historia contemporánea*, 109.

35. Justo Pastor Benítez, *Ensayos sobre el liberalismo paraguayo* (Asunción: n.p., 1932), 36. General Ferreira died in 1920, at the age of seventy-four.

CHAPTER 6

1. Juan Carlos Herken Krauer, *La política económica durante la era liberal* (Asunción: Archivo del Liberalismo, 1989), 70.

2. Gómez Freire Esteves, *Historia contemporánea del Paraguay: luchas de cancillerías en El Plata* (Buenos Aires: n.p., 1921), 91–92; Arturo Bray, *Hombres y épocas del Paraguay* (Asunción: El Lector, 1986), 1:127–28.

3. Bray, *Hombres y épocas*, 1:130, 132–34.

4. For a biography of Albino Jara, see Alfredo L. Jaeggli, *Albino Jara: un varón meteórico* (Buenos Aires: Editorial Lumén, 1963).

5. Rogelio Urizar, *Los dramas de nuestra anarquía* (Asunción: Editorial Fundación Ross, 1989), 1:272.

6. Jaeggli, *Albino Jara*, 220.

7. Urizar, *Los dramas*, 1:274–80.

8. For background on the PCRC's relations with the state, up to 1908, see Harris Gaylord Warren, "The Paraguayan Central Railway, 1889–1907," *Inter-American Economic Affairs* 21 (Summer 1967): 31–48. On the PCRC's role in politics under the Radicals, see Juan Carlos Herken Krauer, *Ferrocarriles, conspiraciones, y negocios en el Paraguay, 1910–1914* (Asunción: Arte Nuevo Editores, 1984).

9. Freire Esteves, *Historia contemporánea*, 120.

10. Ibid.

11. For a description of the Rojas presidency and the second Radical invasion, see Urizar, *Los dramas*, 1:319–51; also Freire Esteves, *Historia contemporánea*, 120–25.

12. On the so-called Portuguese loan, see Teodosio González, *Infortunios del Paraguay* (Buenos Aires: L. J. Rosso, 1931), 124–28; Freire Esteves, *Historia contemporánea*, 121; and Herken Krauer, *Ferrocarriles, conspiraciones y negocios*, 63–71, 81–83.

13. Urizar, *Los dramas*, 1:341, 344–47; Freire Esteves, *Historia contemporánea*, 123.

14. Urizar, *Los dramas*, 1:354–55.

15. Ibid., 1:374.

16. Freire Esteves, *Historia contemporánea*, 130–31, 302–5.

17. Diego Abente, "Foreign Capital, Economic Elites and the State in Paraguay during the Liberal Republic (1870–1936)," *Journal of Latin American Studies* 21, no. 1 (February 1989): 85–86, argues that the creation of the new Exchange Board in 1916 was "the most radical economic decision since the enactment of

the sale of public lands" because it took control of monetary policy out of the hands of the banking and mercantile elites and put it in the hands of the state.

18. Freire Esteves, *Historia contemporánea*, 136.

19. The following sketch of diplomatic relations between Bolivia and Paraguay involving the Chaco is taken from Leslie B. Rout, Jr., *The Politics of the Chaco Peace Conference, 1935–1939* (Austin: University of Texas Press, 1970), chap. 1; David H. Zook, Jr., *The Conduct of the Chaco War* (New York: Bookman Associates, 1960), chap. 1; and Antonio Salúm-Flecha, *Historia diplomática del Paraguay, de 1869 a 1938* (Asunción: Emasa, 1972), 70–76, 84–91, 127–36.

20. Freire Esteves, *Historia contemporánea*, 132–33; Urizar, *Los dramas*, 2:386–89. Besides Gómez Freire Esteves, his brother, Luís, J. Rodolfo Bordón, and Bernardino Caballero, grandson of the Colorado leader, were all involved in the 1936 February Revolution.

21. Urizar, *Los dramas*, 2:396–97.

CHAPTER 7

1. Diego Abente, "Foreign Capital, Economic Elites and the State in Paraguay during the Liberal Republic (1870–1936)," *Journal of Latin American Studies* 21, no. 1 (February 1989): 85–86, views these reforms in a more positive light than I do. Besides weakening the mercantile elites in the all-important area of monetary policy, he argues, the 1916 reform law "also marked the beginning of a process of reversal of the privatisation trend sparked by the wholesale dilapidation of the national patrimony in the 1880s." And it also "set the basis for a permanent role for the state in the management of the foreign trade of the nation."

2. Efraím Cardoso, *23 de octubre: una página de historia contemporánea del Paraguay* (Buenos Aires: Editorial Guayrá, 1956), 21.

3. Alfredo L. Jaeggli, *Albino Jara: un varón meteórico* (Buenos Aires: Editorial Lumén, 1963), 202.

4. Justo Pastor Benítez, "Un tribuno del pueblo: Lisandro Díaz León," in *Ensayos sobre el liberalismo paraguayo* (Asunción: n.p., 1932), 221–24; Carlos R. Centurión, *Historia de la cultura paraguaya* (Asunción: Biblioteca "Ortiz Guerrero," 1961), 2:51–52.

5. Centurión, *Historia de la cultura*, 2:429–34; William Belmont Parker, *Paraguayans of Today* (Buenos Aires: Hispanic Society of America, 1920), 199–200.

6. Rogelio Urizar, *Los dramas de nuestra anarquía* (Asunción: Editorial Fundación Ross, 1989), 2:404–5; Cardoso, *23 de octubre*, 22.

7. Urizar, *Los dramas*, 2:409.

8. Arturo Bray, *Armas y letras* (Asunción: Ediciones Napa, 1981), 1:123.

9. Urizar, *Los dramas*, 2:423–24.

10. *La Prensa*, 6 November 1922, 8.

11. For the Liberal directorate elected 14 May 1922, see Urizar, *Los dramas*, 2:428. Names of leading *schaereristas* can be found in Tomás de los Santos, *La revolución de 1922*, 2 vols. (Asunción: El Lector, 1984), esp. 27.

12. Concerning Peña's tactics, see Cardoso, *23 de octubre*, 22–23; Urizar, *Los dramas*, 2:425, 429, 433; Bray, *Armas y letras*, 1:127; de los Santos, *La revolución de 1922*, 7.

13. Bray, *Armas y letras*, 1:95, 99, 101–2; Juan Speratti, *Política militar paraguaya* (Buenos Aires: ABECE, 1955), 32–34, 97–98, 105.

14. Quoted in Urizar, *Los dramas*, 2:519.

15. Ibid., 2:463–64, 483, 485.

16. Bray, *Armas y letras*, 1:134–35, accuses Ayala of "myopic pacifism."

17. Urizar, *Los dramas*, 1:593. See also Bray, *Armas y letras*, 1:134; and de los Santos, *La revolución de 1922*, 2:58.

18. Having been appointed only *ad interim* to fill out the remainder of Gondra's term, Ayala was eligible. The constitutional restriction against immediate reelection did not apply.

19. This connection to Eusebio Ayala is mentioned in Alfredo M. Seiferheld, *Estigarribia: veinte años de política paraguaya* (Asunción: Editorial Laurel, 1982), 411. Bordenave had once been close to Eduardo Schaerer, serving as his presidential secretary and working on his paper, *El Diario*. This may be why Schaerer believed he could trust Eusebio Ayala as provisional president in 1922. When Schaerer turned against Ayala, Bordenave broke with him.

20. On the controversies surrounding the Benítez and Riart appointments, see Urizar, *Los dramas*, 2:637, 653; and Efraím Cardoso, *Breve historia del Paraguay* (Buenos Aires: Editorial Universitaria de Buenos Aires, 1965), 123.

21. Eligio Ayala, *Migraciones* (Santiago de Chile: n.p., 1941).

22. Ibid., 55.

23. Ibid., 50, 56, 60–61.

24. Teodosio González, *Infortunios del Paraguay* (Buenos Aires: L. J. Rosso, 1931), 168.

25. Lorenzo M. Livieres Guggiari, *El financiamiento de la defensa del Chaco, 1924–1935: un desafío al liberalismo económico* (Asunción: Arte Nuevo Editores, 1983), 83–84; Gómez Freire Esteves, *Historia contemporánea del Paraguay: luchas de cancillerías en El Plata* (Buenos Aires: n.p., 1921), 308–9; Arturo Bray, *Hombres y épocas del Paraguay* (Asunción: El Lector, 1986), 1:143–44.

26. Livieres Guggiari, *El financiamiento*, 33, 83–84.

27. Carlos Pastore, *La lucha por la tierra en el Paraguay* (Montevideo: Editorial Antequera, 1972), 299; Juan Carlos Herken Krauer, *El Paraguay rural entre 1869 y 1913* (Asunción: Centro Paraguayo de Estudios Sociológicos, 1984), 156. According to Pastore, there had been a Homestead Act passed in 1918 that allowed squatters and tenant farmers to acquire up to ten hectares (twenty-five acres) of any unused land. Because the law stipulated that the absentee owners would have to be fully compensated, it had little practical effect. After all, the rural landless had no money and the government's treasury was always empty.

28. Pastore, *La Lucha por la tierra*, 301–6. In the latter case the state would reimburse the owner the price he originally paid for the property, not the current market value. The new peasant owners would have to work their farms themselves and would not be allowed to resell, mortgage, lease, or trade them. Nor

could these farms be subdivided into parcels smaller than six hectares, or merged into cooperatives, or attached for nonpayment of debt. The peasants would repay the state in installments over four years and receive definitive title at the end of that time. In the period 1926–31 some 228,808 hectares (about 572,000 acres) were distributed, mostly from public lands, to some 17,697 families. The average parcel was about thirty-two acres.

29. Ibid., 50–55.

30. George Pendle, *Paraguay: A Riverside Nation* (London: Royal Institute of International Affairs, 1956), 30.

CHAPTER 8

1. See, for example, Rafael Barrett, *El dolor paraguayo* (Caracas: Biblioteca Ayacucho, 1978).

2. Carlos R. Centurión, *Historia de la cultura paraguaya* (Asunción: Biblioteca "Ortiz Guerrero," 1961), 2:425. Efraím Cardoso, *23 de octubre: una página de historia contemporánea del Paraguay* (Buenos Aires: Editorial Guayrá, 1956), 68.

3. Centurión, *Historia de la cultura*, 2:65–66.

4. Juan Speratti, *La revolución de 17 de febrero de 1936* (Asunción: Escuela Técnica Salesiana, 1984), 96–97.

5. Efraím Cardoso, *Breve historia del Paraguay* (Buenos Aires: Editorial Universitaria de Buenos Aires, 1965), 129.

6. Rogelio Urizar, *Los dramas de nuestra anarquía* (Asunción: Editorial Fundación Ross, 1989), 2:690.

7. Cardoso, *23 de octubre*, 33–35.

8. Ibid., 36.

9. Leslie B. Rout, Jr., *The Politics of the Chaco Peace Conference, 1935–1939* (Austin: University of Texas Press, 1970), 13–16.

10. Policarpo Artaza, *Ayala, Estigarribia, y el Partido Liberal* (Buenos Aires: Editorial Ayacucho, 1946), 33–38.

11. Juan Stefanich, *El 23 de octubre de 1931* (Buenos Aires: Editorial Febrero, 1958), 107–11.

12. Urizar, *Los dramas*, 2:600.

13. Arturo Bray, *Armas y letras* (Asunción: Ediciones Napa, 1981), 2:56–58, suggests that Schenoni's reluctance might also have been based on his belief that the Liberals would nominate him for president in 1931. Some Liberals seem to have been hinting as much to him, although the party was officially very opposed to involving military men in politics.

14. Franco still might have marched on the presidential palace after Bray betrayed him, but he was completely fooled by a false report that Bolivia had begun a major attack in the Chaco. Ordered to report immediately to Puerto Casado, he left the other conspirators behind at Campo Grande and, on arriving, was put under arrest. His great popularity still protected him, however, and so he was offered the choice of accepting an extended mission to Europe "to study

military tactics." Proud and indignant, he resigned from the army instead. See Bray, *Armas y letras*, 2:58–68; and Antonio E. González, *Preparación del Paraguay para la Guerra del Chaco* (Asunción: El Gráfico, 1957), 1:151.

15. Urizar, *Los dramas*, 2:699–700.

16. For a description of the political atmosphere in the Colegio Nacional, see Ruperto Resquín, *La generación paraguaya (1928–1932)* (Buenos Aires: Ediciones Paraguay en América, 1978).

17. For the events of 22 and 23 October 1931, see Cardoso, *23 de octubre*, 229–348; and Bray, *Armas y letras*, 2:33–112, for the government's point of view. For the antigovernment view, see Stefanich, *El 23 de octubre de 1931*, 9–23; and Enrique Volta Gaona, *23 de octubre* (Asunción: El Arte, 1957).

18. Justo Prieto, *Llenese los claros* (Buenos Aires: Lucania, 1957). The subtitle of the book is: "An Omission in the Text of the Book *23 de octubre: una página de historia contemporánea del Paraguay*," which suggests that Efraím Cardoso failed to present the whole story of the "23rd of October."

19. Cardoso, *23 de octubre*, 378–89.

20. Alfredo M. Seiferheld, *Estigarribia: veinte años de política paraguaya* (Asunción: Editorial Laurel, 1982), 135.

21. For the basic data about Eusebio Ayala, see Centurión, *Historia de la cultura*, 2:444–48; and William Belmont Parker, *Paraguayans of Today* (Buenos Aires: Hispanic Society of America, 1920), 225–27.

22. George Pendle, *Paraguay: A Riverside Nation* (London: Royal Institute of International Affairs, 1956), 30.

23. Bray, *Armas y letras*, 2:97–98.

24. Ibid., 2:98–99.

25. David H. Zook, Jr., *The Conduct of the Chaco War* (New York: Bookman Associates, 1960), 66–67. Zook cites specific purchases made in Europe to support his argument, but his data actually suggest that most of those happened during Eligio Ayala's administration.

26. Waltrud Q. Morales, "A Comparative Study of Societal Discontent and Revolutionary Change in Bolivia and Paraguay, 1930–1941" (Ph.D. diss., University of Denver, 1977), 81–92.

27. Carlos J. Fernández, *La Guerra del Chaco*, vol. 1 (Buenos Aires: privately published, 1956), 41, 47–48.

28. Quoted in Seiferheld, *Estigarribia*, 31, from an article in *El Liberal*, 6 December 1934, 1.

29. For the Liberal apology on Campo Vía, see Artaza, *Ayala, Estigarribia, y el Partido Liberal*, 79–93. Urizar, *Los dramas*, 2:715–16, is probably closest to the truth in calling the Truce of Campo Vía "an error, not treason."

30. Urizar, *Los dramas*, 2:719. In one of those curious shifts that often happen in Paraguay, Eduardo Schaerer, who had been taken back into the party, had made his peace with his former enemy, Guggiari, and was now helping him to stop Riart. Schaerer himself was too controversial, and also in too poor health, to be considered for the presidency, but his support meant that another obstacle in Ayala's way had been removed.

31. Interview with Federico W. Smith, in Alfredo M. Seiferheld, *Conversaciones político-militares*, vol. 3 (Asunción: El Lector, 1984), 17. Major Eustacio Rojas, another participant in the coup, agreed. He told Seiferheld that there was much hanky-panky involved in promotions and added that "if Estigarribia and Doctor Ayala had been just a little more 'sharp' they would have promoted 500 or 600 officers, with the result that there wouldn't have been the remotest chance of the coup succeeding." See Seiferheld, *Conversaciones político-militares*, vol. 4 (Asunción: El Lector, 1987), 34.

32. Interview with Juan Speratti, in Seiferheld, *Conversaciones*, 3:145–47. See also, Speratti, *La revolución del 17 febrero*, 146–50; and Harris Gaylord Warren, "Political Aspects of the Paraguayan Revolution, 1936–1940," *Hispanic American Historical Review* 30 (February 1950): 2–25.

33. The ceremonies surrounding the "Pantheon of Heroes" are described in Juan Stefanich, *La restauración histórica del Paraguay* (Buenos Aires: Editorial El Mundo Nuevo, 1945).

CHAPTER 9

1. Colonel Smith's assumption that Freire Esteves would be the president gave rise later to a minor controversy when a letter he wrote to a journalist, J. Rodolfo Bordón, suggested that Colonel Franco had usurped the presidency. According to his account, a meeting was held after Franco returned from Argentina to discuss forming a new government. As an honor, Franco was asked to chair the meeting, which he took to mean that he was to be the president. However, Felipe Molas López, a Colorado who participated in the coup, tried to correct this version in a letter he wrote to Smith. According to him, the chief plotters never had anybody in mind for the presidency except Franco and only let Freire Esteves assume the leadership for a few hours until Franco could return. Both letters were published in the appendix to Policarpo Artaza's, *Ayala, Estigarribia, y el Partido Liberal* (Buenos Aires: Editorial Ayacucho, 1946), 240, 243–44. Many years later Smith repeated his story to Alfredo Seiferheld, and added that he had himself refused the plotter's offer of the presidency before he named Freire Esteves. But Juan Speratti, a key coup leader who was designated to receive President Ayala's surrender and resignation, insisted to Seiferheld that Franco was the only man whom the revolutionaries would accept as their president. See Alfredo M. Seiferheld, *Conversaciones político-militares*, vol. 3 (Asunción: El Lector, 1984), 18, 157–58.

2. The text of this Proclamation is from Paraguayan Republic, *La revolución paraguaya* (Asunción: n.p., 1937), 345–49. An English translation can be found in Paul H. Lewis, *The Politics of Exile: Paraguay's Febrerista Party* (Chapel Hill: University of North Carolina Press, 1968), 41–45.

3. Paraguayan Republic, *La revolución paraguaya*, 5–6.

4. The text of Decree Law 152 can be found in Artaza, *Ayala, Estigarribia, y el Partido Liberal*, 155–57; Juan Speratti, *La Revolución del 17 febrero de 1936* (Asun-

ción: Escuela Técnica Salesiana, 1984), 188–89 (though he wrongly gives its date as 10 April); and Saturnino Ferreira Pérez, *Proceso político del Paraguay*, vol. 1 (Asunción: El Lector, 1986), 17–18. As an example of how much Franco was under the influence of the extreme right at this time, Ferreira Pérez quotes him as telling a group of German journalists who visited Paraguay in late February of his admiration for "the brilliant *caudillo* of [the Nazi] revolution, Señor Hitler, one of the purest moral values of postwar Europe" (ibid., 13).

5. Juan Stefanich, *El Paraguay en febrero de 1936* (Buenos Aires: Editorial El Mundo Nuevo, 1946), 42.

6. Roberto Céspedes Ruffinelli, *El febrerismo: del movimiento al partido, 1936–1951* (Asunción: Editorial Luxe, 1983), 49–53.

7. *La revolución paraguaya*, 288–90.

8. Lewis, *Politics of Exile*, 55.

9. Ibid., 50–51.

10. *La revolución paraguaya*, 387–92.

11. Stefanich, *Paraguay en el febrero de 1936*, 104–5, 155–56.

12. Lewis, *Politics of Exile*, 59.

13. The top UNR officers were Stefanich (president); Damián Bruyn, another member of the Liga Nacional Independiente (first vice-president); Pedro Duarte Ortellado, an executive of the ANEC and also minister of health (second vice-president); and Roque Gaona, a former *modestista* deputy and currently editor of the progovernment newspaper, *El Pueblo* (general secretary).

14. Stefanich also defended himself in his memoirs of the Revolution, *La diplomacia de la Revolución* (Buenos Aires: Editorial El Mundo Nuevo, 1945), 68–70, 79–80, 89, 93–94, 98–99.

15. Speratti, *La Revolución*, 276–77, connects Paredes to Justo; but Ferreira Pérez, *Proceso político*, 1:74, mentions only that Schaerer got a loan from the Banco del Hogar Argentino.

16. For the Febrerista view, see Humberto Pérez Cáceres's letter to Alfredo M. Seiferheld, in response to the latter's interview of Sosa Valdéz, in *Conversaciones político-militares*, vol. 1 (Asunción: El Lector, 1984), 186–91, 199. On the other hand, F. Arturo Bordón, a revolutionary who was exiled by Freire Esteves, thinks the government failed in its obligation to supply the troops. He also accepts Paredes's version that Sosa Valdéz was already beginning to march on Asunción and that Paredes went along only to guide the revolt toward saving Franco while ridding him of Stefanich and the other ministers. See his *¡Morínigo! Un paréntesis trágico en la vida democrática del Paraguay* (Asunción: Editora Tavaré, 1975), 14–16. But this is not accepted by most serious writers, who are agreed that Paredes was the prime mover behind the coup. See Arturo Bray, *Armas y letras* (Asunción: Ediciones Napa, 1981), 3:29; and Alfredo M. Seiferheld, *Estigarribia: veinte años de política paraguaya* (Asunción: Editorial Laurel, 1982), 238–39.

17. Amancio Pampliega, interview with Alfredo Seiferheld, in Seiferheld, *Conversaciones*, 3:201.

18. Ferreira Pérez, *Proceso político*, 1:60–67.

19. Sosa Valdéz interview, in Seiferheld, *Conversaciones*, 1:187.

20. Seiferheld, *Estigarribia*, 236.

21. Bordón, *¡Morínigo!*, 15.

22. Céspedes Ruffinelli, *El Febrerismo*, 63. For a history of Febrerismo up to 1964, see Lewis, *Politics of Exile*.

23. Seiferheld, *Estigarribia*, 253–342; and Leslie B. Rout, Jr., *The Politics of the Chaco Peace Conference, 1935–1939* (Austin: University of Texas Press, 1970), 175–209.

24. Seiferheld, *Estigarribia*, 308–15, 332.

25. Ibid., 349.

26. Bray, *Armas y letras*, 3:70–71, 84–86.

27. Ibid., 87–88; Seiferheld, *Estigarribia*, 356–62.

28. Codas was a tax lawyer, Liberal deputy, and general manager of the Banco Agrícola; Dávalos was a physician.

29. Seiferheld, *Estigarribia*, 377–79.

30. Amos J. Peaslee, *Constitutions of Nations* (The Hague: Martinus Nijhoff, 1956), 2:111–31.

31. General Amancio Pampliega, who was present at this meeting, recalled in his memoirs, *Misión cumplida* (Asunción: El Lector, 1984), 25, that "Morínigo never sought nor desired the job of President. Nor had he ever thought about devoting himself to politics. He was a professional [officer, who] . . . received the presidency without struggling for it or even scheming to get it." He was completely surprised by the outcome of the meeting.

32. Augusto Campos Caballero, *Testimonios de un presidente: entrevista al Gral. Higinio Morínigo* (Asunción: El Lector, 1983), 68–70.

33. Pampliega, *Misión cumplida*, 27–36; Ferreira Pérez, *Proceso político*, 1:247–70.

34. Bordón, *¡Morínigo!*, 52, 54.

35. The controversial decree of 25 April 1942 is attacked by Policarpo Artaza in *Ayala, Estigarribia, y el Partido Liberal*, 205–9. For the opposite viewpoint, see Stefanich, *El 23 de octubre*, 238–43; and O. Barcena Echeveste, *Concepción 1947* (Buenos Aires: Juan Pellegrini, 1948), 57–62.

DOCUMENTS, SPEECHES, AND PERIODICALS

Almeida Rojas, Ricardo, ed. *Guía de la Asociación Nacional Republicana*. Asunción: El Arte, 1951.
Asociación Nacional Republicana (Partido Colorado). *Acta de fundación del Partido Colorado y estatutos*. Asunción: Asociación Nacional Republicana, 1969.
————. *Cartillas políticas*. No. 1. Asunción: Junta del Gobierno, 1958.
El estado general de la Nación durante los gobiernos liberales. 2 vols. Asunción: El Archivo del Liberalismo, 1987.
Paraguayan Republic. *La revolución paraguaya*. Asunción: n.p., 1937.
Peaslee, Amos J. *Constitutions of Nations*. Vol. 2. The Hague: Martinus Nijhoff, 1956.
Revista del Paraguay. Buenos Aires, 1891–98.

WORKS BY PARAGUAYAN AUTHORS

Abente, Diego. "Foreign Capital, Economic Elites and the State in Paraguay during the Liberal Republic (1870–1936)," *Journal of Latin American Studies* 21, no. 1 (February 1989): 61–88.
————. "The Liberal Republic and the Failure of Democracy in Paraguay." *The Americas* 45, no. 4 (April 1989): 525–46.
Artaza, Policarpo. *Ayala, Estigarribia y el Partido Liberal*. Buenos Aires: Editorial Ayacucho, 1946.
Ayala, Eligio. *Migraciones*. Santiago de Chile: n.p., 1941.
Ayala, José de la Cruz. *Desde el infierno*. Asunción: Ediciones Napa, 1982.
Báez, Cecilio. *Le Paraguay, son evolution historique*. Paris: Librairie Felix Alcan, 1927.
————. *La tiranía en el Paraguay, sus causas, caracteres y resultados*. Asunción: "El País," 1903.
Bareiro Saguier, Rubén. "El criterio generacional en la literatura paraguaya," *Revista Iberoamericana* 30 (July–December 1964): 293–303.
Basualdo, Arsenio, and Carlos Arza Maldonado, eds. *Forjadores de la democracia*. Asunción: Editorial Clásicos Colorados, 1984.
Benítez, Justo Pastor. *Ensayos sobre el liberalismo paraguayo*. Asunción: n.p., 1932.
Benítez, Luís G. *Breve historia de Grandes Hombres*. Asunción: privately published, 1986.
Bogarín, Juan Sinforiano. *Mis apuntes: memorias de Monseñor Juan Sinforiano Bogarín*. Asunción: Editorial Histórica, 1986.

Bordón, F. Arturo. *Historia política del Paraguay.* Asunción: Orbis, 1976.

———. *Liberales ilustres.* Asunción: Sociedad 18 de Octubre, 1966.

———. *¡Morínigo! Un paréntesis trágico en la vida democrática del Paraguay.* Asunción: Editora Tavaré, 1975.

———. *La verdad en su lugar.* Asunción: Libro del Oro de Liberalismo Paraguayo, 1971.

Bordón, J. Rodolfo. *La revolución del Paraguay del 17 de febrero.* Buenos Aires: Editorial Claridad, 1937.

Bray, Arturo. *Armas y letras.* 3 vols. Asunción: Ediciones Napa, 1981.

———. *Hombres y épocas del Paraguay.* 2 vols. Asunción: El Lector, 1986.

Brugada, Arturo. *La sublevación del 29 de octubre de 1877.* Asunción: Imprenta Sudamericana, 1923.

Brugada, Ricardo. *Benigno Ferreira.* Asunción: El Diario, 1906.

Caballero, Bernardino. *Mensajes presidenciales.* Asunción: Criterio Ediciones, 1987.

Caballero Aquino, Ricardo. *La Segunda República Paraguaya, 1869–1906.* Asunción: Arte Nuevo Editores, 1985.

Calzado, Rafael. *Rasgos bibliográficos de José Segundo Decoud.* Buenos Aires: n.p., 1913.

Campos Caballero, Augusto. *Testimonios de un presidente: entrevista al Gral. Higinio Morínigo.* Asunción: El Lector, 1983.

Cardoso, Efraím. *Breve historia del Paraguay.* Buenos Aires: Editorial Universitaria de Buenos Aires, 1965.

———. *Efemerides de la historia del Paraguay.* Buenos Aires: Ediciones Nizza, 1967.

———. *23 de octubre: una página de historia contemporánea del Paraguay.* Buenos Aires: Editorial Guayrá, 1956.

Centurión, Carlos R. *Historia de la cultura paraguaya.* 2 vols. Asunción: Biblioteca "Ortiz Guerrero," 1961.

———. *Los hombres de la Convención del 70.* Asunción: "El Arte," 1938.

Centurión, Juan Crisóstomo. *Apuntes biográficos de un colonel.* Asunción: Fundación Cultural Republicana, 1988.

Céspedes Ruffinelli, Roberto. *El febrerismo: del movimiento al partido, 1936–1951.* Asunción: Editorial Luxe, 1983.

Decoud, Héctor Francisco. *Los emigrados paraguayos en la Guerra del la Triple Alianza.* Buenos Aires: L. J. Rosso, 1930.

———. *Sobre los escombros de la guerra: una década de la vida nacional, 1869–1880.* Asunción: n.p., 1925.

———. *Tragedia de la cárcel pública: 29 de octubre 1877.* Asunción: Archivo del Liberalismo, 1988.

Decoud, José Segundo. *Cuestiones política y económicas.* Asunción: n.p., 1877.

De los Santos, Tomás. *La revolución de 1922.* 2 vols. Asunción: El Lector, 1984.

Estigarribia, José Félix. *The Epic of the Chaco: Marshal Estigarribia's Memoirs of the Chaco War, 1932–1935.* Translated and edited by Pablo Max Ynsfrán. Austin: University of Texas Press, 1950.

Fernández, Carlos José. *La Guerra del Chaco.* Vol. 1. Buenos Aires: privately published, 1956.

Ferreira Pérez, Saturnino. *Antecedentes del Centro Democrático: El golpe de 18 de octubre de 1891, su fusión con el Partido Liberal Histórico.* Asunción: Ediciones Comuneros, 1988.

————. *Proceso político del Paraguay.* 3 vols. Asunción: El Lector, 1986–87.

Freire Esteves, Gómez. *Historia contemporánea del Paraguay: luchas de cancillerías en El Plata.* Buenos Aires: n.p., 1921.

Ganson de Rivas, Barbara. *Las consequencias demográficas y sociales de la Guerra de la Triple Alianza.* Asunción: Editora Litocolor, 1985.

Gaona, Francisco. *Introducción a la historia gremial y social del Paraguay.* 2 vols. Asunción: Editorial Arandú and R. P. Ediciones, 1967–87.

Garay, Blas. *Paraguay 1899.* Asunción: Editorial Aravera, 1984.

Gill Aguinaga, Juan B. *La Asociación Paraguaya en la Guerra de la Triple Alianza.* Buenos Aires: n.p., 1959.

Gómez Fleitas, José Gaspar. "Ubicación histórica de los partidos tradicionales en el Paraguay." *Revista Paraguaya de Sociología* 7 (September–December 1970): 144–64.

González, Antonio E. *Preparación del Paraguay para la Guerra del Chaco.* 2 vols. Asunción: El Gráfico, 1957.

González, Teodosio. *Infortunios del Paraguay.* Buenos Aires: L. J. Rosso, 1931.

González Erico, Miguel Angel. "Desarrollo de la banca en el Paraguay: 1870–1900," *Revista Paraguaya de Sociología* 9 (September-December 1972): 133–54.

González y Contreras, Gilberto. *J. Natalicio González, descubridor del Paraguay.* Asunción: Editorial Guaranía, 1951.

Herken Krauer, Juan Carlos. *Ferrocarriles, conspiraciones, y negocios en el Paraguay, 1910–1914.* Asunción: Arte Nuevo Editores, 1984.

————. *El Paraguay rural entre 1869 y 1913.* Asunción: Centro Paraguayo de Estudios Sociológicos, 1984.

————. *La política económica durante la era liberal.* Asunción: Archivo del Liberalismo, 1989.

Ibarra, Alonso. *Cién años de vida política paraguaya, posterior a la epopeya de 1865 al 70.* Asunción: Editorial Comuneros, 1973.

Jaeggli, Alfredo L. *Albino Jara: un varón meteórico.* Buenos Aires: Editorial Lumén, 1963.

Livieres Guggiari, Lorenzo N. *El financiamiento de la defensa del Chaco, 1924–1935: un desafío al liberalismo económico.* Asunción: Arte Nuevo Editores, 1983.

Maíz, Fidel. *Etapas de mi vida.* Asunción: El Lector, 1986.

O'Leary, J. E. *Nuestra epopeya.* 1st part. Asunción: Biblioteca Tellechea/Gómez Rodas, 1985.

Pampliega, Amancio. *Misión cumplida.* Asunción: El Lector, 1984.

Partido Liberal. *Historia política del Paraguay: periodo 1870–1904.* Asunción: Ateneo Liberal, n.d.

Pastore, Carlos. *La lucha por la tierra en el Paraguay.* Montevideo: Editorial Antequera, 1972.

Pesoa, Manuel. *Origenes del Partido Liberal Paraguayo, 1870–1887.* Asunción: Criterio Ediciones, 1987.

Prieto, Justo. *Manual del ciudadano liberal paraguayo.* Buenos Aires: Editorial Asunción, 1953.

Prieto Yegros, Leandro, ed. *Enciclopedia Republicana: itinerario colorado de la causa nacional, 1880–1904.* Asunción: Editorial Universo, 1983.

Resquín, Ruperto. *La generación paraguaya (1928–1932).* Buenos Aires: Ediciones Paraguay en América, 1978.

Riquelme García, Benigno. *Cumbre en soledad: vida de Manuel Gondra.* Buenos Aires: Editorial Ayacucho, 1951.

Salúm-Flecha, Antonio. *Historia diplomática del Paraguay, de 1869 a 1938.* Asunción: Emasa, 1972.

Seiferheld, Alfredo M. *Conversaciones político-militares.* 4 vols. Asunción: El Lector, 1984–87.

———. *Estigarribia: veinte años de política paraguaya.* Asunción: Editorial Laurel, 1982.

Sosa, Antonio. *Vida pública.* Buenos Aires: Adolfo Grau, 1905.

Sosa Escalada, Jaime. *El General Ferreira.* Asunción: Jordán y Villaamil, 1906.

Speratti, Juan. *La revolución del 17 febrero de 1936.* Asunción: Escuela Técnica Salesiana, 1984.

Stefanich, Juan. *La diplomacia de la revolución.* Buenos Aires: Editorial El Mundo Nuevo, 1945.

———. *El Paraguay en febrero de 1936.* Buenos Aires: Editorial El Mundo Nuevo, 1946.

———. *Renovación y liberación: la obra del gobierno del febrero.* Buenos Aires: Editorial El Mundo Nuevo, 1946.

———. *La restauración histórica del Paraguay.* Buenos Aires: Editorial El Mundo Nuevo, 1945.

———. *El 23 de octubre de 1931.* Buenos Aires: Editorial Febrero, 1958.

Urizar, Rogelio. *Los dramas de nuestra anarquía.* 2 vols. Asunción: Editorial Fundación Ross, 1989.

Velilla L. de Arrellaga, Julia, and Alfredo M. Seiferheld. *Los ecos de la prensa en 1887.* Asunción: Editorial Histórica, 1987.

Volta Gaona, Enrique. *23 de octubre.* Asunción: El Arte, 1957.

Zubizarreta, Carlos. *Cién vidas paraguayas.* Buenos Aires: Ediciones Nizza, 1961.

FOREIGN SOURCES ON PARAGUAY

García Mellid, Atlio. *Proceso a los falsificadores de la historia del Paraguay.* Vol. 2. Buenos Aires: Ediciones Theoría, 1964.

Grow, Michael. *The Good Neighbor Policy and Authoritarianism in Paraguay.* Lawrence: University of Kansas Press, 1981.

Hilton, Ronald. *Who's Who in Latin America.* Vol. 5: *Argentina, Paraguay, Uru-*

guay. Stanford and Chicago: Stanford University Press and the A. N. Marquis Co., 1950.

Kolinsky, Charles J. *Historical Dictionary of Paraguay.* Metuchen, N.J.: Scarecrow Press, 1973.

———. *Independence or Death! The Story of the Paraguayan War.* Gainesville: University of Florida Press, 1965.

Lewis, Paul H. *The Politics of Exile: Paraguay's Febrerista Party.* Chapel Hill: University of North Carolina Press, 1968.

Morales, Waltrud Q. "A Comparative Study of Societal Discontent and Revolutionary Change in Bolivia and Paraguay, 1930–1941." Ph.D. dissertation, University of Denver, 1977.

Parker, William Belmont. *Paraguayans of Today.* Buenos Aires: Hispanic Society of America, 1920.

Pendle, George. *Paraguay: A Riverside Nation.* London: Royal Institute of International Affairs, 1956.

Raine, Philip. *Paraguay.* New Brunswick, N.J.: Scarecrow Press, 1956.

Rout, Leslie B., Jr. *The Politics of the Chaco Peace Conference, 1935–1939.* Austin: University of Texas Press, 1970.

Warren, Harris Gaylord. "Journalism in Asunción under the Allies and the Colorados." *The Americas* 39 (April 1983): 483–98.

———. *Paraguay and the Triple Alliance: The Postwar Decade, 1869–1878.* Austin: University of Texas Press, 1978.

———. "The Paraguayan Central Railway: 1856–1889." *Inter- American Economic Affairs* 20 (Spring 1967): 3–22.

———. "The Paraguayan Central Railway: 1889–1907." *Inter- American Economic Affairs* 21 (Summer 1967): 31–48.

———. "The Paraguayan Revolution of 1904." *The Americas* 36 (January 1980): 365–84.

———. "Political Aspects of the Paraguayan Revolution, 1936–1940." *Hispanic American Historical Review* 30 (February 1950): 2–25.

———. *The Rebirth of the Paraguayan Republic.* Pittsburgh: University of Pittsburgh Press, 1985.

Williams, John Hoyt. *The Rise and Fall of the Paraguayan Republic, 1800–1870.* Austin: University of Texas Press, 1979.

Zook, David H., Jr. *The Conduct of the Chaco War.* New York: Bookman Associates, 1960.

GENERAL WORKS

Bettleheim, Bruno. "The Problem of Generations." In *Youth: Change and Challenge,* edited by Bruno Bettleheim, pp. 64–92. New York: Basic Books, 1963.

Braungart, Margaret M. "Aging and Politics." *Journal of Political and Military Sociology* 12 (Spring 1984): 79–98.

Braungart, Richard. "The Sociology of Generations and Student Politics: A

Comparison of the Functionalist and Generational Unit Models." *Journal of Social Issues* 30, no. 2 (1974): 31–54.

Burnham, Walter Dean. *Critical Elections and the Mainsprings of American Politics.* New York: W. W. Norton, 1970.

Campbell, Angus, Philip Converse, Warren Miller, and Donald Stokes. *The American Voter.* New York: John Wiley & Sons, 1960.

Chambers, William Nesbit. *Political Parties in a New Nation.* New York: Oxford University Press, 1963.

Chambers, William Nesbit, and Walter Dean Burnham. *The American Party Systems: Stages of Political Development.* New York: Oxford University Press, 1975.

Charles, Joseph. *The Origins of the American Party System.* New York: Harper & Row, 1956.

Duverger, Maurice. *Political Parties.* New York: John Wiley & Sons, 1963.

Eisenstadt, S. N. *From Generation to Generation: Age Groups and Social Structure.* Glencoe, Ill.: Free Press, 1956.

Esler, Anthony. *The Generation Gap in Society and History: A Select Bibliography.* 2 vols. Monticello, Ill.: Vance Bibliographies, 1984.

Ferguson, Gregor. *Coup d'Etat: A Practical Manual.* Dorset, Great Britain: Arms and Armour Press, 1987.

Finer, Samuel. *The Man on Horseback.* New York: Frederick A. Praeger, 1962.

Foner, Anne. "Age Stratification and Age Conflict in Political Life." *American Sociological Review* 39 (1974): 187–96.

Goodspeed, D. J. *The Conspirators: A Study of the Coup d'Etat.* Toronto: Macmillan, 1967.

Hagopian, Mark N. *The Phenomenon of Revolution.* New York: Dodd, Mead, 1974.

Huntingdon, Samuel P. "Generations, Cycles, and Their Role in American Development." In *Political Generations and Political Development,* edited by Richard J. Samuels, pp. 9–28. Lexington, Mass.: Lexington Books, 1977.

———. *Political Order in Changing Societies.* New Haven: Yale University Press, 1968.

Key, V. O. *Politics, Parties, and Pressure Groups.* New York: Thomas Y. Crowell, 1962.

Knoke, David. "Conceptual and Measurement Aspects in the Study of Political Generations." *Journal of Political and Military Sociology* 12 (Spring 1984): 191–201.

Kornhauser, William. *The Politics of Mass Society.* Glencoe, Ill.: Free Press, 1959.

Ladd, Everett C., Jr. *American Political Parties: Social Change and Political Response.* New York: W. W. Norton, 1970.

Laufer, Robert, and Vern L. Bengtson. "Generations, Aging, and Social Stratification: On the Development of Generational Units." *Journal of Social Issues* 30, no. 3 (1974): 181–205.

Lawson, Kay. *The Comparative Study of Political Parties.* New York: St. Martin's Press, 1976.

Luttwak, Edward. *Coup d'Etat: A Practical Handbook.* Cambridge: Harvard University Press, 1979.

Malaparte, Curzio. *Coup d'Etat: The Technique of Revolution.* New York: E. P. Dutton, 1932.

Mannheim, Karl. "The Problem of Generations." In *Essays on the Sociology of Knowledge,* edited by Paul Kecskemeti, pp. 276–320. New York: Routledge & Kegan Paul, 1952.

Marias, Julian. *Generations, A Historical Method.* University: University of Alabama Press, 1970.

Nordlinger, Eric A. *Soldiers in Politics: Military Coups and Governments.* Englewood Cliffs, N.J.: Prentice-Hall, 1977.

Ortega y Gasset, José. *Man and Crisis.* London: Allen & Unwin, 1959.

———. "El tema de nuestro tiempo." In *Obras completas,* 3:145–50. Madrid: Revista de Occidente, 1955.

Panebianco, Angelo. *Political Parties: Organization and Power.* Cambridge: Cambridge University Press, 1988.

Pomper, Gerald. "Classification of Presidential Elections." *Journal of Politics* 29 (August 1967): 535–66.

Post, Jerrold M. "Dreams of Glory and the Life Cycle: Reflections on the Life Course of Narcissistic Leaders." *Journal of Political and Military Sociology* 12 (Spring 1984): 49–60.

Ryder, Norman B. "The Age Cohort as a Concept in the Study of Social Change." *American Sociological Review* 30 (1965): 843–61.

Spitzer, Alan B. "The Historical Problem of Generations." *American Historical Review* 78 (1973): 1353–85.

Abente Haedo, Victor, 100
Aceval, Benjamín, 46, 50, 53, 60–61, 70, 77–78, 80–81, 87, 200 (n. 3), 202 (nn. 6, 17)
Aceval, Emilio, 12, 77–78, 80–81, 85, 87–90, 93–96, 98, 100, 104, 117, 119–20, 186–87, 203 (n. 9)
Airaldi, Tomás, 87
Alcorta, Sinforiano, 26
Alfaro, Miguel, 69, 71
Alvarenga, Juan José, 47
Amarilla, Eduardo, 87
Amarilla, Hilario, 47
Amarilla, Manuel, 77, 187
Antola, Paulino, 175, 180–81
Aponte, Juan Ascenscio, 63, 67
Aramburu, Eduardo, 39
Arbó, Higinio, 115
Arce, Alejandro, 129, 131–32
Argaña, Luís, 171, 174, 178, 180–81, 192
Artaza, Policarpo, 127, 145
Asociación Nacional Republicana. See Colorado Party
Asociación Paraguaya, 18–23, 28–29, 32, 54, 64–66, 186
Audivert, Alejandro, 73, 80, 87–88, 99
Ayala, Elías, 96–97, 101–2, 174, 190
Ayala, Eligio, 100, 131–32, 135–43, 146–53, 157, 187, 191, 209 (n. 25)
Ayala, Enrique, 126
Ayala, Eusebio, 103–4, 117, 119, 121, 131–33, 135, 138, 148, 152–62, 173–74, 176–77, 182, 187, 191, 207 (nn. 18, 19), 210 (nn. 1, 31)
Ayala, José de la Cruz ("Alón"), 58, 60–61, 63, 66, 69–71, 73, 186, 190
Ayala, Juan B., 171

Báez, Cecilio, 60, 63, 66, 69–70, 75, 78–80, 84, 86–88, 94, 96, 98–101, 104, 111, 117–18, 171, 173–74, 186–87, 190, 192
Báez, Federico Guillermo, 20, 23, 28–29
Báez Allende, Isias, 181
Balteiro, J. Manuel, 100, 122
Banks, Benjamín, 154, 161–62
Bareiro, Candido, 23, 25, 27–32, 34–37, 39–43, 45–54, 61, 67–68, 77, 184, 186, 188–90, 198 (n. 4), 199 (nn. 1, 2, 26), 200 (n. 7)
Bareiro, Francisco, 112
Barrett, Rafael, 144
Barthe, Obdulio, 144, 192
Bazaras, José, 200 (n. 3)
Benegas, Ildefonso, 40, 63, 96, 199 (n. 22)
Benítes, Gregorio, 38–39
Benítez, Justo Pastor, 172, 179–80, 192
Benítez, Manuel, 87, 96, 101–2, 108, 138, 187
Benítez Vera, Victoriano, 181
Bertoni, Guillermo Tell, 166
Bobadilla, Pedro, 88, 117
Bogarín, Federico, 77, 93
Bordenave, Enrique, 138, 148, 174, 207 (n. 19)
Bordón, F. Arturo, 127, 145, 211 (n. 16)
Bordón, J. Rodolfo, 17, 145, 165, 206 (n. 20), 210 (n. 1)
Bozzano, José, 171, 173, 175
Bray, Arturo, 150–51, 157, 171–72, 174–75, 208 (n. 14)
Brizuela, Francisco, 120, 127
Brugada, Ricardo, 114
Bruyn, Damián, 211 (n. 13)
Buongermini, Geraldo, 181
Burgos, Manuel, 138

Caballero, Bernardino, 161–63, 165–66, 206 (n. 20)

Caballero, Bernardino (General), 3, 6, 12, 18, 32, 35–37, 40–43, 46–48, 50–71, 74–78, 82, 84–85, 88–90, 93, 95–97, 100, 104, 108, 111, 117, 184–86, 188–93, 199 (n. 26), 201 (nn. 24, 29), 202 (nn. 5, 6)

Caballero, Pedro P., 73–75, 80, 87

Caballero Codas, Marcos, 111, 113, 127

Cabriza, Francisco Lino, 41

Cáceres, Antonio, 94, 97

Calcena, Augusto, 199 (n. 1)

Caminos, José Zacarías, 63, 69, 87–89, 199 (n. 2)

Campos, Francisco, 89, 95–96, 98, 112, 131

Cañete, Agustín, 50, 59, 61, 71, 78, 80–82, 85, 186, 199 (n. 1), 201 (n. 24)

Cardoso, Efraím, 152, 172–73, 175–76, 192

Cardús Huerta, Gualberto, 95, 103–4, 133, 187

Carisimo, Rosendo, 70, 87

Carreras, Cayetano, 93–94, 97–99

Carreras, Fernando, 75, 79, 84, 87

Carvallo, Héctor, 71, 85, 90, 93–94

Casal Ribeiro, Raúl, 100, 136, 150, 161–62, 191

Cavalcanti, Amaro, 78

Centro Democrático. See Liberal Party

Centro Obrero Regional del Paraguay, 145

Centurión, Carlos, 172

Centurión, Juan Crisóstomo, 64, 66, 71, 186, 201 (nn. 24, 29)

Chaco War Veterans' Association (ANEC), 11, 158, 161–66, 211 (n. 13)

Chase Sosa, Luís, 172

Cháves, Federico, 177

Cháves, Francisco, 90, 94

Cháves, Julio César, 172

Chirife, Adolfo, 112, 115–16, 119–21, 125, 127, 129–36, 147

Christian Democratic Movement, 151

Club del Pueblo (Bareiro), 28–30, 34–36, 47, 50, 52, 54, 199 (nn. 1, 2)

Club del Pueblo (Decoud), 23–25, 27–28, 32

Club del Pueblo (Escobar), 60–61, 202 (n. 5)

Club Libertad (Bareiro), 50, 199 (n. 1)

Club Libertad (Caballero), 53, 60, 199 (n. 2), 202 (n. 5)

Club Popular Egusquicista, 76–78, 80, 85, 186–87

Club Unión Republicana, 23–25, 27–28, 32, 50, 52, 198 (n. 4)

Codas, Cipriano, 176, 212 (n. 28)

Collar, José Mateo, 24–25, 34–35, 63, 80–81, 87, 186

Colorado Party, 5–7, 11, 69, 99–100, 108–11, 113–16, 122, 124–25, 130–31, 146, 149, 163, 165–66, 175–77, 182, 184; founding, 3, 17–18, 36, 50, 63–68, 184, 186, 188; factions, 12, 52, 60, 66–67, 69–71, 74–78, 84–85, 89, 92–95, 101, 104, 131–32, 147, 186–89, 191

Communist Party, 144–45, 192

Constitution of 1870, 16, 20, 31, 33, 54, 86, 100, 157, 177–79, 185, 200 (n. 9)

Constitution of 1940, 16, 179–80

Corvalán, Juan León, 47

Corvalán, Miguel, 90, 93

Cotegipe, Baron de, 37–39

Coups, realigning, 90–92

Creydt, Oscar, 144–45, 192

Crosky, Rodney, 82

Dávalos, Alejandro, 176, 212 (n. 28)

Dávalos, Juan Bernardo, 63, 67

Decoud, Adolfo, 40

Decoud, Angel, 19

Decoud, Héctor, 58, 61

Decoud, José Segundo, 20, 22–23, 25–32, 35–37, 40, 45, 47–50, 52–54, 56–61, 63–64, 66, 68, 69–73, 75–78, 80, 87, 89, 100, 104, 117, 186, 188, 190, 192, 200 (n. 3), 201 (n. 24)

Decoud, Juan Francisco, 20–21, 24–26, 28, 30, 38, 40, 186
Decoud, Juan José, 20–21, 24, 26–29
De León, José, 51
Delgado, Nicolás, 174–78
Delmás, Aníbal, 180
Democratic Liberal Party (PLD), 111–12
Díaz de Bedoya, José, 20–21, 23–27, 30
Díaz de Vivar, Emilio, 168
Díaz León, Lisandro, 100, 128, 132, 136, 191
Domínguez, Manuel, 77, 93–94, 104, 111, 113, 132, 187
Duarte, Manuel J., 96–98, 101–2, 119–20, 190, 205 (n. 33)
Duarte, Pedro, 51–52, 54, 61
Duarte Ortellado, Pedro, 161, 192, 211 (n. 13)

Egusquiza, Félix, 23–25, 202 (n. 5)
Egusquiza, Juan Bautista, 12, 20, 23, 40, 54, 70, 73–74, 76–90, 94–95, 101, 104, 106–7, 116, 120, 139, 184–88, 191, 201 (n. 5), 202 (n. 17)
Escobar, Luís, 152
Escobar, Patricio, 35, 40–42, 44, 46, 48, 50–51, 60–61, 66, 68, 70–72, 74, 78, 85, 88–89, 95, 97, 100, 104, 108, 117, 186, 190, 202 (n. 14)
Escobar, Patricio Alejandro, 95, 97, 103, 115, 117, 121, 134, 150, 190
Esculies, Francisco, 178, 180
Escurra, Juan A., 89–90, 93–94, 97, 108
Estigarribia, Antonio de la Cruz, 22
Estigarribia, José Félix, 13, 135–36, 155–59, 172–80, 182, 188, 210 (n. 31)

Falcón, José, 37–38
Farquhar, Percival, 110–11
Febreristas, 7, 151, 168, 170–72, 177, 181–82, 185, 191–92
February Revolution of 1936, 7, 13, 93, 159–66, 168, 170–71, 173, 188, 190, 206 (n. 20)

Fernández, Carlos, 157
Fernández, Francisco, 52
Fernández, Salvador, 100
Ferreira, Benigno, 12–13, 20, 22, 25–26, 28–32, 36–41, 47–49, 52–54, 63, 68–69, 79–80, 84–90, 92, 95–108, 110, 116–17, 131, 137, 147, 153, 184–88, 190–91, 193, 201–2 (n. 5), 205 (n. 35)
Ferrocarril Transparaguayo, 110, 114
Finot, Enrique, 182
Flecha, Juan Cancio, 88
Fleitas, Eduardo, 85, 93–94, 97, 101, 146–47
Francia, José Gaspar Rodríguez de, 15–19, 25, 139
Franco, Manuel, 103–4, 120–21, 126, 139, 153, 187, 191
Franco, Rafael, 149–52, 158–70, 173–74, 176, 181, 188, 191–92, 208 (n. 14), 210 (n. 1), 211 (nn. 4, 16)
Freire Esteves, Gómez, 102, 112, 119, 160–64, 181, 188, 206 (n. 20), 210 (n. 1), 211 (n. 16)
Freire Esteves, Luís, 161, 164, 206 (n. 20)
Frescura, Luís P., 171, 174
Fretes, José Maria, 58–60
Frutos, Juan Manuel, 100
Frutos, Manuel I., 47, 75, 78–79, 87

Gallegos, Miguel, 28, 30
Gaona, Francisco, 145, 164–65, 192
Gaona, Juan B., 78, 82, 95, 97–99, 187, 205 (n. 33)
Gaona, Roque, 145, 211 (n. 13)
Garay, Blas, 84–85, 88, 95, 113, 186
Garay, Eugenio, 97, 115
Garcete, Aniceto, 77
Garcete, Avelino, 63, 75
Garcete, Pablo, 111
García, Carlos, 102
García, Elías C., 98–99, 102, 108, 205 (n. 33)
García Melgarejo, Salvador, 145
Gardel, Emilio, 164, 191

Gasperi, Luís de, 148, 150
Gelly y Obes, Juan Andrés, 24
Generations, theories of, 9–11, 13–14
Genes, Ignacio, 48, 199 (n. 26)
Gill, Emilio, 30, 42, 199 (n. 20)
Gill, José, 108–9, 116
Gill, Juan Bautista, 28–31, 34–37,
   41–48, 50, 52, 68, 87, 108, 184, 186,
   189–90, 201 (n. 24)
Gill, Pedro V., 63–65, 67, 186
Giménez, Juan de la Cruz, 54, 58–59,
   64
Godoi, Juansilvano, 26, 28–30, 38, 40,
   46–47, 51, 69, 80, 186, 197 (n. 19), 199
   (n. 20)
Godoi, Nicanor, 51, 199 (n. 20)
Goiburu, Carlos, 111–13, 115
Goiburu, José J., 63
Goiburu, Matias, 43
Gondim, José Duarte de Araujo, 41–42
Gondra, César, 70–71, 76, 78, 202
   (n. 17)
Gondra, Manuel, 80, 87, 96, 98–100,
   104–11, 113–14, 116–17, 120, 122,
   125–26, 128–33, 135, 137–39, 148,
   153, 172, 185, 187, 189, 191–92, 207
   (n. 18)
González, Antonio Luís, 39–40
González, Emeterio, 80, 87–88
González, Juan Gualberto, 24, 28, 47,
   50, 53–54, 58, 62, 64, 66, 68–72, 75,
   77–78, 84, 86, 188, 199 (n. 1), 202
   (n. 6)
González, Juan Natalicio, 146, 151–52,
   165, 176
González, Rodolfo, 127, 148, 152
González, Teodosio, 87
González Navero, Emiliano, 70, 96,
   98–99, 105, 116, 120–21, 148, 152–53
Gorostiaga, Esteban, 62
Granados, José G., 47, 50–51, 64, 69, 199
   (n. 1)
Gran Club del Pueblo, 27–31, 34–36,
   42, 46–47, 50, 61, 189–90
Guanes, Juan, 48

Guggiari, José P., 100, 122, 128–30,
   134–39, 143, 147–53, 155, 157, 176,
   185, 187, 191–92, 209 (n. 30)
Guggiari, Modesto, 100, 127–28, 135–
   36, 138, 145, 147, 152, 187, 191

Haedo, Miguel, 54, 199 (n. 1)

Ibañez, Cipriano, 100, 112–13
Ibañez, Pastor, 122
Ibarra, Ignacio, 54, 58–60, 63, 69, 71, 87,
   104, 186
Ibarra, Rogelio, 100
Ibarra Legal, Rogelio, 131–32, 136
Ibarra Legal, Sebastian, 111
Industrial Paraguaya, La, 52, 56, 78,
   81–82, 114, 118
Irala, Adriano, 145, 150, 161
Irala, Antolín, 94, 108, 111
Irala, José, 75, 93
Isasi, Carlos Luís, 84, 87, 96
Iturburu, Fernando, 19–25, 28, 30, 70,
   186, 198 (n. 4)
Iturburu, José Toribio, 48

Jara, Albino, 13, 40, 95, 97–100, 103–17,
   126–28, 130, 137, 147, 153, 185, 187,
   191
Jara, Juan Antonio, 23, 28, 35, 47, 50,
   62, 70
Jara, Zacarías, 28, 97, 107
Jefes políticos, 32–33, 53–54, 56, 59, 67,
   71, 86, 124–28, 133–34, 136, 200
   (nn. 8, 9)
Jovellanos, Genaro, 199 (n. 1)
Jovellanos, Salvador, 20, 23, 28, 34–35,
   37, 38–43, 61, 63, 79
Jover Peralta, Anselmo, 145, 150–52,
   161, 163–65, 170, 191
Justo, Agustín P., 167

Land sales, 57–61, 64, 67–68, 72, 82,
   191, 207 (n. 28)
Lara Castro, Ramón, 87, 191
Legal, José Tomás, 87–89, 104, 111, 187

Legión Paraguaya. *See* Paraguayan Legion
Lezcano, Crescencio, 165, 191
Liberal Party, 5–7, 69–70, 89, 99, 107, 120, 122–26, 141–42, 144, 146, 171, 177, 182; Centro Democrático, 3, 11, 17–18, 24, 50, 60, 63–66, 69–70, 72, 75, 79, 86, 113, 117, 184, 186, 190, 199 (n. 2); factions, 12–13, 79, 84–85, 87, 95–96, 98–99, 101–4, 108–11, 113–16, 119–22, 127–39, 171–76, 178, 180, 184–85, 187–89, 191
Liga de la Juventud Independiente, 100, 102–3, 105, 107, 110, 112, 120, 127–28, 136–37, 147, 191
Liga Nacional Independiente, 145–46, 149, 161, 163–66, 168, 189, 211 (n. 13)
Loizaga, Carlos, 19–21, 24–26, 30, 35, 39, 41, 48
López, Carlos Antonio, 15–19, 25, 38, 64, 77, 159, 190, 202 (n. 6)
López, Enrique Solano, 95, 108, 125, 146
López, Francisco Solano, 15–18, 20–22, 23, 25–26, 28, 38, 54, 64, 71–72, 95, 146, 159, 180, 185, 190, 202 (nn. 5, 6)
López, Venancio, 70, 95, 202 (n. 6)
López Decoud, Arsenio, 77, 95, 187
López Moreira, Eduardo, 109, 115, 146–47
Lynch, Eliza, 26, 125

Machaín, Evaristo, 20
Machaín, Facundo, 26–27, 29–31, 37–38, 44, 46–49, 53, 61, 63, 186, 188, 190, 197 (nn. 11, 19), 199 (n. 22), 202 (n. 9)
Machaín, Gregorio, 20
Machaín, Juan José, 202 (n. 9)
Machaín, Juan Pablo, 73–74
Machaín, Serapio, 24, 26
Maciel, Manuel A., 61, 69, 76, 85, 202 (n. 14)
Mallorquín, Juan León, 100, 147

Marín Iglesias, Alejandro, 172, 178, 181, 192
Martincich, Juan, 171
Martínez, Angel, 80–81, 85
Martino, Ramón, 168, 181
Mazó, José Maria, 25
Mazó, Remigio, 71
Mazó, Rufino, 78, 80–81, 187
Méndez Benítez, Narciso, 100
Mendonça, Lucio, 127, 172
Mendoza, Pedro, 112, 127, 136
Mendoza, Tomás, 113
Merles, Artemio, 172
Meza, José M., 199 (n. 2)
Meza, Juan Antonio, 35, 48, 53–54, 61, 63, 68–71, 108, 199 (n. 26)
Miltos, Cayo, 23, 28–31, 34–35, 48, 186
Miltos, Fulgencio, 23, 28, 35, 37
Miranda, José D., 127
Miranda, José del Rosario, 30, 39, 61
Miranda, Pedro, 77
Molas, José A. Dolores, 40, 42–44, 46, 53
Molas López, Felipe, 166, 210 (n. 1)
Montero, José P., 114, 117, 120–22, 126, 138, 153, 191
Moreno, Fulgencio R., 84, 88, 90, 93–95, 113, 115, 186
Morínigo, Higinio, 13, 171, 175, 178, 180–82, 192, 212 (n. 31)
Morínigo, Marcos, 68, 70, 76, 78, 94, 202 (n. 6)

National Confederation of Workers (CNT), 164–65
National Republican Association (ANR). *See* Colorado Party
National Revolutionary Party (PNR), 164–66, 170
National Revolutionary Union. *See* Unión Nacional Revolucionaria
Nuñez, Hipólito, 115

Odriozola, Ricardo, 178
O'Leary, Juan, 100, 146, 150, 154

Ortiz, José A., 109, 111

Paíva, Félix, 13, 103, 117, 120–22, 130, 132–33, 170–77, 187
Palacios, Abdón, 181
Palacios, Miguel, 25–26, 34–35
Pane, Ignacio, 146
Paraguayan Central Railway Company (PCRC), 110–11, 114
Paraguayan Confederation of Workers (CPT), 165
Paraguayan Legion, 18–19, 21–24, 28–29, 32, 38, 52, 54, 64–66, 71, 107, 146, 186, 189, 197 (n. 6)
Paraguayan Students' Federation (FEP), 164–65
Paranhos, José Maria Silva, 24–26
Paredes, Ramón, 167–71, 173–75, 178, 180–81, 211 (nn. 15, 16)
Partido Liberal (1871), 36, 39, 41–42, 53
Partido Nacional, 36–37, 41–42, 52–53, 68, 93, 189–90
Patri, Luigi, 82
Pavón, Rogelio, 172
Peña, Manuel, 138
Peña, Pedro, 94, 115, 130, 132, 146–47, 178
Peña, Pío Otoniel, 19–20, 69
Pereira Casal, Gerónimo, 88
Pérez, José del Carmen, 74
Pérez, José Emilio, 94, 97–99, 101
Political parties, theories of development, 2–9, 32–33
Prieto, Justo, 17–18, 52, 161, 172, 175–76, 192

Queirolo, Fabio, 63, 66, 73–74, 79–80, 87–89, 186, 190
Quintana, Susana Rodrígues Viana de, 204 (n. 23)

Ramírez, J. Isidro, 100
Ramos, Alfredo, 171, 181
Ramos Giménez, Leopoldo, 118
Recalde, Bernardo, 28

Recalde, Camilo, 149, 151, 158, 161
Recalde, Facundo, 158, 165
Recalde, Juan Francisco, 174
Recalde, Pedro, 35, 37, 39, 198 (n. 4)
Resquín, Ruperto, 192
Riart, Gerónimo, 127, 136, 177
Riart, Luís, 120–21, 127, 136, 138, 143, 148, 152–53, 157, 161–62, 172, 174–76, 187, 191, 209 (n. 30)
Ríos, Guillermo de los, 80–82, 85, 88–90, 95–96, 98, 101, 104, 187
Riquelme, Adolfo, 87, 96, 100, 103–4, 108–12, 187, 191
Rivarola, Belisario, 87, 127, 132, 135, 138, 146, 148, 153, 161–62, 191
Rivarola, Cirilo Antonio, 24–26, 30–31, 33–38, 42–43, 45–46, 48–49, 53, 63, 91, 127, 135, 186, 190, 199 (n. 26), 200 (n. 7)
Rivarola, Juan Bautista, 73
Rivarola, Salvador, 47
Rivarola, Vicente, 93
Rivas Ortellado, Aristides, 167, 169
Riveros, Benigno, 77, 187
Rodrígues, Manuel, 111, 114
Rojas, Emiliano, 114
Rojas, Esteban, 69, 71, 73
Rojas, Eustacio, 210 (n. 31)
Rojas, Liberato Marcial, 87, 110, 113–15, 127, 142, 191
Rojas, Manuel, 131–32
Rojas, Victor, 152, 161–62
Rojas Silva, Adolfo, 142, 145
Rolón, Francisco, 111, 171
Romero Pereira, Cayo, 109
Romero Pereira, Tomás, 114–15
Rosa, J. Eliseo da, 100, 120, 127, 131–32, 138, 148, 153, 191

Saguier, Adolfo, 23, 30, 47–52, 60, 77, 82, 90, 188
Saguier, Carlos, 25
Saguier, Emilio, 95–96
Saguier, Fernando, 60–61
Saguier, Rodolfo, 77

Salamoni, Tomás A., 178, 180
Sánchez Palacios, Francisco, 145, 192
Schaerer, Eduardo, 87, 96, 104–5, 110,
    114, 116–17, 119–22, 125–33, 138–39,
    145, 147, 149, 153, 167–68, 170, 185,
    189, 191, 193, 207 (n. 19), 209 (n. 30),
    211 (n. 15)
Schenoni, Manlio, 112, 121, 129, 131,
    133–36, 138–39, 147, 149–50, 208
    (n. 13)
Serrano, Germán, 35, 40–42, 44
Smith, Federico W., 157–58, 160–62,
    181, 210 (n. 1)
Sociabilidad Paraguaya, 47–48, 50–51
Sociedad Libertadora, 12, 18–19, 28, 32,
    64–66, 186
Solalinde, Cirilo, 51–53, 60, 63, 186, 199
    (nn. 1, 2)
Soler, Adolfo, 84, 87, 96–99, 101–2, 104,
    108, 186–87, 190
Soler, Germán, 164–65
Soler, Victor M., 63, 69–70, 79, 86–87
Sosa, Antonio, 77, 85, 108
Sosa, Guillermo, 130
Sosa, Ignacio, 25, 27
Sosa, José Tomás, 41, 47, 69–70
Sosa Escalada, Jaime, 20, 22, 24, 26,
    28–30, 38–39, 41, 43–44, 190
Sosa Gaona, Francisco, 120–21
Sosa Valdéz, Damaso, 168–71, 175, 178,
    180–81, 211 (n. 16)
Soteras, Francisco, 37, 39, 52, 63
Speratti, Juan, 210 (n. 1)
Stefanich, Juan, 145, 149–52, 161–70,
    188, 211 (nn. 13, 16)
Stroessner, Alfredo, 179, 182, 192

Taboada, Antonio, 24–25, 28, 35, 40, 52,
    58–60, 62–63, 65, 67, 69–70, 72–75,
    78–79, 87, 96, 98, 102, 104, 117, 131,
    186–87, 190

Taboada, Rufino, 24–25, 28–30, 34–35,
    48, 186, 197 (n. 11)
Tiempistas, 174, 178, 180, 192
Torreani Vera, Eduardo, 176, 178,
    180–81
Torrents, Felipe, 52, 62–63, 199 (n. 2)
23rd of October incident, 150–52, 162,
    166, 171, 190

Unión Nacional Revolucionaria (UNR),
    7, 11, 166, 170, 185, 211 (n. 13)
Unión Obrera Paraguaya, 141
Urdapilleta, José, 46–47, 53, 87–89
Uriarte, Higinio, 29, 37, 41, 43, 46, 53,
    64, 68, 87, 186, 201 (n. 24)
Urizar, Rogelio, 115
Usher, Mario, 100, 109–11, 127

Valdovinos, Arnaldo, 165, 192
Valiente, Bernardino, 25
Varela, Mariano, 22
Velásquez, Ernesto, 117, 120, 127, 129
Velásquez, Héctor, 80–81, 187
Velilla, Benjamín, 127
Velilla, Pascual, 96
Vera, Eduardo, 40, 52, 72–73, 92, 96,
    191
Villagra Maffiodo, Salvador, 178,
    180
Villasboa, Mushuito, 174

Yegros, Elpidio, 162, 166, 170, 192
Ynsfrán, Facundo, 78–81, 84, 93–94,
    176, 186, 202 (nn. 6, 17)
Ynsfrán, Pablo Max, 176, 178–79, 181,
    192

Zayas, Antonio, 52, 63, 199 (n. 2)
Zubizarreta, Gerónimo, 117, 148,
    152–53, 172–74, 187